I0975637

# The How

*of*

# Happiness

THE PENGUIN PRESS

*New York*

*2008*

# The How

## *of*

## Happiness

A Scientific Approach to
Getting the Life You Want

*Sonja Lyubomirsky,* Ph.D.

THE PENGUIN PRESS
Published by the Penguin Group
Penguin Group (USA) Inc., 375 Hudson Street, New York, New York 10014, U.S.A. •
Penguin Group (Canada), 90 Eglinton Avenue East, Suite 700, Toronto, Ontario, Canada M4P 2Y3
(a division of Pearson Penguin Canada Inc.) • Penguin Books Ltd, 80 Strand, London WC2R 0RL,
England • Penguin Ireland, 25 St. Stephen's Green, Dublin 2, Ireland (a division of Penguin Books Ltd)
• Penguin Books Australia Ltd, 250 Camberwell Road, Camberwell, Victoria 3124, Australia (a division
of Pearson Australia Group Pty Ltd) • Penguin Books India Pvt Ltd, 11 Community Centre,
Panchsheel Park, New Delhi – 110 017, India • Penguin Group (NZ), 67 Apollo Drive, Rosedale,
North Shore 0632, New Zealand (a division of Pearson New Zealand Ltd) • Penguin Books
(South Africa) (Pty) Ltd, 24 Sturdee Avenue, Rosebank, Johannesburg 2196, South Africa

Penguin Books Ltd, Registered Offices:
80 Strand, London WC2R 0RL, England

First published in 2007 by The Penguin Press,
a member of Penguin Group (USA) Inc.

Copyright © Sonja Lyubomirsky, 2007
All rights reserved

Grateful acknowledgment is made for permission to reprint "The Journey" from *Dream Work* by
Mary Oliver. Copyright © 1986 by Mary Oliver. Reprinted by permission of Grove/Atlantic, Inc.

Library of Congress Cataloging-in-Publication Data

Lyubomirsky, Sonja.
The how of happiness : a scientific approach to getting the life you want / Sonja Lyubomirsky.
p. cm.
Includes bibliographical references and index.
ISBN-13: 978-1-59420-148-6
1. Happiness. I. Title.
BF575.H27L98 2008            2007039942
158—dc22

Printed in the United States of America
1  3  5  7  9  10  8  6  4  2

*Designed by Meighan Cavanaugh*

*To Gabriella and Alexander,*

*the biggest hows behind*

*my happiness*

~

# THE JOURNEY

One day you finally knew
what you had to do, and began,
though the voices around you
kept shouting
their bad advice—
though the whole house
began to tremble
and you felt the old tug
at your ankles.
"Mend my life!"
each voice cried.
But you didn't stop.
You knew what you had to do,
though the wind pried
with its stiff fingers
at the very foundations,
though their melancholy
was terrible.
It was already late
enough, and a wild night,
and the road full of fallen
branches and stones.
But little by little,
as you left their voices behind,
the stars began to burn
through the sheets of clouds,
and there was a new voice
which you slowly
recognized as your own,
that kept you company
as you strode deeper and deeper
into the world,
determined to do
the only thing you could do—
determined to save
the only life that you could save.

—*Mary Oliver*

# CONTENTS

## Part Two

## Happiness Activities

## Part Three

⌒

# Secrets to Abiding Happiness

# The How

*of*

# Happiness

# FOREWORD

All of us want to be happy, even if we don't admit it openly or choose to cloak our desire in different words. Whether our dreams are about professional success, spiritual fulfillment, a sense of connection, a purpose in life, or love and sex, we covet those things because ultimately we believe that they will make us happier. Yet few of us truly appreciate just how much we can improve our happiness or know precisely how to go about doing it. To step back and consider your deep-seated assumptions about how to become a happier person and whether it's even possible for you—what I hope this book will spur you to do—is to understand that becoming happier is realizable, that it's in your power, and that it's one of the most vital and momentous things that you can do for yourself and for those around you.

What are the meanings and mysteries of happiness? Is it possible to acquire more of it, and can new happiness ever endure? These are foundational questions to which I have devoted my entire career as a research psychologist. When I was beginning my investigations, as a twenty-two-year-old psychology graduate student, the study of well-being wasn't a well-regarded choice, the subject matter considered elusive, unscientific, "soft," and "fuzzy." But recently happiness has exploded as a hot topic in the social science community, a symptom, perchance, of the Western twenty-first-century individualistic zeitgeist.

Alas, has happiness today become a fad, like hula hoops, big hairdos, and Fonzie? It can certainly appear so, with the market saturated with newspaper and magazine pieces, television documentaries, books, quotes, blogs, and podcasts on the topic, the vast majority of which are relatively uninformed by empirical data. Not infrequently, this frenzy drives researchers like myself to want to keep a distance, yet I think it's essential to engage in the national discussion about happiness and insist that it abide by strict scientific standards. Why? Because I believe deeply in the importance of the scientific study of happiness and well-being. The majority of people in the world, across vast continents and cultures, profess that being happy is one of their most cherished goals in life—for themselves and, above all, for their children. What's more, happiness offers myriad rewards, not just for the happy person but for his or her family, workplace, community, nation, and society. Working on how to become happier, the research suggests, will not only make a person *feel* better but will also boost his or her energy, creativity, and immune system, foster better relationships, fuel higher productivity at work, and even lead to a longer life.[1] Happiness, in my humble opinion, is the Holy Grail, "the meaning and the purpose of life," as Aristotle famously said, "the whole aim and end of human existence."

The science of happiness deserves to be more than a fad. Striving to be happy is a serious, legitimate, and worthy aim. If you consult the ancient texts in history, literature, or philosophy, you'll also find that it's eternal. Many of us suffer, and many more feel empty and unfulfilled, yet to attain more joy, less anguish, more tranquillity, and less insecurity is a venerable goal. I have been conducting research in this field for eighteen years, initially as a doctoral student at Stanford University and then and now as a professor at the University of California, Riverside. In the intervening years I have seen the science of happiness grow as part of a movement called positive psychology, the psychology of what makes life worth living. The label comes from the conviction that empowering people to develop a positive state of mind—to live the most rewarding and happiest lives they can—is just as important as psychology's traditional focus on repairing their weaknesses and healing their pathologies. The focus on flourishing and fulfillment may seem like a wise and obvious choice, yet psychology for the last half of the twentieth century was fixated on disease, disorder, and the negative side of life.[2]

The goals of today's psychologists are grander and more ambitious. During the past ten years psychological science has made tremendous advances in knowledge about not only how to treat depression—that is, how to lift people from feeling terrible to feeling good—but how to elevate them to feeling great. We're in a new era, each month witnessing hot-off-the-press publications about how to achieve and sustain happiness, how to make life more fulfilling, more productive, and more enjoyable. Unfortunately, these findings are typically disseminated formally and informally only among scientists or else published in technical academic journals subscribed by universities and lying beyond the reach of the nonexpert. In this book I have assembled and interpreted the discoveries about how to become happier, using them as jumping-off points to teach skills that people can use to shift to a higher and sustainable level of well-being.

Allow me temporary license to make some lofty claims. First, the star of *The How of Happiness* is science, and the happiness-increasing strategies that I and other social psychologists have developed are its key supporting players. My story is that of a research scientist, not a clinician, life coach, or self-help guru. To my knowledge, this is the first how-to-become-happier book authored by someone who has actually conducted research revealing how people can achieve a greater sense of happiness in their lives. Friends and colleagues have urged me to write this book for many years, but only now do I believe that the scientific advances in the field are solid and rigorous enough to interpret and translate into specific recommendations. As a result, *The How of Happiness* is different from many self-help books inasmuch as it represents a distillation of what researchers of the science of happiness, including myself, have uncovered in their empirical investigations.

Every suggestion that I offer is supported by scientific research; if evidence is mixed or lacking on a particular subject, I plainly say so. Notes and references are provided for all theories, statistics, and original research. If you are interested in any specific topic area in these pages and aspire to pursue it more deeply, the notes will tell you where to go. If you find such interruptions distracting, feel free to disregard them.

Why should readers care about whether the advice they read in self-help books is supported by science? Because empirical research holds multiple advantages over anecdotal or clinical observations. By applying the scientific method, researchers have the ability to disentangle cause and effect and to study a phenomenon systematically, without biases or preconceptions. Thus, if a magazine article proclaims that daily meditations make people happier or that a natural herb alleviates headaches, only a true double-blind experiment in which participants are randomly assigned to the meditation (or natural herb) condition and others to a control group can determine if these claims are true. Although science is imperfect, we can be much more confident in its conclusions than in those of a single individual proffering advice based on his or her limited experience and assumptions.

A newspaper reader once wrote the following eloquent letter to the editor, on the subject of science:

> There are questions of faith, such as "Does God exist?" There are questions of opinion, such as "Who is the greatest baseball player of all time?" There are debate questions, such as "Should abortion be legal?" And then there are questions that can be answered to a degree of certainty by the application of the scientific method, which are called empirical questions—in other words, those that can be largely settled by the evidence.[3]

Whether it's possible to learn how to become lastingly happier and how exactly you can go about doing so turns out to be just such an empirical question. My friend and research collaborator Ken Sheldon and I received a grant for more than one million dollars from the National Institute of Mental Health to fund research on the possibility of becoming happier. Along with a team of gifted graduate students, Ken and I have been using this grant to conduct so-called happiness interventions, a scientific term we use to refer not to confrontations with addicts but to experiments that aim to find out which happiness-boosting strategies are effective—and how and why. (Incidentally, both types of "interventions" share the notion that for major change to happen, a break with the status quo must be achieved.) Our research from such experimental interventions suggests, as you will soon learn in these pages, that enjoying a real increase in your own happiness is in fact attainable, *if* you are prepared to do the work. If you make a decision to be happier in your life, and you understand that this is a weighty decision that will take effort, commitment, and a certain amount of discipline, know that you can make it happen.

*Merriam-Webster's Collegiate Dictionary* (11th ed.) lists the first, second, and third definitions of the adverb *how* as follows: "1a: in what matter or way b: for what reason: why c: with what meaning: to what effect." *The How of Happiness* embraces each of these definitions in full. Above all, this is a book about *how* to become a happier person, supplying you a road map—a dozen happiness-increasing strategies—for the *matter or way* to get there and for *how* to choose the strategies that fit you best. Further, understanding the precise *reasons* that the strategies are successful (i.e., *why* they work) is just as important as knowing what they are and how to apply them optimally. Finally, the *meaning* and *effects* of being happier—the multiple benefits and consequences for yourself, your family, and your community—is another vital theme that I address.

Backed by the results of our work with thousands of research participants, I deliver in *The How of Happiness* a theory of the determinants of happiness, a unifying theory of a sort, which encapsulates for you in one take everything that scientists currently know about what makes people happy and the implications for attaining ever-greater well-being. In a sense, the many drips and drabs you may have picked up about the subject of happiness from other sources converge meaningfully in this book into a single integrated whole. And essential to my idea that we can maximize our own happiness is the notion of the 40 percent solution.

As it happens, "The 40 Percent Solution" was one of this book's original titles, because it is effectively the tool that underlies the promise of becoming happier, the answer to the question of how the realization of greater happiness is possible and what this book is essentially all about. Why 40 percent? Because 40 percent is that part of our happiness that it's in our power to change through how we act and how we think, that portion representing the potential for increased lasting happiness that resides in all of us. It's not a small number, and it's not a huge number, but it's a reasonable and realistic number. *The How of Happiness* shows you *how* to apply that number to your own circumstances. However, instead of showing you how to move from the negative range toward a neutral point, the aim of most therapies and treatments for depression, I shall spotlight how to advance from your current (perhaps unrewarding) state (be it −8, −3, or +3) toward +6 or +8 or even higher.

This is how to read this book. Chapters 1 and 2 introduce you to the foundations of the how-to-be-happier program described here, the theory behind the 40 percent solution. These chapters lay out the principles and empirical evidence behind two fundamental questions that we ask ourselves: How can we decide what will make us happier, and how precisely should we go about making it happen? You will learn what most of us believe will make us happier, and in what ways we're wrong, and what scientists have shown *actually* determines happiness. In the 40 percent solution lies a bounty of possibilities. Remaking yourself as a happier person, a new person, is entirely in your hands, if you are willing to bring to bear some effort and commitment, *if* you are ready, and only if you understand how to proceed. Part I of the book will deliver you to that starting line.

At that point you'll be geared up to begin introducing the thoughts and behaviors that will make you happier, but where to start? This is where Chapter 3 plays a decisive role. In this brief but important chapter, you will complete a diagnostic test that will flag which particular strategies will work to make you happier. Establishing this outright will direct you to what to take away from the next part of the book, from Part II, which presents detailed analyses and concrete illustrations of twelve specific happiness-enhancing activities. The fit diagnostic will lead you to those chapters detailing activities that apply specially to your personality, resources, goals, and needs. Contrary to popular belief, there is no one secret to happiness, just as there is no one miracle diet that works for all. Each of us needs to determine which strategy, or set of strategies, will be most valuable, and once you have completed the fit diagnostic in Chapter 3, you are prepared and equipped to carry on. Find your best-fitting activities in Part II, and begin the challenging but rewarding process of becoming a happier person.

That's not all. The last part of the book contains two vital chapters. Chapter 10 describes five important hows behind abiding happiness, offering you insight into how and why the happiness strategies "work." We know from the field of medicine that patients who have a good understanding of the thinking behind treatments are more likely to comply with them and benefit from them. The same logic applies here. Some of you might be tempted to skip this chapter, but you will be more successful in improving your own happiness, not to mention more erudite, if you read on. A final chapter worth reading—"Postscript: If You Are Depressed"—is reserved for those of you who have been feeling sad or down during the last weeks. If this describes you, you may even want to read this first.

Before I leave you, I must preempt an observation I made while writing about the twelve happiness-enhancing strategies, and it is this: Why do many of the most powerful happiness activities sound so . . . well, hokey? To be sure, some of us find exhortations to "count your blessings," "live in the present," "commit random acts of kindness," "look on the bright side" or "smile!" trivial at best and corny at worst. Yet as I shall plainly illustrate, these strategies, when practiced in effortful and optimal ways, have been borne out in numerous studies to be incredibly effective. Why aren't they hip then? Why don't people shout them from mountain peaks and rooftops?

One reason, perhaps, is that such potent and complex happiness recommendations are not easily condensed or drawn down to their essence. *Of course*, we all would be happier if we truly and sincerely felt gratitude for our health, our families, friends, homes, and jobs, even when those things are imperfect. But somehow, boiling down this behavior to "Honey, you'd be so much more content if you just counted your blessings" makes the suggestion sound like a silly platitude. Alternatively, it may be that when we translate into a universal maxim something so personal, so close to the bone as how we wish to be or how we behave toward loved ones, the outcome sounds watered down, hackneyed, and clichéd.

Last but not least, some people associate happiness-enhancing strategies with people who seem to be too cheery and blissed out to be real. When I was in high school, I had a friend whose bedroom was adorned (to the horror of my fifteen-year-old self) with Pollyanna-like assertions ("I ♥ Life," "Never Give Up," etc.) beneath photos of cuddly kittens and dazzling sunsets. Of course, now I look at some of those quotes, which I used to think were so trite, and notice that they are powerful enough to include in my book. My point is that you don't have to hang quotations about happiness on your walls or agree with the exact locution of some of the phrases I employ here to experience the impact of what I am trying to impart. Above all, understand that there are many faces of happiness aside from the ubiquitous smiley face and the inspirational poster. The face of happiness may be someone who is intensely curious and enthusiastic about learning; it may be someone who is engrossed in plans for his next five years; it may be someone who can distinguish between the things that matter and the things that don't; it may be someone who looks forward each night to reading to her child. Some happy people may appear outwardly cheerful or transparently serene, and others are simply busy. In other words, we all have the potential to be happy, each in our own way. Yet what I hope you'll come to appreciate from reading this book is the notion that the basic strategies for improving happiness in our day-to-day lives are less daunting than you might once have thought.

*Foreword*

Growing up in both Russia and the United States, I've known some very unhappy people in my life. I've also witnessed more than one friend become, and remain, genuinely happier as she grew, changed, and matured. This book is the product of years of thinking, reading, and conducting research on how we can accomplish this feat. Whether you personally yearn to become happier or know someone who does, or you are intellectually curious about what scientists currently understand about the causes and potential for abiding well-being, I hope you will be enriched and enlightened by these pages.

## Part One

~

# How to Attain Real and Lasting Happiness

# 1.

# Is It Possible
# to Become Happier?

To change one's life, start immediately,
do it flamboyantly, no exceptions.

—*William James*

W hat do you think would make you happier? Take a moment to consider. Might it be . . .

- A relationship?
- More flexibility at work?
- A new job that better provides for you and your family?
- An extra bedroom?
- A more attentive spouse?
- A baby?
- Looking younger?
- Relief from your bad back?
- Losing weight?
- Your child excelling at school?
- Knowing what you really want to do with your life?
- More supportive, loving parents?
- Cure from a chronic illness or disability?

- More money?
- More time?

If your answers look anything like these, all of which friends have confided to me over the years, you're in for a surprise. None of these things will make you substantially happier. But this doesn't mean that the goal of finding lasting happiness is unrealistic or naive. The catch is that we tend to look for happiness in the wrong places. What we *believe* would make a huge difference in our lives actually, according to scientific research, makes only a small difference, while we overlook the true sources of personal happiness and well-being.

In almost every nation, from the United States, Greece, and Slovenia to South Korea, Argentina, and Bahrain, when asked what they want most in life, people put happiness at the top of their lists.[1] Learning how to be happier is critical for those of us who are currently depressed or low, and it may be invaluable to everyone. In this book, I shall show you why our desire to be happier isn't just a pipe dream.

# A Program for Lasting Happiness

You may have picked up this book because you believe that you are not living up to your potential in your personal or working life, or perhaps you are not as happy and fulfilled as you yearn to be. Nationally representative samples of U.S. adults indicate that slightly more than half of us (54 percent) are "moderately mentally healthy" yet not flourishing—that is, we lack great enthusiasm for life and are not actively and productively engaged with the world.[2] This explains why the desire to be happier is felt not just by the clinically depressed but by a wide range of us, from those of us who are not as happy as we'd like to be, who sense that we're not quite thriving, to those who may be doing quite well yet want more— more joy, more meaning in life, more stimulating relationships and jobs. Finally, some of us may have once known true happiness but feel powerless to bring that moment back.

This sense of languishing or having fallen in a hole or being trapped in a rut can be daunting. We may think that it would take a staggering amount of energy and stamina to pull ourselves up. But I have hopeful news. The "work" to heave yourself out of the hole and onto higher ground can start out very small and will often yield immediate results. In one study, the University of Pennsylvania professor Martin Seligman taught a single happiness-enhancing strategy to a group of severely depressed people—that is, those whose depression scores put them in the most extremely depressed category. Although these individuals had great difficulty even leaving their beds, they were instructed to log on to a Web site and engage in a simple exercise. The exercise involved recalling and writing down three good things that happened every day—for example, "Rosalind called to say hello," "I read a chapter of a book my therapist recommended," and "The sun finally came out today." Within fifteen days their depressions lifted from "severely depressed" to "mildly to moderately depressed," and 94 percent of them experienced relief.[3]

So you see, research suggests that the initial steps to becoming happier can be implemented straightaway. The first step involves recognizing that our yearning to increase our happiness is not just wishful thinking. It is a vitally important goal, one that we all have a right to pursue and the wherewithal to achieve. Happiness isn't a knock of good fortune that we must await, like the end of rainy season. Neither is it something that we must find, like a freeway exit or a lost wallet, if only we knew the secret path and if only we could acquire the right job or the right boyfriend. Interestingly, the notion that happiness must be found is so pervasive that even the familiar phrase *pursuit of happiness* implies that happiness is an object that one has to chase or discover. I don't like that phrase. I prefer to think of the *creation* or *construction* of happiness, because research shows that it's in our power to fashion it for ourselves.

You will learn in these pages that achieving lasting happiness does not necessarily require, as a psychotherapist might tell you, digging deep into your childhood, psychoanalyzing your past traumatic experiences, or dissecting your habitual ways of relating to others. Nor is it essential to secure a bigger paycheck, to obtain a cure from illness, or to recapture youth or beauty. In this book, I describe strategies that you can start doing right away and that will immediately boost your feelings of well-being, even if you are deeply despondent. To *continue* accruing happiness-boosting benefits, you will need to embark on a longer-term program. The good news about a lifelong plan to build and sustain personal happiness is that the effort to do so is greatest when the new behaviors and practices you'll learn don't yet feel natural, but with time the required effort diminishes, as such strategies become habitual and self-reinforcing. *The How of Happiness* describes an ongoing happiness-enhancing program that you might choose to begin today and undertake for the rest of your life. The only person who has the power to make it happen is *you.*

A final note: If you've been diagnosed with depression, this happiness program isn't meant to replace established treatments such as cognitive-behavioral therapy and antidepressant medication. But you should consider it a potent complement, which might help you feel better sooner, stronger, and longer. See the "Postscript: If You Are Depressed" for more.

## Do You Know What Makes You Happy?

At this point you may be feeling skeptical about the happiness program I'm describing. If permanently boosting our happiness is so attainable, so within reach, why, you might ask, are we so poor at it? Why do we try so often and fail? The prime reason, I suspect, is that we have been conditioned to believe that the wrong things will make us lastingly happy. Psychological scientists have amassed persuasive evidence that we are routinely off base about what will bring us pleasure and fulfillment, and as a result, we sometimes work to make things happen that don't actually make us happy.[4] Perhaps the most common error is that we assume that positive events, be they promotions at work, clean bills of health, hot dates, or victories by our preferred presidential candidates or football teams, will provide much more happiness than they really do. Take materialism, the pursuit of money and possessions, as an example. Why is it so hard for us (even myself!) to believe that money really doesn't make us happy? Because the truth is that money *does* make us happy. But our misunderstanding, as one happiness researcher eloquently explains, is that "we think money will bring lots of happiness for a long time, and actually it brings a little happiness for a short time."[5] Meanwhile, in our effortful pursuit of such dead ends to pleasure, we end up ignoring other, more effective routes to well-being.

Consider the cases of two people I interviewed who realized that the things most of us think create happiness—wealth, fame, beauty—don't really matter all that much.


## ROCK STAR

I was introduced to Neil one summer during the filming of a documentary about the lives of very happy people.[6] Neil had wanted to be a rock star when he was young, and against all odds, he actually achieved his dream. As the drummer for a successful folk-rock group, he made a fortune, appeared on *Saturday Night Live*, was nominated for several Grammy awards, and, for a decade, traveled the continents, touring with the band. Then his world abruptly collapsed. The band broke up, the touring stopped, he lost the big house, and his wife left him.

We spent an entire afternoon interviewing Neil at his new modest ranch-style house, with a big pile of dirt blocking the front. The single father and his two small children live on the outskirts of Winnipeg, in sparsely settled prairie country, miles away from the nearest shop or school. Even in July the wind was brisk when we visited, setting the tall, dry grasses blowing. It struck me as the kind of place that must be bitter cold and desolate during the long Manitoba, Canada, winters. A trip for milk, let alone a playdate, must be hard to manage.

Neil immediately struck me as a person completely comfortable and at peace with himself, genuine and at ease with his children, and fully engaged in his music. Did being a wealthy rock star make Neil very happy? "I had it, the money and fame," he said, "and now I don't, but my happiness level is the same. There is no difference."

## EXTREME MAKEOVER

I met Denise on the set of a talk show where she came to tell her story. Denise lives in St. Petersburg, Florida. She used to teach high school kids with learning disabilities, and now she stays home with her three school-age children. It's not easy to be a full-time mother of three kids. Moreover, as she was turning forty, Denise felt that she had let herself go: didn't wear makeup, stopped working out, looked tired all the time. Years spent under the scorching Florida sun had made her look wrinkly, she believed, and much older than her age. She put in an application for *Extreme Makeover* and, to her delight, made it on the show.

The surgery took twelve hours. Denise had an eye lift, an upper and lower forehead lift, and a full face-lift. A bump was taken out of her nose, liposuction done under her chin, and laser resurfacing on her face. The cosmetic changes were so well executed and seamless that the show's makeup artist, who spent at least a half hour working on Denise's face, was floored when I told her that Denise had been on *Extreme Makeover*. She hadn't noticed anything unusual about her reconstructed face.

After the surgical makeover, Denise felt that she had traveled back in time; she looked ten years younger. She received a lot of attention—from family, friends, strangers, media. "I think I was caught up with that," she said. "I had lived like a movie star, and my confidence went overboard." She considered leaving her husband and starting a new life.

A year later Denise came to her senses and realized that giving up her marriage would have been a huge mistake. Did the plastic surgery make her happier? "I do have to say it's nice to have less wrinkles," Denise confessed. But it didn't make her happier in the long run. "The makeover is nothing compared to *real* happiness."

Neil and Denise may have once thought, "If only I were rich . . . If only I were famous . . . If only I were beautiful, I would be happy." They would have been wrong. Intuitions such as theirs, combined with an avalanche of research evidence, have been formalized by my colleagues and me into a theory of the causes of happiness, a theory that has decisive implications for what *you* can do about your happiness, starting today. The story begins in an unlikely Mayan Riviera village.

# Discovering the Real Keys to Happiness

## POSITIVE PSYCHOLOGY IN AKUMAL

In January 2001 I traveled to a beautiful, serene resort in a small town in Mexico, two hours outside Cancún, called Akumal. There, under a palapa and warm breezes, about a dozen or so researchers in the then budding field of positive psychology gathered to share their latest findings and brainstorm new ideas. It was hard for me to concentrate at first; I had left my twenty-month-old daughter behind with her dad in Los Angeles and had just found out that I was pregnant again. Nevertheless, several conversations that I had in Akumal ended up transforming the shape and direction of my work. One of those conversations was with fellow professors Ken Sheldon and David Schkade. I had e-mailed them before the trip and asked if we could meet to talk about writing an article that would categorize the different ways that people pursue happiness. Sitting together, however, we rapidly realized that almost no empirical research existed on this subject. Not only were researchers generally unaware of what strategies people use to become happier, but it became apparent to us that most psychologists were pessimistic about the very notion of permanently increasing happiness. Two findings had caught the imagination of the academic community at that time: first, that happiness is heritable and extremely stable over the course of people's lives, and second, that people have a remarkable capacity to become inured to any positive changes in their lives. Consequently, the logic went, people cannot be made lastingly happier because any gains in happiness would be temporary, and in the long term, most cannot help returning to their original, or baseline, levels of well-being.

## THE 40 PERCENT SOLUTION

Ken, David, and I were skeptical of the conclusion that lasting happiness was impossible and determined to prove that it was wide off the mark. The result of our discussions over the next few years was a discovery about the causes of well-being. Together we were essentially able to identify the most important factors determining happiness, represented in the following simple pie chart.[7]

### *What Determines Happiness?*

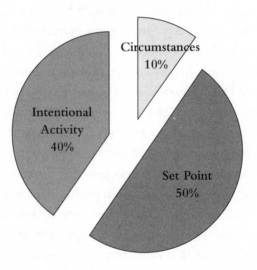

Imagine a movie theater full of a hundred people. These hundred individuals represent the full continuum of happiness: Some are exceptionally happy, others less so, and still others are terribly unhappy. The lower right slice of the pie shows that an astounding 50 percent of the differences among people's happiness levels can be accounted for by their genetically determined *set points*. This discovery comes from the growing research done with identical and fraternal twins that suggests that each of us is born with a particular happiness set point that originates from our biological mother or father or both, a baseline or potential for happiness to which we are bound to return, even after major setbacks or triumphs.[8] This means that if with a magic wand, we could turn all hundred theatergoers into genetic "clones" (or identical twins) of one another, they *still* would differ in their happiness levels, but those differences would be reduced by 50 percent.

The set point for happiness is similar to the set point for weight. Some people are blessed with a skinny dispositions: Even when they're not trying, they easily maintain their weight.[9] By contrast, others have to work extraordinarily hard to keep their weight at a desirable level, and the moment they slack off even a bit, the pounds creep back on. The implication of this finding for happiness is that like genes for intelligence or cholesterol, the magnitude of our innate set points—that is, whether it is high (a six on a seven-point scale) or low (a two) or in between (a four)—governs to a large extent how happy we will be over the course of our lives.

Perhaps the most counterintuitive finding is that as the chart shows, only about 10 percent of the variance in our happiness levels is explained by differences in life circumstances or situations—that is, whether we are rich or poor, healthy or unhealthy, beautiful or plain, married or divorced, etc.[10] If with a magic wand, we could put all hundred moviegoers into the same set of circumstances (same house, same spouse, same place of birth, same face, same aches and pains), the differences in their happiness levels would be reduced by a measly additional 10 percent.

A great deal of science backs up this conclusion. For example, a well-known study demonstrated that the richest Americans, those earning more than ten million dollars annually, report levels of personal happiness only slightly greater than the office staffs and blue-collar workers they employ.[11] And although married people are happier than single ones, the effect of marriage on personal happiness is actually quite small; for example, in sixteen countries, 25 percent of married people and 21 percent of singles described themselves as "very happy."[12] This discovery that the circumstances of our lives (like income and marital status) have such little bearing on our well-being is astonishing to many of us, though Neil and Denise would probably not be surprised. It may be hard to believe that such things as riches, beauty, and perfect health have only a short-term and limited influence on achieving happiness, but the evidence is formidable, and I offer several intriguing explanations for it later in this book. If we can accept as true that life circumstances are *not* the keys to happiness, we'll be greatly empowered to pursue happiness for ourselves.

To get back to the pie chart: Even if all hundred people in the theater were identical twins and all had identical life situations, they *still* would differ in how happy they are. This finding suggests to me that even after we take into account our genetically determined personalities (i.e., who we are) and the rich and complex circumstances of our lives (i.e., what we face), 40 percent of the differences in our happiness levels are still left unexplained. What makes up this 40 percent? Besides our genes and the situations that we confront, there is one critical thing left: our behavior. Thus the key to happiness lies *not* in changing our genetic makeup (which is impossible) and *not* in changing our circumstances (i.e., seeking wealth or attractiveness or better colleagues, which is usually impractical), but in our daily intentional activities. With this in mind, our pie chart illustrates the potential of the 40 percent that is within our ability to control, the 40 percent for room to maneuver, for opportunities to increase or decrease our happiness levels through what we *do* in our daily lives and how we *think*.[13]

This is terrific news. It means that all of us *could* be a great deal happier if we scrutinized carefully what precise behaviors and thoughts very happy people naturally and habitually engage in. Our untapped potential for increasing our own happiness is precisely what much of my research has focused on: systematically observing, comparing, and experimenting on very happy and unhappy people. Below is a sample of my observations, as well as those of other researchers, of the thinking and behavior patterns of the happiest participants in our studies.

- They devote a great amount of time to their family and friends, nurturing and enjoying those relationships.
- They are comfortable expressing gratitude for all they have.
- They are often the first to offer helping hands to coworkers and passersby.

- They practice optimism when imagining their futures.
- They savor life's pleasures and try to live in the present moment.
- They make physical exercise a weekly and even daily habit.
- They are deeply committed to lifelong goals and ambitions (e.g., fighting fraud, building cabinets, or teaching their children their deeply held values).
- Last but not least, the happiest people do have their share of stresses, crises, and even tragedies. They may become just as distressed and emotional in such circumstances as you or I, but their secret weapon is the poise and strength they show in coping in the face of challenge.

As I discuss at greater length in Chapters 4 through 9, a massive literature reveals what kinds of attributes, thoughts, and behaviors characterize the happiest people.[14] In my laboratory and the laboratories of a few others, ways of harnessing the power of our own thoughts and behaviors—that is, our intentional activities—have been tested. We have conducted formal happiness-increasing intervention studies devised to increase and maintain a person's happiness level *over and above his or her set point.*[15] In Part II of this book I introduce a dozen happiness-increasing strategies and practices in detail, showing how they work in everyday life and describing the scientific evidence supporting them. The list of things that very happy people do every day, sampled above, may look intimidating, but that is because you do not, and should not, try to be all those things. No one can do it all, and it is the rare person who can achieve the greater part. What you *can* do is select just one strategy (or a few) that will work for you. *You* are in control and can influence your life from this day forward in a significant and meaningful way. This is where you can begin.

To fashion a successful set of strategies for your individualized happiness program, a vital requirement is wise selection. As with any life-changing endeavor, some programs will be more effective and more appropriate for particular individuals than for others. In Chapter 3, I introduce an important self-diagnostic test, essentially, a questionnaire that will help you identify which strategies will work best for you. Chapter 3 will assist you in choosing the four happiness-boosting strategies that fit your individual personality, your strengths, your goals, and your current situation. Remember that the endeavor to become happier is about *you*—your interests, your values, and your needs. Once you learn which activity will work best for you, you're more than halfway there.

# The Most Rewarding "Work" You'll Ever Do

It may be obvious that to achieve anything substantial in life—learn a profession, master a sport, raise a child—a good deal of effort is required. But many of us find it difficult to apply the notion of effort to our emotional or mental lives. Without effort, we might "get lucky," but like a long-forgotten New Year's resolution, the success will be short-lived.

Consider how much time and commitment many people devote to physical exercise, whether it's going to the gym, jogging, kickboxing, or yoga. My research reveals that if you desire greater happiness, you need to go about it in a similar way. In other words, becoming lastingly happier demands making some permanent changes that require effort and commitment every day of your life. Pursuing happiness takes work, but consider that this "happiness work" may be the most rewarding work you'll ever do.

# Why Be Happy?

Why should we put forth all this effort in order to be happier? In case anyone needed convincing, the scientific evidence reveals many compelling reasons to aspire for greater happiness and fulfillment. My collaborators Ed Diener and Laura King and I have documented a large and growing psychological literature showing that becoming happier doesn't just make you *feel good*.[16] It turns out that happiness brings with it multiple fringe benefits. Compared with their less happy peers, happier people are more sociable and energetic, more charitable and cooperative, and better liked by others. Not surprisingly then, happier people are more likely to get married and to stay married and to have richer networks of friends and social support. Furthermore, contrary to Woody Allen's suggestion in *Annie Hall* that happy people are "shallow and empty, and . . . have no ideas and nothing interesting to say," they actually show more flexibility and ingenuity in their thinking and are more productive in their jobs. They are better leaders and negotiators and earn more money. They are more resilient in the face of hardship, have stronger immune systems, and are physically healthier. Happy people even live longer.

Consider just two of the examples from above: money and marriage. Comedian Henny Youngman once quipped, "What good is happiness? It can't buy money." He was very funny, but he was wrong. One study has shown that those who were happy as college freshmen had higher salaries *sixteen years later* (when they were in their mid-thirties) without an initial wealth advantage.[17] In another study, which also followed undergraduates over time, women who expressed sincere joy in their college yearbook photos were relatively more likely to be married by age twenty-seven and more likely to have *satisfying* marriages at age fifty-two.[18]

Indeed, happiness is so important that an entire country—admittedly a very small country, the size of Switzerland—has made its goal to increase the well-being of its citizens. The king of Bhutan, the last Buddhist kingdom in the Himalayas, nestled between India and China, decided that the best way to foster economic development would be to boost his nation's gross domestic happiness—that is, to focus on the GDH rather than on the GDP. Bhutan's emphasis on the happiness of its people above all else appears to have produced society-wide benefits. Although most people in this tiny country are subsistence farmers, they have what they need—food on the table and universal health care—and have refused to make money from commercial ventures that might compromise the health and beauty of their environment and their egalitarian existence.

In sum, across all the domains of life, happiness appears to have numerous positive by-products that few of us have taken the time to really understand. In becoming happier, we not only boost experiences of joy, contentment, love, pride, and awe but also improve other aspects of our lives: our energy levels, our immune systems, our engagement with work and with other people, and our physical and mental health. In becoming happier, we bolster as well our feelings of self-confidence and self-esteem; we come to believe that we are worthy human beings, deserving of respect. A final and perhaps least appreciated plus is that if we become happier, we benefit not only ourselves but also our partners, families, communities, and even society at large.

# 2.

# How Happy Are You and Why?

Have you ever known someone who is deeply and genuinely happy? A person who truly has the ability to see the world through rose-colored glasses? Someone who appears composed and untroubled even in the face of adversity? Perhaps it is a friend or a coworker or even a member of your family. It's hard not to envy such people. How do they do it? Why aren't they bothered or distraught by the strains and ordeals of everyday life, like most of us?

It's especially frustrating and perplexing to be around such individuals when they're in the same difficult or troubling situation as we are but seem happy in spite of it. Say, for example, that you both share a tormenting boss, a screamer who is never satisfied with your work. Or you both are in the first year of law school and are loaded down with a crushing amount of reading and homework. Or you both are new parents and overwhelmed with the sleep deprivation, anxiety, and drudgery of caring for a newborn. Such situations drag you down, making you moody, nerve-racked, and sometimes even terribly unhappy and low. But this happy person you know seems able to brush off the frustrations, the stresses, the hardships, and the disappointments, to pick herself up each time and to put on a positive face. She sees challenge where you see only threat. She takes an uplifting, optimistic perspective when you feel distrustful and beaten down. She is galvanized to take action, while you are sluggish and passive.

Such individuals may be mind-boggling and intimidating and, yes, even off-putting at times. They can be demoralizing because they make us wonder about our own dispositions. How can we be more like them? Can we ever be as happy as they are? I've asked myself these questions too and decided that the only way to find out is to do some research, to study genuinely happy people systematically and intensively. By closely observing them, we can learn a great deal not just about them but about ourselves.

In my interviews and experiments with very happy people, I've even found a few who remain happy or are able to recover their happiness fairly quickly after tragedies or major setbacks. Take the cases of Angela and Randy.

## ANGELA

Angela is thirty-four and one of the happiest people that I ever interviewed.[1] You wouldn't guess it, however, from all she's had to bear. When Angela was growing up in Southern California, her mother was emotionally and physically abusive to her, and her father did nothing to intervene. In addition to what she endured at home, she was overweight as a teenager and stigmatized at school. When Angela was in eleventh grade, her mother was diagnosed with breast cancer, and the physical abuse ended. However, the emotional abuse got only worse, until Angela couldn't stand it any longer and moved out to marry a man she'd known for just three months. She and her husband moved up north and lived there for four years. Soon after the birth of their daughter, Ella, they divorced, and Angela moved back to California, where she still lives.

Angela is currently a single mother. Things are hard financially. Her ex-husband doesn't visit his daughter and pays no child support. To provide for her small family, Angela has taken a crack at several careers. During her last career change she felt as though she had finally found her dream job (as an aesthetician), but she was fired unexpectedly, her hopes and finances in ruins. She had to file for bankruptcy and go on welfare for a time. Right now she is back in college full-time, working toward a degree in nursing.

Still, with all that has happened and all the challenges that have come to pass, Angela considers herself a very happy person. Her daughter, Ella, to whom she is extremely close, brings her endless joy. They relish reading *The Chronicles of Narnia* together, going to free concerts, and snuggling in bed watching videos. As Angela sees it, Ella doesn't always have what the other kids have, but she gets more love than she could possibly want. Angela also has an infectious sense of humor, and when she laughs about her troubles—the time on welfare, the day she lost her beloved job—it's impossible not to laugh along with her. She has made many friends— indeed, formed a whole community of like-minded people—and they are a pleasure and a support to her. She finds deep satisfaction in helping others heal from their own wounds and traumas, for as she reasons, "It's virtually impossible to face one's shadows alone."

## RANDY

Like Angela, Randy endured a lot as a child. He lost two people close to him to suicide, at age twelve his father and at age seventeen his best friend. When he was in fifth grade, his mother left his father and moved the family out of state and away from everyone he knew in order that she could live with her boyfriend, Roy. Although Randy's bond with his mother was, and still is, strong, Roy belittled Randy, and their relationship was strained. Interestingly, much like Angela, Randy escaped his home life by marrying too soon and too young. His marriage was fraught with difficulty and finally ended when he discovered the extent of his wife's infidelities. Still, he was devastated initially by the breakup and felt that he had had more than his share of loss and death.

Today Randy is one of those happy people who make everyone around them smile and laugh. He picked himself up after his divorce, moved to another city, found work as a safety engineer, and eventually remarried. He is now forty-three, remarried for three years, and step-father to three boys. How did he do it? Randy is an eternal optimist and claims that seeing the "silver lining in the cloud" has always been his key to survival. For example, although some of his coworkers find their jobs frustrating and stressful, he says that his allows him "to think outside the box." Moreover, while a friend of his struggles with stepchildren, Randy is overjoyed by "the opportunity to be a dad." Indeed, one of his favorite activities is watching his sons play football. Others might look back on their childhoods with bitterness, but he remembers the good times.

# Where Do You Fit In?

Although they may appear unique, there are quite a few Randys and Angelas around. Of course, there are many very unhappy individuals as well. All of us can identify people who are exactly the opposite—that is, people who never seem to be happy, even during the good times, who are chronically sullen and sour, who accentuate the negative and focus on the downside of everything, and appear to be unable to find much joy in life.

## SHANNON

One such person I interviewed is Shannon. At twenty-seven Shannon is studying for a certificate to teach English as a second language. She has a boyfriend, who's in school in Italy, and when he returns in two months, they plan to move in together. Growing up, Shannon had an uneventful childhood, a stable and modest home, and several close friends. Her family did a lot of traveling all over the United States. Shannon told me that when she was in eighth grade, her mother gave her a dog, Daisy, still alive today. Shannon considers the dog one of her best friends.

But despite the lack of tragedy or trauma in her life, Shannon seems to turn everything into a crisis. She found the transition from high school to college extremely stressful and often felt crushed and overwrought about the harder and less familiar workload. In the dormitory, she shared a room with a roommate, who was generally a nice person but who had irritating habits, like turning up the volume on the TV. Shannon was incredibly bothered by this and grew more and more distant and hostile toward her roommate. When Shannon finally was able to switch to a new roommate whom she liked and admired, she was ecstatic at first but then became hurt that the other girl "was never around."

Today Shannon is very active. She rock climbs and Rollerblades in the summer and snowboards and skis in the winter. She also told me that she enjoys teaching and thinks there is mutual growth between the children she currently tutors and herself. On the surface, her life is quite good. She has a promising and enjoyable career ahead of her, a boyfriend, a stable family life, even a dog she loves. However, Shannon sees herself as a generally unhappy person. Although she is pleased with her academic achievements, she believes that she can't truly enjoy those achievements because of a lack of self-confidence. Indeed, she minimizes any success by explaining it away as caused by luck or persistence. Sometimes she even is haunted by the feeling that she should have chosen a different career. Overall, Shannon feels very alone and believes her life to be unsteady and her relationships unreliable. She remembers her childhood fondly, as the only time she knew "true happiness" and felt self-assured and carefree. Today she depends a great deal on her boyfriend for positive feelings of self-worth, and she experiences life as "very lonely" when he's not around. She is prone to overspend and overeat at such times. When Shannon feels particularly insecure and hopeless, everything seems dark, and she finds herself sinking into dejection and gloom.

## THE HAPPINESS CONTINUUM

Human happiness, like height or temperature or IQ, lies on a continuum, a numerical scale that ranges from very, very low to very, very high. Shannon represents the lower end of the happiness continuum. Randy and

Angela are at the high end. All of us fit somewhere on that scale, and it is critical to find out where exactly that may be. No matter whether you are deeply depressed or are simply not as happy as you'd like to be, before you can begin the process of becoming happier, you need to determine your present personal happiness level, which will provide your first estimate of your happiness set point.

From the Greek philosopher Aristotle to the father of psychoanalysis Sigmund Freud to *Peanuts* creator Charles Schulz, writers and thinkers have offered wide-ranging definitions of happiness. Aristotle wrote that happiness is "an expression of the soul in considered actions," Freud noted that it's a matter of *lieben und arbeiten*—to love and to work—and Schulz famously proclaimed, "Happiness is a warm puppy." Most of us, however, are well aware of what happiness is and whether we are happy. To paraphrase the late U.S. Supreme Court Justice Potter Stewart, happiness is like obscenity: We can't define it, but we know it when we see it.

I use the term *happiness* to refer to the experience of joy, contentment, or positive well-being, combined with a sense that one's life is good, meaningful, and worthwhile. However, most of us don't need a definition of happiness because we instinctively know whether we are happy or not. Academic researchers prefer the term *subjective well-being* (or simply *well-being*) because it sounds more scientific and does not carry the weight of centuries of historical, literary, and philosophical subtexts.[2] I use the terms *happiness* and *well-being* interchangeably.[3]

So, how do you measure the degree to which you are a happy or an unhappy person? Because no appropriate happiness thermometer exists, researchers generally rely on self-reports. In much of my research with human participants, I have used a popular simple four-item measure of overall happiness that I developed and call the Subjective Happiness Scale.[4] The title is fitting, inasmuch as happiness is inherently subjective and must be defined from the perspective of the person. No one but you knows or should tell you how happy you truly are. So reply to the four items opposite to determine your current happiness level, which you need to know before you can estimate your set point. (More on that later.)

## SUBJECTIVE HAPPINESS SCALE

INSTRUCTIONS: For each of the following statements or questions, please circle the number from the scale that you think is most appropriate in describing you. (Carefully take note of the labels, or anchors, for the 1 to 7 scales, as they differ for each of the four items.)

(1) In general, I consider myself:

| 1 | 2 | 3 | 4 | 5 ✓ | 6 | 7 |
|---|---|---|---|---|---|---|
| not a very happy person | | | | | | a very happy person |

(2) Compared with most of my peers, I consider myself:

| 1 | 2 | 3 | 4 | 5 | 6 ✓ | 7 |
|---|---|---|---|---|---|---|
| less happy | | | | | | more happy |

(3) Some people are generally very happy. They enjoy life regardless of what is going on, getting the most out of everything. To what extent does this characterization describe you?

| 1 | 2 | 3 ✓ | 4 | 5 | 6 | 7 |
|---|---|---|---|---|---|---|
| not at all | | | | | | a great deal |

(4) Some people are generally not very happy. Although they are not depressed, they never seem as happy as they might be. To what extent does this characterization describe you?

| 1 | 2 | 3 | 4 | 5 ✓ | 6 | 7 |
|---|---|---|---|---|---|---|
| a great deal | | | | | | not at all |

### HOW TO CALCULATE YOUR SCORE:

STEP 1: Total = Item 1:__5__ + Item 2:__6__ + Item 3:__3__ + Item 4:__5__ = __19__

STEP 2: Happiness score = Total (from above)__17__ divided by 4 = __4.25__

9/4/30 - 4.7

Date: _____

Happiness score (2nd administration): _____ Date: __4.25_____

Happiness score (3rd administration): _____ Date: __4.7_____

As you may have gathered, the highest happiness score that you can get is 7 (if you give yourself a 7 on all four items) and the lowest is 1 (if you rate yourself 1 on all four items). I have administered this scale to many different groups of people, as have other researchers, and the average score runs from about 4.5 to 5.5, depending on the group. College students tend to score lower (averaging a bit below 5) than working adults and older, retired people (who average 5.6).[5]

Now you have determined the value of your current happiness score. If you're past college age, and your happiness score is lower than 5.6, then you're less happy than the average person. To put it another way, more than 50 percent of people in your age group rate themselves higher on the scale. If your score is greater than 5.6, then you're happier than the average person. Of course, what the "average person" is for you will depend on your gender, your age, your occupation, ethnicity, etc. But what's important to remember is that *no matter what your score is*, you can become happier.

## COULD YOU BE DEPRESSED?

Some of us are likely to be not just slightly unhappy but clinically or sub-clinically depressed. If your happiness score is 4 or lower or if you've been feeling down for more than a couple of weeks, I encourage you to complete a depression scale. (If not, you may choose to skip this subsection.) The depression scale takes less than ten minutes, and those minutes may turn out to be invaluable.

Opposite is a standard, commonly used depression questionnaire called the Center for Epidemiologic Studies Depression Scale, or CES-D.[6] There are many measures of depression, but this one is recommended for use with the general (i.e., nonclinical or nonpsychiatric) population.[7] Follow the instructions to complete the scale and determine your overall depression score.

## CENTER FOR EPIDEMIOLOGIC STUDIES DEPRESSION SCALE

INSTRUCTIONS: This set of questions is related to how you *felt or behaved* in the *past week*. Using the scale below, please write the number which best describes how often you felt or behaved this way *during the past week*.

| 0 | 1 | 2 | 3 |
|---|---|---|---|
| rarely or none of the time (less than 1 day) | some or a little of the time (1–2 days) | a moderate amount of the time (3–4 days) | most or all of the time (5–7 days) |

\_\_\_\_ 1. You were bothered by things that usually don't bother you.

\_\_\_\_ 2. You did not feel like eating; your appetite was poor.

\_\_\_\_ 3. You felt that you could not shake off the blues even with help from your family and friends.

\_\_\_\_ 4. You felt that you were just as good as other people. (X)

\_\_\_\_ 5. You had trouble keeping your mind on what you were doing.

\_\_\_\_ 6. You felt depressed.

\_\_\_\_ 7. You felt that everything you did was an effort.

\_\_\_\_ 8. You felt hopeful about the future. (X)

\_\_\_\_ 9. You thought your life had been a failure.

\_\_\_\_ 10. You felt fearful.

\_\_\_\_ 11. Your sleep was restless.

\_\_\_\_ 12. You were happy. (X)

_____ 13. You talked less than usual.

_____ 14. You felt lonely.

_____ 15. People were unfriendly.

_____ 16. You enjoyed life. (X)

_____ 17. You had crying spells.

_____ 18. You felt sad.

_____ 19. You felt that people disliked you.

_____ 20. You could not get "going."

## HOW TO CALCULATE YOUR SCORE:

STEP 1: Your scores on Items 4, 8, 12, and 16 (the ones marked with an X) should be "reverse-scored"—that is, if you gave yourself a 0, cross it out and change it to a 3; if you gave yourself a 1, change that to a 2; change a 2 to a 1; and change a 3 to a 0.

STEP 2: Using the changed scores for those four items, now add your scores for *all* the 20 items.

Your total depression score is _____.    Date: _____

Your total depression score is _____.    Date: _____

Your total depression score is _____.    Date: _____

The lowest score that you could possibly get is 0 and the highest is 60. Psychologists use the cutoff score of 16 to differentiate depressed persons from nondepressed ones. So, if your score is 16 or higher, you would be classified as depressed. Exactly *how* depressed depends on how high your score is; depression can range from quite mild (a score of 16 to 20) to moderate (a score of 21 to 25) to severe (a score of 26 to 60).[8] Furthermore, unlike the happiness scale, the depression scale is acutely sensitive to your moods and to your general mental state, so that you would be expected to obtain different depression scores at different times, even as close as two weeks apart.

If you are currently depressed or if you've ever been depressed, you are not alone. Studies show that 15 percent of people in the United States (and 21 percent of women[9]) will become clinically depressed at some point during their lifetimes.[10] Of the rest, half report experiencing mild depression occasionally, usually as a result of a major setback or crisis, be it a broken heart, the death of a loved one, a career failure, or a financial loss. Furthermore, the age at which people experience their first depressive episode has decreased dramatically during the last several decades.[11] Incredibly, of *all* diseases, depression places the largest burden on society in the United States (and the fourth-largest disease burden in the world in terms of reduced years of healthy life, after perinatal conditions, lower respiratory diseases like chronic obstructive pulmonary disease, and HIV/AIDS).[12] The World Health Organization predicts that by the year 2020 depression will be the second-leading cause of mortality in the entire world, affecting 30 percent of all adults.[13]

Many experts believe that depression has become an epidemic.[14] By some estimates, clinical depression is ten times more likely to torment us now than it did a century ago.[15] Several forces may be behind this development. First, our expectations about what our lives should be like are greater than ever before; we believe that we can do anything, and we are profoundly disappointed when reality doesn't meet or even come close to perfection. Second, our increasingly individualistic culture leaves us all alone to manage our everyday stresses and problems, compelling us to blame only ourselves for our shortcomings and failures. Increasing job insecurity also contributes to the many stressors of modern life. And perhaps most important may be the unraveling of the social fabric. Compared with previous generations, we feel far less belonging and commitment to our families and communities and are thus less buffered by social support and strong meaningful connections to others. All these factors may combine to make more of us clinically depressed than ever before.

If you have scored as depressed, I encourage you to see a mental health professional—a psychiatrist, clinical psychologist, or licensed counselor with whom you can discuss your options for treatment, including psychotherapy and antidepressant medication. Moderate to severe depression, especially, requires urgent attention from a professional. If you are depressed, you will also likely greatly benefit from the happiness-increasing strategies described in Part II of this book. Additionally, if you have scored in the depressed range, be sure to skip ahead and read the "Postscript" chapter ("If You Are Depressed") before continuing to learn about those strategies, as you will need to know how to adapt the happiness program to your unique symptoms, feelings, and needs.

# Happiness Myths

No matter where you fall on the happiness and depression scales—whether you are rarely happy, occasionally happy, or even fairly happy—you will learn how to apply to your own strengths and weaknesses the happiness-enhancing strategies that I teach you, in order to make yourself permanently happier and more fulfilled. But before you can start incorporating those strategies into your own life, I need to dispel a number of myths surrounding happiness.

One of the great obstacles to attaining happiness is that most our beliefs about what will make us happy are in fact erroneous. Yet they have been drummed into us, socialized by peers and families and role models and reinforced by the stories and images ever present in our culture. Many of the presumed sources of happiness seem so intuitive and so commonsensical that all of us—even happiness researchers!—are prone to fall under their spell. This is where science can shine a clear and vivid light. The three major myths about happiness that we tend to fall for are plainly illuminated by the happiness pie chart, which I here reproduce.

### *What Determines Happiness?*

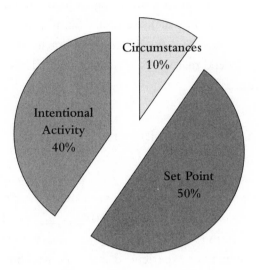

## MYTH NO. 1: HAPPINESS MUST BE "FOUND"

The first myth is that happiness is something that we must *find*, that it's out there somewhere, a place just beyond our reach, a kind of Shangri-la. We could get there, yes, but only if the right things would come to pass: if we'd marry our true loves, secure our dream jobs, purchase elegant houses. Don't be the person who is waiting for this, that, or the other thing to happen before she can be happy. There's a cartoon in which a little boy on a tricycle says to a playmate holding a kite, "I can't wait to grow up and be happy."[16] If you're not happy today, then you won't be happy tomorrow unless you take things into your own hands and take action. To understand that 40 percent of our happiness is determined by intentional activity is to appreciate the promise of the great impact that you can make on your own life through intentional strategies that *you* can implement to remake yourself as a happier person.

Happiness is not out there for us to find. The reason that it's not *out* there is that it's *inside* us. As banal and clichéd as this might sound, happiness, more than anything, is a state of mind, a way of perceiving and approaching ourselves and the world in which we reside. So, if you want to be happy tomorrow, the day after, and for the rest of your life, you can do it by choosing to change and manage your state of mind. These steps lie at the heart of this book.

## MYTH No. 2: HAPPINESS LIES IN CHANGING OUR CIRCUMSTANCES

Another big fallacy is the notion that if only something about the circumstances of our lives would change, then we would be happy. This kind of thinking is what I call "I would be happy IF _____" or "I will be happy WHEN _____." This logic is shared by some of us who remember periods in our lives when we experienced real happiness but think that we could never recapture the exact set of circumstances that brought this real happiness about. Perhaps these were the college years (as they were for me, at least in hindsight), or when we fell in love for the first time, or when our children were young, or when we lived abroad. The reality is that the elements that determined our happiness in the past, and can make for future happiness, are with us right now and are right here waiting to be taken advantage of. As we can see from the pie chart, changes in our circumstances, no matter how positive and stunning, actually have little bearing on our well-being.

## MYTH No. 3: YOU EITHER HAVE IT OR YOU DON'T

One day my brother, who's an electrical engineer, told me that he had read an article about Buddhist monks who taught themselves to be happy through meditation. "What a new concept!" he exclaimed. "I never thought you could *teach* yourself to be happy. I thought you either have it or you don't." This notion—that we are born happy or unhappy—is ubiquitous. Many of us, especially those of us who are not very happy, believe that our unhappiness is genetic and there's really nothing we can do about it. To the contrary, growing research demonstrates persuasively that we can overcome our genetic programming.

In the rest of the chapter we'll consider each of these fallacies more deeply. Let's start by examining exactly what it is that scientists have learned about the ways that the circumstances of our lives do and do not influence us.

# The Limits of Life Circumstances

Life circumstances include, to quote Herman Melville, "the wife, the heart, the bed, the table, the saddle, the fire-side, the country." Consider the incidental but stable facts about your life: your gender, age, and ethnicity; where you grew up; which significant events shaped your childhood and adolescence (e.g., on the negative side: parental divorce, car accident, stigma, bullying; on the positive side: family harmony, winning an award, being popular); and which significant events have taken place in adulthood. Are you married, single, divorced, widowed, or separated? What are your occupation, income, and religious affiliation? What kind of living conditions and neighborhood do you live in? Have you ever been diagnosed with a chronic or acute illness? Or, as Shakespeare might ask, have you suffered the slings and arrows of outrageous fortune?

As significant as our major life events are to each of us, studies suggest that they actually determine, as the pie chart shows us, a tiny percentage of our happiness. The 10 percent figure represents an average from many past investigations, which reveal that all life circumstances and situations put together account for only about 10 percent in how happy different people are. So, although you may find it very hard to believe, whether you drive to work in a Lexus hybrid or a battered truck, whether you're young or old, or have had wrinkle-removing plastic surgery, whether you live in the frigid Midwest or on the balmy West Coast, your chances of being happy and becoming happier are pretty much the same.[17] How could this be?

## MATERIAL WEALTH

Consider material wealth—your monthly income, nest egg, assets, and possessions. For the moment, let's assume that by virtue of your being able to afford to buy this book and to have the leisure time to read it, your household stands above the U.S. national median in income.[18] A compelling case can be made that the level of material comfort (or lack thereof) you are experiencing today is equivalent to how the top 5 percent lived a half century ago![19] Recently, while reading *No Ordinary Time*, Doris Kearns Goodwin's fine book about the Roosevelts, I ran across a description of what life was like in the United States in 1940.[20] Approximately one-third of all homes in 1940 did not have running water, indoor toilets, or bathtub/showers, and more than half had no central heating. If you were twenty-five years or older in 1940, you would have stood only a 40 percent chance of having completed the eighth grade, a 25 percent chance of having graduated from high school, and only a 5 percent chance of having finished college.

When asked to rate their overall satisfaction with life, Americans in 1940 reported being "very happy," with an average score of 7.5 out of 10.[21] However, times have changed. The typical house today not only has running water, two or more baths, and central heating but is twice the size, with an average of two rooms per person, not to mention being equipped with microwave ovens, dishwashers, color TVs, DVD players, iPods, and personal computers. And real monthly personal income has more than doubled. So what is the average score for Americans' happiness today? It's 7.2.[22]

Apparently, all that extra space and those gadgets and appliances don't really make us happy, even if we think they will.[23] How many of us have ever said, "If only I had [fill in blank here], I would be so happy!" I have said that many times myself, as a teenager before owning my first car, as a student before I could afford to live alone, and as a parent before each of my kids had his or her own bedroom. (They still don't.)

Very wealthy people have a great deal more than the average person, but the research shows that they are not much happier. Consider Michael Ovitz, former president of the Walt Disney Company. In the *Los Angeles Times*, columnist Steve Lopez reported on Ovitz's plans to build a 28,059-square-foot mansion for his wife and him. This home will have the world's largest basement (13,974 square feet), a separate 4,997-square-foot office with guest quarters, a 2,407-square-foot covered tennis pavilion, a garage big enough to accommodate thirteen cars, a yoga room, and an art gallery.[24] I would bet that if Mr. Ovitz were to complete the Subjective Happiness Scale and e-mail it to me, his overall score would be no higher than that of my neighbor who teaches middle school and lives in a pleasant but tiny studio apartment.

**Materialism and its costs.** As I write this, the high-end department store Macy's is unleashing its newest advertising campaign. Each of its full-page full-color advertisements features a single beautiful model—dressed in a new cashmere sweater, holding a spanking new handbag, wearing tight jeans—with the tagline "What makes you happy?" If only we could acquire the sweater, handbag, or jeans, the ad suggests, we all would be bursting with joy! Frank Lloyd Wright observed: "Many wealthy people are little more than the janitors of their possessions."[25] You too could become a janitor of your possessions, if your goals primarily revolved around material things. Indeed, not only does materialism not bring happiness, but it's been shown to be a strong predictor of *unhappiness*. Researchers examined the attitudes of twelve thousand college freshmen at elite colleges and universities in 1976, when they were eighteen years old on average, and then measured their life satisfaction at age thirty-seven.[26] Those who had expressed materialistic aspirations as freshmen—that is, making money was their primary goal—were less satisfied with their lives two decades later. Furthermore, materialists are more likely than nonmaterialists to suffer from a variety of mental disorders![27]

One of the reasons for the failure of materialism to make us happier may be that even when people finally attain their monetary goals, the achievement doesn't translate into an increase in happiness.[28] Also, materialism may distract people from relatively more meaningful and joyful aspects of their lives, such as nurturing their relationships with family and friends, enjoying the present, and contributing to their communities. Finally, materialistic people have been found to hold unrealistically high expectations of what material things can do for them.[29] One father confided to me that he believed that purchasing a forty-two-inch flat-panel TV would improve his relationship with his eleven-year-old son. It didn't.

Few of us would own up that a wide-screen television, a Sub-Zero refrigerator, and a seven-foot-high SUV have noticeably improved their lives. (My husband, who is chopping vegetables while I write this, just shouted to say that he would be really, really happy if only he had a kitchen island!) Yet most people still report that "more money" would definitely enhance the quality of their lives.[30] Since 1967 an annual study called the American Freshman Survey has probed the attitudes and plans of freshmen all around the United States. In its last year—2005—263,710 students at 385 colleges and universities responded. A record high number of freshmen, 71 percent, said it's very important to be "very well off financially," compared with 42 percent in 1967.[31] Interestingly, only 52 percent of current freshmen admitted that it was very important or essential for them to "develop a meaningful philosophy of life," compared with 86 percent in 1967.

Of course the more those college freshmen attain, the more they'll want. Those with salaries of under $30,000 per year claim that $50,000 would thrill them, whereas those who earn more than $100,000 say they need $250,000 to be satisfied.[32] If they only knew how the wealthy truly felt. In a study of 792 well-off adults, more than half reported that wealth didn't bring them more happiness, and a third of those with assets greater than $10 million said that money bought more problems than it solved.[33] Indeed, although those with higher incomes report being somewhat more satisfied with their lives, studies of how they actually spend their days find that they don't spend time in any more enjoyable activities than their less prosperous peers and, in fact, are more likely to experience daily anxiety and anger.[34] A wise (and rich) person once said, "I've never borrowed a significant amount of money in my life . . . [because] I never thought I would be way happier when I had 2X instead of X."[35]

## BEAUTY

Before I explain why having a huge amount of money isn't going to make most of you sustainably happy, I'd like to mention one other life circumstance that does not correlate with happiness, and that is physical attractiveness. Even I, as a seemingly objective scientist, have trouble believing that being very beautiful wouldn't make me happier. But would it?

The American Society for Aesthetic Plastic Surgery reports that more and more of us are remaking our appearances every year. The year 2004 saw an increase of 44 percent in the number of cosmetic procedures over 2003, including a record 2.8 million Botox injections, 1.1 million chemical peels, and hundreds of thousands of breast augmentations, eyelid surgeries, nose reshapings, and liposuctions.[36] Most people report being satisfied with their postsurgery physical appearances—but only for short periods of time.[37] The happiness boost is not likely to endure.

One explanation for why a cosmetic enhancement doesn't bring abiding happiness—and, in general, why being beautiful doesn't have a stronger effect on our well-being—is that we simply don't focus on our appearance when thinking about how happy we are. A fascinating study that investigated how people in the Midwest versus California were affected by their local weather backs up this argument. Researchers were interested in whether people who live in California are truly happier (as many believe) than those who live in the Midwest.[38] To this end, they asked college students at two California colleges and two midwestern ones to rate their satisfaction with their lives overall and their satisfaction with *the weather*. The former is a judgment of deep, overall well-being, and the latter is a judgment of a more transient feeling. It turned out that *both* the Californians and the midwesterners believed that people in California were happier. But they were not. There was absolutely no difference in the overall satisfaction of the two groups of students.

However, an enormous difference emerged in the students' ratings of their satisfaction with the weather. Midwesterners were much less happy with the summer weather they experienced and much, *much* less happy with their winter weather. Indeed, the midwesterners were significantly less satisfied than Californians with a number of other aspects of their lives, such as personal safety, outdoor activities, and the natural beauty of their surroundings. So why weren't they less happy overall? Because, the researchers explained, people don't focus on such things as the weather or their personal safety—or any single aspect of their lives, for that matter—when they try to figure out how happy they are overall. While it's not fun to be cold and wet, being cold and wet doesn't make you believe that you're unhappy. I submit that the same phenomenon occurs with regard to physical attractiveness. If beautiful people were asked if they were happy with their looks, they'd say "sure." But if they were asked if they were happy overall, their looks would have a minimal, if any, effect on their judgment.

My assertion that there's no link between beauty and happiness implies that beautiful people are no happier than their plain-looking relatives, colleagues, and friends. That happens to be true. Ed Diener and his coinvestigators did a series of very nice studies that, in my opinion, definitively resolve this issue.[39] Using a multimethod approach, dragging happy and unhappy undergraduate volunteers into the lab, Diener and others photographed and videotaped them and then showed the photos and videos to a panel of judges to rate them on physical attractiveness. In some of the studies Diener and colleagues instructed participants to come "as they are," and in others, they were asked to come "unadorned," removing all cosmetics and jewelry and with their clothing and hair covered. The latter was accomplished by having the unwitting participant don a white shower cap (to cover all hair) and a white laboratory coat (to conceal clothing) or to insert her head in an oval cutout of a big piece of cardboard, kind of like the ones in cheesy amusement parks that offer the chance to be photographed with the body of a muscleman or princess, but the cardboard in this study was just blank and white.

If you are thinking that this is an odd setup for a laboratory study, it is. But it allowed Diener to study the happiness/attractiveness link. Are happier participants actually "objectively" more attractive (as rated by judges who saw their photos or videos), or do they simply have higher opinions of their own handsomeness or beauty?

The results were revealing. Although the happiest participants tended to believe that they were attractive, the objective judges did not regard them as any nicer-looking than their less happy peers. Interestingly, this finding was even more pronounced when the participants were "unadorned," suggesting that happy people may be particularly skilled at enhancing their natural beauty.

So, the bottom line is that good-looking people aren't any happier. Of course this brings up the question of which comes first, the chicken or the egg, thinking you're beautiful or being happy. There's evidence that happy people are somewhat more likely to perceive *everything* about their lives, including their appearances, in more positive, optimistic ways.[40] But other people don't rate them as more physically striking, at least when viewed in a photograph or a ten-minute video, and especially not when their faces are sticking through a cardboard cutout!

So beauty is not associated with happiness. Becoming objectively more beautiful will not make most of you happier. Coming to *believe* that you are beautiful is another story, and research suggests that this may be one of many happiness boosters.

## THE CURIOUS AND POWERFUL PHENOMENON OF HEDONIC ADAPTATION

> When I am in New York, I want to be in Europe, and when
> I am in Europe, I want to be in New York.
>
> —*Woody Allen*

One of the great ironies of our quest to become happier is that so many of us focus on changing the circumstances of our lives in the misguided hope that those changes will deliver happiness. In an attempt to allay unhappiness, a recent college graduate may choose a high-paying job in a distant city, a middle-aged divorcée may undergo beautifying cosmetic surgery, or a retired couple may buy a condominium with a view. Unfortunately, all these individuals will likely become only temporarily happier. An impressive body of research now shows that trying to be happy by changing our life situations ultimately will not work.

Why do life changes account for so little? Because of a very powerful force that psychologists call hedonic adaptation.[41]

Human beings are remarkably adept at becoming rapidly accustomed to sensory or physiologic changes. When you walk in from the bitter cold, the warmth of the crackling fire feels heavenly at first, but you quickly get used to it and may even become overheated. When a mild but conspicuous odor dwells in your apartment, you may completely fail to notice it until you have left for a while and returned. This experience is labeled physiological or sensory adaptation. The same phenomenon, however, occurs with hedonic shifts—that is, relocations, marriages, job changes—that make you happier for a time, but only a short time. To give a concrete example, I had laser eye surgery at age thirty-six, after a lifetime of near blindness, discomfort with contact lenses, and loathing of glasses. The result was miraculous. For the first time in memory, I could read street signs, tell time when waking in the middle of the night, and see my toes in the shower. The surgery made me wonderfully happy. Remarkably, however, after about two weeks I was completely and perfectly adapted to my new 20/20 vision, and it no longer provided the happiness boost it had on that memorable first day. Nearly everyone has stories like this: about moving into a bigger house, securing a promotion or a pay raise, getting a makeover, or flying first class. Research psychologists have even tried to bottle this experience by investigating it systematically—for example, asking whether people show hedonic adaptation to such significant life events as marriage, sudden wealth, or chronic illness. It turns out they do.

## THE ALTAR, THE LOTTERY, AND A HOUSE IN THE 'BURBS

Any happy newlywed will wonder how it could be possible to adapt to the benefits of matrimony. Indeed, every married person reading this has undoubtedly grasped the enormous, life-changing impact of marriage. In fact, studies show that married people are significantly happier than their single peers.[42] Numerous anecdotal examples, including mine, prove the point: Getting married was one of the best things that I have ever done, and I am absolutely convinced that I am happier now than before.

Yet psychological researchers have evidence to prove me wrong. In a landmark study, residents of West Germany and East Germany, including citizens, immigrants, and foreigners—25,000 in all—were surveyed every year for fifteen years.[43] Over the course of the study, 1,761 individuals got married and stayed married. Using this spectacular data set, scientists showed that alas, marriage has only a temporary effect on happiness. It appears that after the wedding husband and wife get a happiness boost for about two years and then simply return to their baseline in happiness, their set point. It seems wise not to share this bit of news with newlyweds.

Several lines of research suggest that a similar phenomenon occurs with the attainment of money and possessions. In a classic study conducted back in the 1970s, psychologists interviewed some lucky individuals who had won between fifty thousand and one million dollars (in 1970s dollars) in the Illinois State Lottery.[44] Strikingly, less than a year after receiving the potentially life-changing news of winning the lottery, they reported being no more happy than regular folks who had not experienced the sudden windfall. Indeed, the lottery winners mused that they now derived less enjoyment from day-to-day activities, such as watching television or going out to lunch, relative to the nonwinners.

Why does hedonic adaptation occur? The two biggest culprits are rising aspirations (e.g., the bigger house you buy after your windfall feels natural after a while; you experience a sort of "creeping normalcy" and begin to want an even bigger one) and social comparison (e.g., your new friends in the new neighborhood are driving BMWs and you feel you should too). As a result, even as people amass more of what they want with every year, their overall happiness tends to stay the same. To paraphrase the Red Queen in *Through the Looking-Glass*, "We're running faster and faster, but we seem to end up in exactly the same place."

My friend Dianna is a walking case study in hedonic adaptation. When she married her husband, he was still a graduate student, and for a year they shared a single tiny dormitory room, lacking a kitchen, with their new baby and Dianna's mother. I remember thinking how insanely difficult this must have been: her husband laboring to finish his dissertation, the baby crying in the middle of the night, a mother-in-law sleeping a couple of feet away. Years later the family, now with three beautiful girls, moved to a tidy bedroom community north of San Diego, with a neighborhood pool and an excellent public school. Their house is lovely and new—two stories, four bedrooms, family room, enormous yard with playground set. A few months after they settled in, Dianna called to tell me about a house three doors down from them that had just gone on the market. It was identical to theirs, but it had an extra bedroom and an extra patio where one could mount a barbecue. She was obsessed with this house, ruminating about every possible way that it was superior to theirs. Could they afford to buy it? Maybe they could. Could they? Maybe somehow they could. . . .

So the bad news about hedonic adaptation is that it ultimately dampens your happiness and satisfaction after any positive event or uplift. But there is good news too. I would argue that human beings are actually lucky to have the ability to adapt quickly to changing circumstances, as it's extremely useful when *bad* things happen. Some studies of hedonic adaptation show, for instance, that we have a phenomenal ability to recover much of our happiness after a debilitating illness or accident.

Do you think that having end-stage kidney disease would reduce your capacity for happiness? Imagine having to endure *nine hours* of hemodialysis per week, during which you are attached to a machine filtering your blood. Imagine having to adhere to a strict diet, limiting meat, salt, and even daily fluids. Most people are positive that this situation would make them quite unhappy. Researchers put their belief to empirical test.[45] Two groups of people—healthy participants and dialysis patients—were asked to carry for a week PalmPilots that would beep them randomly every ninety minutes. After each beep, the participant was required to punch in the mood that he happened to be experiencing at that very moment (pleased? joyful? anxious? unhappy?). The average of a person's mood ratings gathered over the course of a week happens to be an excellent indicator of his general well-being because such ratings are unlikely to be edited, filtered, or otherwise biased. It turned out that the renal disease patients were just as happy as the healthy controls. It seems that they adapted quite well to their condition. But the healthy participants truly believed that they would be less happy if they had to undergo regular dialysis, and even the patients themselves lacked insight into their own miraculous capacity for hedonic adaptation; they were certain they'd be happier if they had not had to endure the disease.

Amazing as it may seem, people show a great deal of adaptation to disabilities like paralysis and blindness and other conditions that involve losing an important capacity or function. Consider a multiple sclerosis patient whose disease, as it developed, was transformed from something frightening to something manageable. Although with time Ernest could no longer drive, run, walk, or even stand, these things "lost much of their importance. . . . [They] are no longer within the sphere of possibility and are therefore not missed as though they were possible." He explained his change in perspective this way: "Gradual changes have taken place in my outlooks, in my likes and dislikes, in what I feel to be a natural part of my life and in what I had always regarded as a necessity for happiness. . . . Probably had I known in 1956 what would be the symptoms that have appeared by now, I would have been anxious about and discouraged by the prospect of the future. Now that I actually find myself here, however, it seems that things are not nearly so bad as I would have thought then."[46]

## SUMMING UP

We cannot and will not adapt to everything. But the evidence for hedonic adaptation, especially with regard to positive events, is very strong. Human beings adapt to favorable changes in wealth, housing, and possessions, to being beautiful or being surrounded by beauty, to good health, and even to marriage. The only exception that I would argue is the effects of having children. As a mother of two I can attest that the first time you cuddle with your child, it feels wonderful. The thousandth time, it feels—oh, maybe 95 percent as wonderful.

# The Happiness Set Point

I hope that you have now accepted the fact that the specifics of your life circumstances, unless they are truly dire, are really not the crux of your unhappiness. If you're unhappy with your job, your friends, your marriage, your salary, or your looks, the first step you should take toward reaching greater lasting happiness is to put those things aside in your mind for now. Hard as it is, try not to reflect on them. Keep reminding yourself that these things are really not what is preventing you from getting happier. It will take a great deal of discipline and self-control, and you may lapse, but it's important to unlearn this commonly held but false belief.

One of my guilty pastimes is reading newspaper advice columns. Some months ago a woman wrote in to my local paper, complaining about every job that she's ever had. At her first job she was plagued by spiteful, gossipy coworkers, at her second it was an overbearing boss, at her third it was utter monotony, and so on. She appealed for help in finding a job she likes. The wise advice columnist's blunt reply was something like this: "It's not the colleagues or the boss or the nature of the work; it's something that *you're* doing!"

If the cause of your unhappiness is really not your circumstances, then surely it must be that you were just born this way. This is also a fallacy, the myth of "you either have it or you don't." Challenging the veracity of this belief is trickier because you see, it is partly true. As the pie chart illustrates, your genetically determined predisposition for happiness (or unhappiness) accounts for 50 percent of the differences between you and everyone else. Notably, a susceptibility to clinical depression has also been found to be partly rooted in our genetic makeups. Before we get depressed about being born depressed, however, I'd like to highlight one vital implication of these findings: that those of us who wish we were a great deal happier should be a little less hard on ourselves. We are, after all, dealing with a stacked deck to some extent. Another critical step in clearing the way to committing to becoming happier is to appreciate the fact that 50 percent is a long way from 100 percent, and that leaves ample room for improvement. So how exactly do we know that the happiness set point accounts for 50 percent?

## HELEN AND AUDREY

The strongest evidence for the set point comes from a series of fascinating studies done with identical and fraternal twins. The reason that studying twins reveals so much about the genetics of happiness is that twins share specifically known portions of their genetic material; identical twins share 100 percent, and fraternal twins (like regular siblings) 50 percent. So, by measuring the degree to which twins are similar in their happiness levels, we can infer how much of their happiness is likely rooted in their genes.

One of the most famous twin studies, the Happiness Twins study, was carried out by behavior geneticists David Lykken, Auke Tellegen, and colleagues at the University of Minnesota. Using data from the Minnesota Twin Registry, they have followed a large number of mostly Caucasian twins born in Minnesota.[47] Let's consider two participants from their study, Helen and Audrey, who are thirty years old and identical twins, born in St. Paul.[48] Suppose our task was to guess how happy Audrey is, and we are given information about her life during the past ten years. A lot happened: She graduated from Carleton College in Northfield, Minnesota, and launched a career in graphic design; she had a long-term relationship that didn't work out, then started another one with the man who is now her husband of two years. The couple recently moved to Chicago and live together in a two-bedroom apartment. She's not religious, but she considers herself a spiritual person.

If we wanted to figure out (or "predict," as psychologists would say) how happy Audrey is from examining her life over the last decade, we wouldn't do very well. The correlation between happiness and income (or occupation or religiosity or marital status) is very small. In the Happiness Twins study, for example, income accounted for less than 2 percent of the variance in well-being, and marital status accounted for less than 1 percent. However, if we tried to guess how happy Audrey is by considering the happiness level of her twin sister, Helen, who still lives in St. Paul, we'd be much more accurate. In fact, if we considered Helen's happiness level ten years ago—at age twenty!—that level would be very close to Audrey's happiness today.

In other words, the average happiness of your identical twin (even if assessed ten years earlier) is a much more powerful clue to your happiness today than *all the facts and events* of your life!

However, to be completely sure of their striking findings of the comparable levels of the happiness of identical twins, researchers had to compare the happiness of fraternal twins as well. Recall that fraternal twins are one-half as genetically similar to each other as are identical twins. Interestingly, the researchers found that if Helen and Audrey had been fraternal twins and thus no more alike than any two sisters, you could *not* guess Audrey's happiness from knowing Helen's. Whether or not your fraternal twin (or any other sibling) is happy or unhappy implies nothing about how happy or unhappy you might be. This fact—that identical twins (but not fraternal ones) share similar happiness levels—suggests that happiness is largely genetically determined. Indeed, the present-day consensus among researchers, based on a growing number of twin studies, is that the heritability of happiness is approximately 50 percent; hence the 50 percent slice of the pie on my pie chart.

## SEPARATED AT BIRTH

There's a significant problem with such twin studies, however. To make conclusions from them, the researchers must assume that both types of twins—identical and fraternal—experience similar family environments. But is this really true? Unlike identical twins, fraternal twins of the same sex often look and behave quite differently. Thus their parents, teachers, and friends are likely to treat them differently, and the twins themselves are likely to emphasize their uniqueness. So the environment and upbringing of fraternal twins are not really as closely shared as those of identical twins.

Fortunately, this problem can be addressed by doing a different kind of study altogether. Researchers can compare twins raised together with twins separated in infancy and raised apart. This is a tough-to-find sample, but one researcher managed to assemble a set of such twins who had already reached middle age and asked them to complete measures of well-being.[49] Their findings have been deemed a classic in psychology. The identical twins were extremely similar to each other in their happiness scores, and remarkably, the similarity was no smaller if the twins had been raised apart! The happier one identical twin was, the happier the other was—no matter whether they grew up under the same roof or on different coasts. Interestingly, however, regardless of whether they were raised together or apart, the happiness levels of the *fraternal* twins were completely uncorrelated. Like any siblings, fraternal twins do not resemble each other in their average levels of happiness. Again, these findings are fascinating, underscoring the conclusion that happiness is, to a large extent, influenced by genetic factors, that each one of us inherits a pre-programmed set point. But the research also shows us that yes, while 50 percent of the differences among our happiness levels is determined by set points (and 10 percent, let's not forget, by circumstances), fully 40 percent is still available to us to mold.

I've probably come across the twins data a dozen times, yet they freshly surprise me each time I see them. I picture two little identical twin boys separated at birth and growing up to be teenagers and then men with different parents and siblings, in different homes, schools, and cities. I imagine them meeting each other for the first time in their thirties or forties and being floored at how similar they are. The Minnesota Twin Registry has documented many such meetings, and the stories are probably familiar enough to have entered the national consciousness. The most famous case is that of two men—both named James—who encountered each other for the first time at age thirty-nine.[50] The day they met, both were six feet tall and weighed exactly 180 pounds. Each smoked Salems, drank Miller Lite, and habitually bit his fingernails. When they discussed their life histories, some incredible coincidences emerged. Both had married women named Linda, had divorced them, and then remarried women named Betty. Each James enjoyed leaving love notes to his wife throughout the house (though perhaps both Lindas didn't appreciate it enough). Their firstborn sons were also named James, one James Alan and the other James Allen, and both men had named their dogs Toy. Each James had owned a light blue Chevrolet and had driven it to the same beach in Florida (Pass-a-Grille Beach) for family vacations. I would bet anything that they were equally happy (or unhappy).

## Do Genes Predestine Us to Be Happy or Unhappy?

No matter which way we look at it, the empirical data from the Happiness Twins study led to the conclusion that the genetic basis for happiness is strong—very strong. It appears that each of us is born with a happiness set point, a characteristic potential for happiness throughout our lives. The magnitude of that set point may originate from the sunny maternal side of our family or our depressive paternal side, or roughly equally from both; we'll never know. The essential point is that even if major life changes, like a new relationship or a car accident, might push our happiness level up or down, we tend to revert to this genetically determined set point. Evidence for this phenomenon comes from studies that follow people over time as they react to good and bad things happening in their lives. For example, one study tracked Australian citizens every two years from 1981 to 1987 and found that positive and negative life events (e.g., "made lots of new friends," "got married," "experienced serious problems with children," or "became unemployed") influenced their feelings of happiness and satisfaction as we would expect. But after the events had passed, their feelings returned to their original baselines.[51] Another study conducted in the United States with undergraduates showed essentially the same thing. The big and small events experienced by these students boosted or deflated their well-being, but only for about three months.[52] So, although you may be made temporarily ecstatic or miserable by what comes to pass, it seems that you can't help eventually returning to your set point. And as far as anyone knows, this set point *cannot be changed*. It is fixed, immune to influence or control.

*But just because your happiness set point cannot be changed doesn't mean that your happiness level cannot be changed.*

In *The African Queen*, Katharine Hepburn declares to Humphrey Bogart, "Nature, Mr. Allnut, is what we are put in this world to rise above!" We can rise above our happiness set points, just as we can rise above our set points for weight or cholesterol. Although on the face of it, the set point data appear to suggest that we all are subject to our genetic pro-gramming, that we all are destined to be only as happy as that "program-ming" allows, in actuality they do not. Our genes do not *determine* our life experience and behavior. Indeed, our "hard wiring" can be dramatically influenced by our experience and our behavior. This is illustrated, as I describe in detail later, by the notion that there's a great deal of room to improve our happiness by the things we *do*, our intentional activities. Even the most heritable traits like height, which has a heritability level of .90 (relative to about .50 for happiness), can be radically modified by environ-mental and behavioral changes. For example, since the 1950s the average height of Europeans has been growing at a rate of two centimeters per decade, in part because of better overall nutrition.[53]

Or take the case of a rare condition known as phenylketonuria. PKU stems from a mutation in a single gene on chromosome 12 and, without treatment, leads to brain damage, resulting in mental retardation and pre-mature death.[54] PKU is said to have a heritability of 1, because it is *entirely* genetically determined. But this doesn't mean that an infant born with the gene that causes PKU is doomed to its lethal effects. If the parents ensure that the infant's diet is free of an amino acid called phenylalanine, which is found in such common foods as eggs, milk, bananas, and NutraSweet, the brain damage may be entirely prevented. It's important to note that the infant's genetic endowment doesn't change—she will always carry the mutant gene—but the expression of her genetic endow-ment *can* change.

I make much the same case for happiness. If you are born with a low set point for happiness, the genes coding for that set point will always be a part of you. However, for those genes to be fully expressed, they must encounter the appropriate, fitting environment, much the way a seed requires a particular soil to grow. In fact, there is a powerful study that shows just what a dramatic effect one particular environmental factor can have on whether or not people who have a "depression gene" actually succumb to depression. That environmental factor is severe stress.

## THE CASE OF THE "DEPRESSION GENE"

When I was an undergraduate, I was a research assistant for a psychology professor named Paul Andreassen. Paul was a good friend of another professor, Avshalom Caspi, who dropped by our lab on a regular basis. At the time I was in awe of research, of professors, indeed of anything having to do with Harvard, and I remember Avshalom as a dark, striking figure with long hair and an Israeli accent. Little did I know that years later and a continent away, along with his future wife and collaborator, Terri Moffitt, he would conduct a truly groundbreaking study.[55] Caspi, Moffitt, and their colleagues at King's College in London were interested in the relationship between stress and depression. Why do stressful life experiences, like being evicted from one's apartment or losing a pregnancy, trigger depression in some people but not in others?

It turns out that depression is associated with a particular gene, called the 5-HTTLPR, which comes in two forms, the long and the short. The short allele is undesirable to have, because it rids the brain of a substance needed to fend off depressive symptoms.[56] Caspi tracked the presence of this so-called bad gene in a sample of 847 infants born in New Zealand and learned that more than half carried it. At the time of the study, because those infants were now twenty-six years old, the researchers were able to identify the number of stressful or negative life events the participants had experienced during the past five years (since age twenty-one), as well as evidence of depression during the past year (at age twenty-six). A quarter (26 percent) reported having experienced three or more adverse life events, and 17 percent had had major depressive episodes.

Not surprisingly, overall the more stress and trauma the New Zealanders had experienced during their last five years, the more likely they were to become depressed. The critical finding, however, was that the stressful experiences led to depression *only* among those participants who carried the "bad" short allele of the 5-HTTLPR gene. Interestingly, the same result was found for stress suffered in childhood. Those participants who were maltreated between ages three and eleven were more likely to become depressed at age twenty-six, but again, *only* if they carried the ill-fated short allele.

So, our genes play an important role in depression, as they do in happiness, but they need to be "expressed"—or turned on or off. The findings of the New Zealand study, which was voted by the editorial board of *Science* magazine as the second-biggest finding of that year (the biggest was on the origins of life!), suggest that the short allele variant of the 5-HTTLPR gene is activated by an environmental trigger—namely, stress. Similarly, the long "good" allele appears to *protect* us from responding to a stressful experience by becoming depressed—that is, by making us resilient. The fact that many of us may carry genes for a particular vulnerability (be it PKU or cardiovascular disease or depression or happiness) therefore does not mean that we will express that vulnerability in our lives. If the New Zealanders with the short "bad" allele of the 5-HTTLPR gene were able to avoid highly stressful situations or to engage psychotherapists or supportive confidants when they anticipated stress, their genetic propensity for depression might never be triggered. Furthermore, new research has shown that individuals unfortunate enough to possess the "bad" gene yet fortunate to have had either supportive family environments *or* several present-day positive life experiences do *not* become depressed.[57] In order to express or *not* to express themselves, genes need a particular environment (e.g., a happy marriage or job layoff) or a particular behavior (e.g., seeking out social support). This means that no matter what your genetic predisposition, whether or not that predisposition is expressed is in *your* hands.

## WHAT ELECTRODES CAN TEACH US

A better understanding of the happiness set point comes from perhaps the most exciting laboratory right now in the area of well-being, that of Richard Davidson at the University of Wisconsin–Madison. Like the behavior geneticists, Davidson argues that each of us has a natural set point, which he defines as a baseline of activity in the prefrontal cortex (front part) of the brain. In a fascinating discovery, he noticed that happy people show greater activity in one side of their brain than the other, and unhappy people show the reverse pattern.

Davidson uses the procedure called electroencephalography (EEG) to measure a person's brain activity.[58] He finds that happy people, those who smile more, and who report themselves to be enthusiastic, alert, and engaged in life show a curious asymmetry in their brain activity; they have more activity in their *left* prefrontal cortex than in the right.[59] Although no researcher would claim that the left side of the front region of the brain is the "happiness center," clearly this region is associated with positive emotion. Even newborns who are given something nice to suck display increased activation in the left sides of their brains, and so do adults who are shown funny film clips. The right prefrontal region, by contrast, is activated during unpleasant states and negative emotions.

What does it mean to any of us that the left side of a happy person's brain lights up more than the right side? Perhaps only something as seemingly ineffable as the fact that happiness appears to be hardwired in the neural circuitry. Thus, although Davidson's work doesn't offer proof for the notion of a happiness set point, it certainly supports it. If the set point is genetically determined, it's presumably rooted in our neurobiology.

## IMPLICATIONS FOR YOU

Some of us simply possess higher set points for happiness, more cheerful dispositions, and higher potentials for well-being. Perhaps "the sun shines more brightly for some persons than others."[60] Having a high set point may feel as if more of our days were sunny ones. It may mean never having to work very hard at being happy. But this is not the situation facing most of us. So let's start with the premise that we may have a disappointingly *low* set point and then ask ourselves: First, precisely how low *is* that set point, and second, what can we do about it?

To address the first question, it's impossible to know exactly what your set point is unless you evaluate it over time. You need to record the date that you first completed the Subjective Happiness Scale (see p. 33). Your score on that scale is your *preliminary estimate* of your set point. The reason it's preliminary is that it's somewhat sensitive to what's happening around you. For example, your score could have been influenced by a recent event, by your stress level that day, even by the weather. You will need therefore to fill out the Subjective Happiness Scale again, ideally at least two weeks after initially taking it but *before* you begin the happiness building program described in this book. If you intend to begin straightaway, then retake the scale the day before you start; the *average* of your two scores (or three scores, if you take it three times, and so on) will serve as the estimate of your set point. The more often you take the Subjective Happiness Scale, and the further apart in time you take it, the more reliable the estimate of your set point.

What can you do if your happiness set point is lower than you like? (Although the average is around five, your own hoped-for yardstick may be a lot higher or a lot lower.) To begin with, I must stress that if you desire to become lastingly happier, the answer is not to try to change your set point. By definition, the set point is constant, immune to influence, and wired in your genes. Analogously, if you are born with brown eyes, your eyes will forever remain truly brown. However, as you saw earlier, you are not doomed to obey the directives of your genes, because your genes need a specific environment, a particular set of life experiences, in order to be expressed. Many of these life experiences are indeed under your control, and their potential for influencing your happiness lies in the activities and strategies that make up the large 40 percent of our happiness "pie." Through these activities we can change our happiness *levels,* if not our set points, much as we can change our eye colors (through tinted contact lenses), if not the innate colors of our eyes.

# The Promise of Intentional Activity

*Happiness consists in activity. It is a running stream, not a stagnant pool.*

—*John Mason Good*

Many are familiar with the Serenity Prayer, written by German philosopher Reinhold Niebuhr and widely adopted for use in twelve-step programs: "God, grant me the serenity to accept the things I cannot change, the courage to change the things I can, and the wisdom to know the difference." But how *can* you know the difference?

It should be obvious by now where the secret to happiness does *not* lie. The fountain of happiness lies *not* in changing our genetically determined set points, for they are, by definition, resistant to change, influence, or control. We are also unlikely to find lasting happiness by changing our life circumstances. Although we may achieve temporary boosts in well-being by moving to new parts of the country, securing raises, or changing our appearances, such boosts are unlikely to be long-lasting. The primary reason, as I have argued, is that people readily and rapidly adapt to positive circumstantial changes. I would furthermore be remiss if I failed to point out other reasons why circumstantial changes may prove unsuccessful in making us permanently happier: because they can be very costly, often impractical, and sometimes even impossible. Does everyone have the money, resources, or time to change her living situation, her job, her spouse, her physical appearance?

If the secret to happiness does not lie in increasing our set points or in positively impacting the circumstances of our lives, what is left? Is it possible to attain greater happiness and sustain it? To be sure, most of us do become happier at some point during our lives. Indeed, contrary to popular belief, people actually get happier with age. A twenty-two-year study of about two thousand healthy veterans of World War II and the Korean War revealed that life satisfaction increased over the course of these men's lives, peaked at age sixty-five, and didn't start significantly declining until age seventy-five (see p. 64).[61]

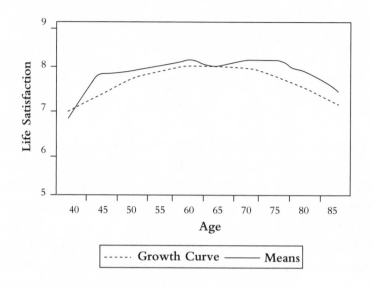

This is heartening news. But what precisely can we do to hasten or bolster such increases in happiness? The answer lies in the pie chart theory of happiness. Recall that 50 percent of individual differences in happiness are governed by genes, 10 percent by life circumstances, and the remaining 40 percent by what we *do* and how we *think*—that is, our intentional activities and strategies. The secret of course lies in that 40 percent. If we observe genuinely happy people, we shall find that they do not just sit around being contented. They make things happen. They pursue new understandings, seek new achievements, and control their thoughts and feelings. In sum, our intentional, effortful activities have a powerful effect on how happy we are, over and above the effects of our set points and the circumstances in which we find themselves. If an unhappy person wants to experience interest, enthusiasm, contentment, peace, and joy, he or she can make it happen by learning the habits of a happy person.

## MARKUS AND ROLAND: THWARTING ADAPTATION

Let's return, for a moment, to the massive German study in which researchers followed 1,761 people over the course of fifteen years, starting when they were single, then continuing after they became married and stayed married. On average, as this remarkable study found, people were no happier during the years after marriage than before marriage, and the average "marriage boost" in happiness lasted for only two years. Notably, however, there was significant variability in people's responses to tying the knot. Consider Markus and Roland, two somewhat unusual participants who both happened to wed their girlfriends while the study was going on. Markus's happiness increased more than average when he got hitched, and eight years later he is *still* happier being married (just declining a tiny bit from his high point) than when he was single. Roland, on the other hand, ended up *less* happy during the first two years of marriage and has become even less happy in the five years since.

What is unique about these two men? Well, Markus didn't want the effects of marriage to "wear off"; he didn't want to adapt to the rewards of marriage and take it for granted. So he decided to dedicate himself to be the best husband he could be and *not* take his wife and their relationship for granted. He consciously remembers to say, "I love you," to bring her flowers, to initiate plans, trips, and hobbies, to take an interest in his wife's challenges, successes, and feelings. In contrast, Roland was disappointed at the outset that matrimony did not live up to his idealistic expectations and since then has failed to observe the slow and steady deterioration of his relationship.

The lesson from Markus and Roland is that while it's true that we tend to adapt to positive changes in our lives, it's in our power to apply effort to try to inhibit or slow down the adaptation process. Markus tried to inhibit adaptation to his marriage by actively and creatively behaving in ways that preserved his and his wife's love and affection for each other, a strategy that we can learn from as an example of a conscious goal that we can undertake and commit to practice. For example, I have argued that moving to a new location, however magnificent it may be initially, eventually leads to a dampening of enthusiasm. This will undoubtedly occur, but only if you passively accept your situation. It doesn't have to be that way. When I moved to California from New England, I recall waking up every morning and saying to myself, What a beautiful day! But just like Steve

Martin's parody of the weatherman in *L.A. Story* announcing every day that "it's going to be sunny . . . again!," this recognition of beauty eventually grew old. Like most people around me, I became accustomed to the splendor of my surroundings and the serenity and blueness of my skies, no longer deriving the extra boost in happiness they initially afforded me. However, in the last few years, still living in California, I have been taking my own research advice to heart. Most mornings I go running on a path overlooking the Pacific Ocean, and I make a conscious decision to take a moment and look at the beach and the mountains in the distance more attentively, to breathe extra deeply the salty air. The other day some Swedish tourists asked me in the middle of a run to take a photograph of them in front of the ocean view. Instead of being annoying, the interruption made me thankful to these tourists for unknowingly deepening my appreciation for the singular special lovely place where I live.

## JUDITH: CHOOSING TO BE HAPPY

Judith was born and raised in Indiana, but has been living in Edmonton, Alberta, for more than thirty years. I interviewed her outdoors, at one of her favorite neighborhood restaurants. She is sixty years old, divorced, with a grown daughter. Once upon a time in life Judith was deeply unhappy. She grew up in a dysfunctional, abusive family. Her mother used to beat her with anything she could get her hands on—a paddle, a hairbrush—and wouldn't stop until the object broke. As an adult Judith illustrated perfectly the toxic triangle of food, alcohol, and depression that Susan Nolen-Hoeksema describes in her book *Eating, Drinking, Overthinking*[62]: She had a major weight problem, turned to alcohol, and was clinically depressed and insecure.

Today Judith admits to being "an incredibly happy person." She has a fulfilling job, volunteers widely, and cares for a fourteen-year-old foster boy. She decided to return to college at age fifty-two. She is spiritual, and she is forgiving, now referring to her troubled mother as "poor thing."

"I chose to be happy," Judith said. "I learned to simply change my mind. What a concept." Indeed, she purely exemplifies the value of focusing on the 40 percent of our happiness that we have the power to control. "The beginning for me was to look into the mirror and say (in Barbra Streisand's accent): 'Hellooo, gorgeous!' I kept saying it until I didn't burst into laughter every time I said it." This may seem easy or trivial, but it's not when you appear ugly and worthless to yourself. "I also worked very hard," Judith told me, "to stop the negative thoughts (I called them the bad thoughts) by simply saying in my mind, STOP! and then I would say to myself, You are okay right now."

Judith was likely born with a low set point for happiness, and starting early in life, she was saddled with difficult life circumstances and damaging experiences. Even today there are trying times. Recently a dear friend of hers committed suicide, and she failed to get her job renewed. But Judith has risen above both her circumstances and her nature by striving for a life-transforming goal—to change how she thought about herself and the world around her, to build her self-esteem and nurture optimistic thinking—by choosing to be happy.

# Conclusion

The media are constantly telling us about the latest newfangled strategy shown to "really" work in boosting health and well-being. These strategies keep changing, each one evidently bested by the next, such that every new pronouncement becomes harder to believe. If the new kind of yoga or meditation or marital therapy technique were as effective as the reports claim, then wouldn't everyone be doing it and benefiting from it? Well, no. Any major life-changing endeavor must be accompanied by considerable sustained effort, and I would speculate that the majority of people do not or cannot continue putting out that kind of effort. What's more, all new happiness-enhancing or health-boosting strategies have something in common; each one bestows on the person a specific *goal,* something to do and to look forward. Moreover, as I explain later on, having goals in and of themselves is strongly associated with happiness and life satisfaction. That's why—at least for a time—any new happiness strategy does work!

In a nutshell, the fountain of happiness can be found in how you behave, what you think, and what goals you set every day of your life. "There is no happiness without action."[63] If feelings of passivity and futility overcome you whenever you face up to your happiness set point or to your circumstances, you must know that a genuine and abiding happiness is indeed within your reach, lying within the 40 percent of the happiness pie chart that's yours to guide.

# 3.

# How to Find Happiness Activities That Fit Your Interests, Your Values, and Your Needs

*Different men seek after happiness in different ways and by different means, and so make for themselves different modes of life. . . .*

*—Aristotle*

I f 40 percent of our happiness is rooted in intentional activity, then pre-cisely which activities or strategies can help you reach your desired level of well-being? Many of us persist in searching for "the one" true secret path to happiness (or to career success or to spiritual fulfillment and so on), like the one diet that will work when all others have failed. In truth, there is no one magic strategy that will help every person become happier. All of us have unique needs, interests, values, resources, and inclinations that undoubtedly predispose us to put effort into and benefit from some strate-gies more than others. For example, an extravert may be more likely to stick with an activity that brings her into regular contact with other people, and a very nurturing person may benefit more from an activity that grants him opportunities to take care of others. Furthermore, some people are best served by working on an area of specific weakness (whether it's pessimism or overthinking or problems with friendship), and others profit from engag-ing in a happiness strategy that meshes with their personal ideal of happiness (be it positive thinking or gratifying relationships or fulfilling work). This general "matching" notion is supported by much recent research.[1]

It is also fairly intuitive. If you want to become physically fit or chuck an addiction, there are many programs and strategies you can try, and you would be prudent to choose one that fits your goals, resources, and lifestyle best. Interestingly, although the importance of good fit is widely recognized, even obvious, in the domains of diet and fitness, it is rarely considered in regard to a person's emotional life. Yet fit is absolutely critical. So much so that I'll go out on a limb here and say that if there's any "secret" to becoming happier, the secret is in establishing which happiness strategies suit you best. Once you have done so, half the battle is won; the way to greater happiness is in your hands.

# Three Ways That Strategies Can Fit

When it comes to determining which happiness strategies will work best for a particular individual, I believe in taking an idiographic, or personalized, approach. The goal is person-activity fit. When you choose wisely, you will feel motivated to try a particular happiness activity, persist at it, and experience its rewards. It goes without saying that a person needs to make an honest effort in trying a new strategy in order to achieve any benefit. However, even the most ardently pursued activities won't bring happiness for every single individual. One of the chief reasons that many of us fail in our efforts to become happier is unfortunate choosing, picking a strategy or approach that is either inherently fruitless (like pursuing wealth, approval, or beauty, as discussed in the previous chapter) or not well suited to us. A good person-activity fit can be achieved in a number of ways. These ways, described below, can work independently or in concert. Let's consider all the options.

**Fit with the source of your unhappiness.** The first approach is to contemplate what underlies your own unhappiness. Leo Tolstoy famously opened *Anna Karenina* by declaring: "Happy families are all alike; every unhappy family is unhappy in its own way." As a psychologist who studies individuals, not families, I prefer the following restatement, which has its own truth: "Happy people are all alike; every unhappy person is unhappy in his or her own way." The research bears this out; there are many varieties and sources of unhappiness. Each individual is unhappy for a unique constellation of reasons. Some of us feel apathetic and powerless over our lives, whereas others are convinced that the future is bleak. The crux for some is an inability to obtain much pleasure from daily activities. For others, it's being too shy to join in social events or being traumatized and unsettled by past experiences. This means that particular happiness-enhancing activities may uniquely address our specific problems or areas of weakness. The pessimist may benefit from cultivating optimism, the pleasure-lacking individual from savoring, the traumatized person from learning coping skills, and so on.

**Fit with your strengths.** Person-activity fit, however, does not have to be based on repairing your specific weaknesses. Alternatively, you can start by identifying your strengths, talents, or goals. For example, an achievement-oriented person may do well at pursuing significant life goals or taking up competitive sports as a way to boost his happiness, while a creative person may choose to express gratitude or forgiveness through painting or writing. Indeed, different people can attain happiness in different ways, so it makes sense that some of us should focus on a particular set of happiness-increasing activities, while others should focus on an entirely different set of activities.

**Fit with your lifestyle.** Think about the extent to which the activities you choose can be adapted to your needs and lifestyle. For example, if your life is stressful and hectic, then you can choose activities (like counting blessings) that don't take any extra time out of your day. If you are satisfied with your relationships, but not with your work, then you can choose activities (like increasing flow or striving for new goals) that can help you enjoy your job more and pursue novel opportunities. If you're not spiritual or religious, then you can pass on the religion strategy. If you're a lifelong practitioner of concentrative meditation, then you can opt out of the happiness activity that involves meditating. Much like a diet that you can individualize to fit your food preferences, you can tailor the happiness strategies to fit your personality and your way of life. There are probably as many ways to achieve happiness as there are to lose it.

# Corniness, Again

Finally, I have to raise the issue of corniness again. It's possible that you will read over the list of the dozen happiness activities and observe that some of these activities, perhaps many of them, appear hokey or undoable to you. You may even react with distaste: "This is not for me!" I myself have had this experience. It's not uncommon, and it doesn't mean that you are destined never to become happier. The reality is that some of us have an aversion to advice that seems overly sentimental or simplistic. We can't picture ourselves "counting blessings" or "savoring life's joys" or "learning to forgive," because these suggestions smack of mawkishness and even naiveté to us. Such reactions are authentic, and I can't dispute them. Fortunately, if this reaction describes you, you have a choice. Other activities are available that may be a better fit for your interests, needs, and values. However, even the corniest-sounding exercise can grow on you and end up being practiced sincerely and from the heart. Chris Peterson, professor at the University of Michigan and one of the founders of positive psychology, admitted once that he couldn't bring himself to write gratitude letters, which he regularly assigned to his own students. When he finally forced himself to do it, he wound up masking any embarrassing sentiments with humor and ended up feeling insincere. Needless to say, the exercise did not succeed in boosting his happiness. So he tried again, and this time he says, "I spoke from the heart."

# Person-Activity Fit Diagnostic

Learning that there are several ways to make a strategy fit makes it all seem very complicated. How do you go about selecting the set of activities that are the optimal fit for you? Which *type* of fit is best? Fortunately, the answer is simple and straightforward. I have developed a self-diagnostic test that conveniently incorporates all the different ways of measuring fit, whether it is fit with your weaknesses, your strengths and goals, or your needs and lifestyle. This test of person-activity fit uses a systematic, empirically based approach to determine which set of happiness activities (out of twelve) will be most valuable for you to try. Set aside fifteen to thirty minutes to complete it in a quiet setting—the test requires effort and concentration—and be sure to rate all twelve activities presented. How you answer this diagnostic is crucial to everything else that you will learn in this book. But that having been said, it's not a test in the sense that there are right or wrong responses but rather an opportunity to define yourself, so the only prerequisite is to be honest and true.

## PERSON-ACTIVITY FIT DIAGNOSTIC
### (adapted from Sheldon)

INSTRUCTIONS: Consider each of the following 12 happiness activities. Reflect on what it would be like to do it *every week* for an extended period of time. Then rate each activity by writing the appropriate number (1 to 7) in the blank space next to the terms *NATURAL, ENJOY, VALUE, GUILTY,* and *SITUATION.*

People do things for many different reasons. Rate why you might keep doing this activity in terms of each of the following reasons. Use this scale:

| 1 | 2 | 3 | 4 | 5 | 6 | 7 |
|---|---|---|---|---|---|---|
| not at all | | | somewhat | | | very much |

NATURAL:    I'll keep doing this activity because it will feel "natural" to me and I'll be able to stick with it.

ENJOY:    I'll keep doing this activity because I will enjoy doing it; I'll find it to be interesting and challenging.

VALUE:    I'll keep doing this activity because I will value and identify with doing it; I'll do it freely even when it's not enjoyable.

GUILTY:    I'll keep doing this activity because I would feel ashamed, guilty, or anxious if I didn't do it; I'll force myself.

SITUATION:    I'll keep doing this activity because somebody else will want me to or because my situation will force me to.

1. Expressing gratitude: Counting your blessings for what you have (either to a close other or privately, through contemplation or a journal) or conveying your gratitude and appreciation to one or more individuals whom you've never properly thanked.

\_\_\_\_NATURAL    $\underline{1}$ENJOY    \_\_\_\_VALUE    \_\_\_\_GUILTY    \_\_\_\_SITUATION

2. Cultivating optimism: Keeping a journal in which you imagine and write about the best possible future for yourself or practicing to look at the bright side of every situation.

\_\_\_\_NATURAL    \_\_\_\_ENJOY    $\underline{5}$VALUE    \_\_\_\_GUILTY    \_\_\_\_SITUATION

3. Avoiding overthinking and social comparison: Using strategies (such as distraction) to cut down on how often you dwell on your problems and compare yourself with others.

___NATURAL    ___ENJOY   _5_VALUE    ___GUILTY    ___SITUATION

4. Practicing acts of kindness: Doing good things for others, whether friends or strangers, either directly or anonymously, either spontaneously or planned.

___NATURAL    ___ENJOY    ___VALUE    ___GUILTY   _4_SITUATION

5. Nurturing relationships: Picking a relationship in need of strengthening, and investing time and energy in healing, cultivating, affirming, and enjoying it.

___NATURAL    ___ENJOY    ___VALUE   _5_GUILTY    ___SITUATION

6. Developing strategies for coping: Practicing ways to endure or surmount a recent stress, hardship, or trauma.

___NATURAL    ___ENJOY    ___VALUE    ___GUILTY   _6_SITUATION

7. Learning to forgive: Keeping a journal or writing a letter in which you work on letting go of anger and resentment toward one or more individuals who have hurt or wronged you.

___NATURAL    ___ENJOY    ___VALUE    ___GUILTY   _4_SITUATION

8. Doing more activities that truly engage you: Increasing the number of experiences at home and work in which you "lose" yourself, which are challenging and absorbing (i.e., flow experiences).

___NATURAL   _7_ENJOY    ___VALUE    ___GUILTY    ___SITUATION

9. Savoring life's joys: Paying close attention, taking delight, and replaying life's momentary pleasures and wonders, through thinking, writing, drawing, or sharing with another.

___NATURAL   _6_ENJOY    ___VALUE    ___GUILTY    ___SITUATION

10. Committing to your goals: Picking one, two, or three significant goals that are meaningful to you and devoting time and effort to pursuing them.

____NATURAL   ____ENJOY   ____VALUE   _3_GUILTY   ____SITUATION

11. Practicing religion and spirituality: Becoming more involved in your church, temple, or mosque or reading and pondering spiritually themed books.

____NATURAL   ____ENJOY   _5_VALUE   ____GUILTY   ____SITUATION

12. Taking care of your body: Engaging in physical activity, meditating, and smiling and laughing.

____NATURAL   _6_ENJOY   ____VALUE   ____GUILTY   ____SITUATION

## HOW TO CALCULATE YOUR "FIT" SCORE AND DETERMINE YOUR SET OF BEST-FITTING ACTIVITIES:

STEP 1: For *each* of the 12 activities, subtract the average of the GUILTY and SITUATION rating from the average of the NATURAL, ENJOY, and VALUE ratings. In other words, for each of the 12 activities:

FIT SCORE = (NATURAL + ENJOY + VALUE)/3 − (GUILTY + SITUATION)/2

STEP 2: Write down the four activities with the highest FIT SCORES:

1) _____   3) _____

2) _____   4) _____ .

Date: _____

As you can see, the Person-Activity Fit Diagnostic yields a short list of four happiness activities for you to undertake as you begin the happiness-increasing program described here. Some of you will be surprised by your short list and thus will have learned something valuable about yourself. Others will find their short lists to be exactly what they expected. In any case, depending on your level of energy and motivation, you may choose initially to engage in only *one* of the four activities or up to two or three simultaneously. *Feel free to jump ahead after this chapter and only read about the activities in Part II of this book that suit you best.* With time, as you make progress, you can add more activities or even advance to trying out those that yielded somewhat lower fit scores. The six chapters making up Part II will give you the "goods" on each of the twelve happiness activities, describing in detail how precisely to implement them and why.

The rationale behind the Person-Activity Fit Diagnostic is that a particular happiness-increasing strategy will match you better if it feels natural to you and you are truly motivated to pursue it—that is, you want to do it because you value doing it and because you find it enjoyable and *not* because you feel forced or pressured into doing it, out of either guilt or a desire to please. The fit score is in large part a measure of what Ken Sheldon and his coauthors call self-determined motivation—that is, a commitment to pursue a goal that's grounded in one's genuine interests and deeply held fundamental values.[2] Research suggests that if you have this kind of motivation in striving for greater happiness, you will continue to put effort into the endeavor and be ultimately more likely to succeed.[3] In other words, where there is a good fit, you will try harder and feel right about what you're doing.

The results of a recent study by one of my graduate students confirm these benefits of person-activity fit.[4] We randomly assigned participants to carry out a single happiness strategy (in this case, practicing either gratitude or optimism) over a two-month period; they also completed the Person-Activity Fit Diagnostic. As we anticipated, participants who were lucky to be assigned the activities that fitted them were more likely (1) to report finding their practice "natural" and "enjoyable" after the fact, (2) to continue engaging in the activities even after the study was over, and (3) to derive greater happiness as a result of practicing them.[5] So, there you have it: the significance of fit!

# P.S. More Options

There are several reasons why I present exactly twelve activities in this book. First, I chose only evidence-based happiness-increasing strategies whose practice is supported by scientific research. Second, I sought to include a wide variety of activities, so that every individual could find a set right for him or her. This is why there are twelve and no fewer. Nonetheless, there's a risk that even an activity with a high fit score may not at first work for you. In that case, you need to persist at it, or attempt a different activity, or try a combination. Research has shown that when it comes to changing something fundamental about themselves, people often need to make multiple attempts. For example, one study recruited hundreds of individuals who were successful at losing weight and maintaining the weight loss for at least five years.[6] Most recounted trying several different diets and forms of exercise to lose the weight, and it took four or five tries (sometimes more) for them finally to succeed. This is another reason why it is worthwhile to choose from a range of strategies.

Don't be constrained, however, by your list of four best-fitting activities. I have found that people who find a particular well-fitting activity tend to find several other complementary activities to fit as well[7]—that is, certain happiness strategies "go together" with other strategies. So, in Part II, after the description of each one of the twelve happiness activities, I suggest a set of two others, based on research evidence from my lab, that you might find valuable to try even if you did not establish it as one of your four primary activities. For example, the very first strategy I describe is expressing gratitude. If this activity has yielded a high fit score for you, you should give it your best shot. If you feel yourself becoming happier, continue to express gratitude on a regular basis. At this point, however, you may also add one or more activities to undertake from your set of four best-fitting ones. And if gratitude appeals to you and seems to be especially effective, there are two others that you might consider trying: practicing kindness and learning to forgive. To this end, skip ahead to the kindness or forgiveness sections if you like.

For you convenience, I've created a grid in the Appendix that shows which happiness-increasing strategies go together. Again, use this grid to help you find additional helpful happiness activities besides your list of four best-fitting ones, but generally it's a good idea to first exhaust that list of four.

# Final Words

Aiming for greater happiness is no small endeavor, requiring effort and commitment. Taking these first steps may be a bit daunting, but it is also empowering because the control in how you undertake this path (or whether you choose to do so) resides entirely in you. The Person–Activity Fit Diagnostic has this power. Selecting an appropriate activity to undertake vastly increases the chances that you will succeed. On the other hand, if the wrong strategy is chosen, it is likely to fail, and you may give up altogether. The fit diagnostic has been developed to help prevent you from feeling frustrated and to optimize the way you determine the happiness-enhancing strategies that will be most effective for *you*—that is, the four strategies that fit your current values, goals, and needs. Again, I encourage you to start with that set of strategies. Jump ahead now to your best-fitting activity. Alternatively, many people may benefit from opting to read about them all. Finally, it's critical to your success to read about *how* and *why* such happiness-enhancing activities work. This important material is presented in "The Five Hows Behind Sustainable Happiness" (Chapter 10).

*Part Two*

~

Happiness Activities

# Foreword to Part Two

## *Before You Begin*

I n Part II you will learn about and embark on one or more of the happiness activities that best fit you, as determined by the Person-Activity Fit Diagnostic from the last chapter. Before you begin, however, it's important to determine your initial happiness score by completing the happiness scale below. You will revisit this scale, the Oxford Happiness Questionnaire, on a regular basis in order to track your progress—that is, to establish whether (and how successfully) the happiness activities are "working" to boost your happiness. Your initial and future scores on the Oxford scale, I should note, reflect your happiness level, not your happiness set point. The set point, as I have argued, is fixed at birth and constant. Your happiness level, by contrast, can shift up or down depending on what you *do* and how you *think*—in other words, by the activities embodied by the 40 percent of the happiness pie chart.

# THE OXFORD HAPPINESS QUESTIONNAIRE[1]

INSTRUCTIONS: Below are a number of statements about happiness. Please indicate how much you agree or disagree with each statement by entering a number alongside it according to the scale below.

| 1 | 2 | 3 |
|---|---|---|
| strongly disagree | moderately disagree | slightly disagree |

| 4 | 5 | 6 |
|---|---|---|
| slightly agree | moderately agree | strongly agree |

_2_ 1. I don't feel particularly pleased with the way I am. (X)

_4_ 2. I am intensely interested in other people.

_5_ 3. I feel that life is very rewarding.

_6_ 4. I have very warm feelings towards almost everyone.

_2_ 5. I rarely wake up feeling rested. (X)

_2_ 6. I'm not particularly optimistic about the future. (X)

_3_ 7. I find most things amusing.

_3_ 8. I am always committed and involved.

_1_ 9. Life is good.

_2_ 10. I don't think that the world is a good place. (X)

_3_ 11. I laugh a lot.

INSTRUCTIONS: Below are a number of statements about happiness. Please indicate how much you agree or disagree with each statement by entering a number alongside it according to the scale below.

___3___ 12. I am well satisfied with everything in my life.

___1___ 13. I don't think I look attractive. (X)

___5___ 14. There's a gap between what I would like to do and what I have done. (X)

___5___ 15. I am very happy.

___6___ 16. I find beauty in some things.

___2___ 17. I always have a cheerful effect on others.

___4___ 18. I can find time for everything I want to do.

___3___ 19. I feel that I'm not especially in control of my life. (X)

___4___ 20. I feel able to take anything on.

___2___ 21. I feel fully mentally alert.

___4___ 22. I often experience joy and elation.

___4___ 23. I don't find it easy to make decisions. (X)

___2___ 24. I don't have a particular sense of meaning and purpose in my life. (X)

___5___ 25. I feel I have a great deal of energy.

___5___ 26. I usually have a positive influence on events.

___1___ 27. I don't have fun with other people. (X)

INSTRUCTIONS: Below are a number of statements about happiness. Please indicate how much you agree or disagree with each statement by entering a number alongside it according to the scale below.

_2_  28. I don't feel particularly healthy. (X)

_1_  29. I don't have particularly happy memories of the past. (X)

## HOW TO CALCULATE YOUR SCORE:

STEP 1: Your scores on the 12 items marked with an X should be "reverse-scored"— that is, if you gave yourself a 1, cross it out and change it to a 6; if you gave yourself a 2, change that to a 5; change a 3 to a 4; change a 4 to a 3; change a 5 to a 2; and change a 6 to a 1.

STEP 2: Using the changed scores for those 12 items, now add your scores for *all* the 29 items.

STEP 3: Happiness score = Total (from Step 2)_____ divided by 29 = _____

Your total happiness score is _____.        Date: _____

Your total happiness score is _____.        Date: _____

Your total happiness score is _____.        Date: _____

Your total happiness score is _____.        Date: _____

Your total happiness score is _____.        Date: _____

Your total happiness score is _____.        Date: _____

The lowest possible score on the Oxford Happiness Questionnaire is 1 (if you gave yourself a 1 for all 29 items) and the highest possible score is 6 (if you gave yourself a 6 for all 29 items). The average is around 4.30.[2]

Keep a record of your happiness score and the date you complete the scale. As you engage in the happiness activities, you will want to complete the scale on a regular basis—for example, on the first day of each month or after a particular goal has been met. Either way, you will be able to observe how your happiness changes, and increases, as you continue the happiness program.

# 4.

# Practicing Gratitude and
# Positive Thinking

I t is a truism that how you *think*—about yourself, your world, and other people—is more important to your happiness than the objective circumstances of your life. "The mind is its own place, and in itself / Can make a Heaven of Hell, a Hell of Heaven," John Milton wrote in *Paradise Lost.* The three happiness-increasing activities in this chapter all aim to transform the way we think about our lives: making a heaven of hell, finding something to be glad about, and not sweating the small stuff.

Philosophers, writers, and great-grandmothers of times past have long extolled the virtues of the three happiness activities I describe here, expressing gratitude, cultivating optimism, and avoiding overthinking and social comparison. Such exhortations as "Try to be more optimistic," "Don't dwell on it too much," and "You'd feel better if you were more appreciative" have been around for generations. So what makes them important for us today? Why should you spend your valuable time and energy in learning them, in turning them into habits? Furthermore, how do we know, first, that these habits are even learnable (as opposed to inborn) and second, that even if you could train yourself to do them, you'd be happier? The answers to these questions are found within these pages. I have selected for this book only those activities (from among many) that have been shown to be successful through science, rather than conjecture. What's more, I describe *why* these strategies work and *how* precisely they should be implemented to maximize their effectiveness using evidence from the latest research. In every grandmotherly bit of advice lies a kernel of truth. I've chosen the biggest kernels, established what the data show, and sought to determine for whom these truths might work best and how and why. Apply these activities to your own life, and you will harness the promise of the 40 percent solution, for such is the amount of wiggle room you have to remake yourself.

# Happiness Activity No. 1: Expressing Gratitude

The expression of gratitude is a kind of metastrategy for achieving happiness. Gratitude is many things to many people. It is wonder; it is appreciation; it is looking at the bright side of a setback; it is fathoming abundance; it is thanking someone in your life; it is thanking God; it is "counting blessings." It is savoring; it is not taking things for granted; it is coping; it is present-oriented. Gratitude is an antidote to negative emotions, a neutralizer of envy, avarice, hostility, worry, and irritation. The average person, however, probably associates gratitude with saying thank you for a gift or benefit received. I invite you to consider a much broader definition.

The world's most prominent researcher and writer about gratitude, Robert Emmons, defines it as "a felt sense of wonder, thankfulness, and appreciation for life."[1] You could strive to feel grateful by noticing how fortunate your circumstances are (and how much worse they could be), by calling an old mentor and thanking him for guiding you through one of life's crossroads, by relishing moments with your child, or by recalling all the good things in your life at present. By definition, the practice of gratitude involves a focus on the present moment, on appreciating your life as it is today and what has made it so.

Expressing gratitude is a lot more than saying thank you. Emerging research has recently started to draw attention to its multiple benefits. People who are consistently grateful have been found to be relatively happier, more energetic, and more hopeful and to report experiencing more frequent positive emotions. They also tend to be more helpful and empathic, more spiritual and religious, more forgiving, and less materialistic than others who are less predisposed to gratefulness. Furthermore, the more a person is inclined to gratitude, the less likely he or she is to be depressed, anxious, lonely, envious, or neurotic.[2] All these research findings, however, are correlational, meaning that we cannot know conclusively whether being grateful actually causes all those good things (or inhibits bad things), or whether possessing traits like hopefulness, helpfulness, and religiosity simply makes people feel grateful. Fortunately, several experimental studies have now been done that solicit expressions of gratitude from unsuspecting individuals and then record the consequences.

In the very first such set of studies, one group of participants was asked to write down five things for which they were thankful—namely, to count their blessings—and to do so once a week for ten weeks in a row.[3] Other groups of participants participated in the control groups; instead of focusing on gratitude every week, these individuals were asked to think about either five daily hassles or five major events that had occurred to them. The findings were exciting. Relative to the control groups, those participants from whom expressions of gratitude were solicited tended to feel more optimistic and more satisfied with their lives. Even their health received a boost; they reported fewer physical symptoms (such as headache, acne, coughing, or nausea) and more time spent exercising.

Other studies have prevailed on both students and adults with chronic illnesses to try the count your blessings strategy, with similar results. These studies have shown that on the days that individuals strive to express their gratitude, they experience more positive emotions (that is, feelings like interest, excitement, joy, and pride) and are more likely to report helping someone, to feel connected with others, and even to catch more hours of quality sleep.

These investigations show for the first time that expressions of gratitude are causally linked to the mental and physical health rewards that we have seen. However, the goal of this research has been to determine the extent of gratitude's *real-time* influence on positive affect and health—that is, whether you feel happier on a day that you are trying to be more grateful. My laboratory, by contrast, is interested in the question of how people can become happier over time. When my graduate students and I were deciding what to do for our very first happiness "intervention" (that is, an experiment aimed to make people happier), testing the strategy of counting one's blessings seemed like the obvious choice. Building on these findings, we conducted a new experiment, in which we measured participants' happiness levels, then implemented our gratitude intervention, and, once it was over, measured their happiness levels again immediately. The gratitude intervention was very similar to the one I just described. We directed our participants to keep a sort of gratitude journal—that is, to write down and contemplate five things for which they were grateful. Their exact instructions were as follows: "There are many things in our lives, both large and small, that we might be grateful about. Think back over the events of the past week and write down on the lines below up to five things that happened for which you are grateful or thankful." Five blank lines followed, headed by "This week I am grateful for:"

The participants engaged in this happiness exercise over the course of six weeks. Half of them were instructed to do it once a week (every Sunday night), and half to do it three times a week (every Tuesday, Thursday, and Sunday). The things that our participants recorded covered quite a wide range, from "mom," "a healthy body," and "having a Valentine" to "getting tested on only three chapters for my midterm" and "AOL instant messenger."

As we expected, our simple exercise was effective in producing higher levels of thankfulness and appreciation. More important, those participants who counted their blessings on a regular basis became happier as a result. Compared with a control group (i.e., people who did not practice any kind of exercise), the gratitude group reported significantly bigger increases in their happiness levels from before to after the intervention. Interestingly, this effect was observed only for those who expressed gratitude every Sunday night. The participants who counted their blessings three times a week didn't obtain any benefit from it. This finding might seem puzzling at first, but we believe there is an explanation: The average person made to express his or her gratitude every Tuesday, Thursday, and Sunday appeared to have become bored with the practice, perhaps finding it a chore, whereas the person made to express gratitude only once a week likely continued to find it fresh and meaningful over time. We'll return to this specific finding later; it has important implications for *how* to carry out the gratitude activity—or any happiness-increasing activity for that matter—with success.

## Eight Ways That Gratitude Boosts Happiness

It may sound corny, but the research clearly demonstrates that you *would* be happier if you cultivated an "attitude of gratitude."[4] However, instead of your following this advice blindly, it's important to understand why and how expressing gratitude works to make you happier. Indeed, there are no fewer than eight reasons for why I advise people to practice it.

First, grateful thinking promotes the savoring of positive life experiences. By relishing and taking pleasure in some of the gifts of your life, you will be able to extract the maximum possible satisfaction and enjoyment from your current circumstances. When my first child was only a few months old, an older woman approached me while I was struggling with the stroller. "Your baby is so beautiful," she said. "Appreciate this age; it goes by so fast!" At the time I was feeling overwhelmed and sleep-deprived and, to be honest, didn't much appreciate her glib intrusion, but it had a powerful effect. Taking time to feel grateful for this small child allowed me to step outside the dreariness of my long days caring for her and to savor the magic of the small moment I shared with my daughter.

Second, expressing gratitude bolsters self-worth and self-esteem. When you realize how much people have done for you or how much you have accomplished, you feel more confident and efficacious. Unfortunately, for many people, it comes more naturally to focus on failures and disappointments or on other people's slights and hurts. Gratefulness can help you unlearn this habit. Instead of automatically thinking, "Woe is me," in response to any setback, the practice of gratitude encourages you instead to consider what you value about your current life or how you are thankful that things aren't worse.

Third, gratitude helps people cope with stress and trauma. That is, the ability to appreciate your life circumstances may be an adaptive coping method by which you positively reinterpret stressful or negative life experiences.[5] Indeed, traumatic memories are less likely to surface—and are less intense when they do—in those who are regularly grateful.[6] Interestingly, people instinctively express gratitude when confronted with adversity. For example, in the days immediately after the September 11, 2001, terrorist attacks on the United States, gratitude was found to be the second most commonly experienced emotion (after sympathy).[7]

Expressing gratefulness during personal adversity like loss or chronic illness, as hard as that might be, can help you adjust, move on, and perhaps begin anew. Although it may be challenging to celebrate your blessings at moments when they seem least apparent to you, it may be the most important thing that you can do. In one of my recent courses, I had a severely disabled older student named Brian. He has some mobility, but not much, in his hands and is able to control a wheelchair by pressing on a lever located near his shoulder with his bent right hand. One day the class was going around the room and talking about their happiest moments in life. This is what Brian said: "My happiest moment is kind of a perverse one. It was the day that I came home from the hospital, after my accident. I felt *defiant*. I said, 'Ha! I'm still alive! I beat you!' I don't know who exactly I beat. But I felt grateful that I was home. It seemed like a little thing, but being home from the hospital after four months was so good." Echoing this perspective, sixty-seven-year-old Inger, who had been given a short time to live, described her illness this way: "When you can hear the minutes ticking and you know the buzzer is going to go off in any minute and your time will be up, you see things so clearly. You just know without a doubt where your values are and why you're alive, and you're so grateful for each moment."[8] Inger and Brian have a remarkable capacity for gratitude, a capacity that undoubtedly serves them well in both sickness and health.

Fourth, the expression of gratitude encourages moral behavior. As I mentioned earlier, grateful people are more likely to help others (e.g., you become aware of kind and caring acts and feel compelled to reciprocate) and less likely to be materialistic (e.g., you appreciate what you have and become less fixated on acquiring more stuff). To wit, an Auschwitz survivor was once described this way: "His life was rooted in gratitude. He was generous, because the memory of having nothing was never far from his mind."[9] In one study, people induced to be grateful for a specific kind act were more likely to be helpful toward their benefactor, as well as toward a stranger, even when the helping involved doing an unpleasant, tedious chore.[10]

Fifth, gratitude can help build social bonds, strengthening existing relationships and nurturing new ones.[11] Keeping a gratitude journal, for example, can produce feelings of greater connectedness with others. Several studies have shown that people who feel gratitude toward particular individuals (even when they never directly express it) experience closer and "higher-quality" relationships with them.[12] As Robert Emmons argues, when you become truly aware of the value of your friends and family members, you are likely to treat them better, perhaps producing an "upward spiral," a sort of positive feedback loop, in which strong relationships give you something to be grateful for, and in turn fortifying those very same relationships. In addition, a grateful person is a more positive person, and positive people are better liked by others and more likely to win friends.[13]

Sixth, expressing gratitude tends to inhibit invidious comparisons with others. If you are genuinely thankful and appreciative for what you have (e.g., family, health, home), you are less likely to pay close attention to or envy what the Joneses have.

Seventh, the practice of gratitude is incompatible with negative emotions and may actually diminish or deter such feelings as anger, bitterness, and greed.[14] As one psychiatrist has argued, "gratitude . . . dissolves negative feelings: anger and jealousy melt in its embrace, fear and defensiveness shrink."[15] Indeed, it's hard to feel guilty or resentful or infuriated when you're feeling grateful. My friend's sister is one of the few working moms I know who feel not an ounce of guilt. The reason is that she is a prodigy at asking friends and family for help and thanking them so profusely and sincerely afterward that they feel like rock stars.

Last but not least, gratitude helps us thwart hedonic adaptation. If you recall, hedonic adaptation is illustrated by our remarkable capacity to adjust rapidly to any new circumstance or event. This is extremely adaptive when the new event is unpleasant, but not when a new event is positive. So, when you gain something good in your life—a romantic partner, a genial office-mate, recovery from illness, a brand-new car—there is an immediate boost in happiness and contentment. Unfortunately, because of hedonic adaptation, that boost is usually short-lived. As I've argued earlier, adaptation to all things positive is essentially the enemy of happiness, and one of the keys to becoming happier lies in combating its effects, which gratitude does quite nicely. By preventing people from taking the good things in their lives for granted—from adapting to their positive life circumstances—the practice of gratitude can directly counteract the effects of hedonic adaptation.

## HOW TO PRACTICE GRATITUDE

If you learned in Chapter 3 that gratitude is one of the happiness activities that fit you best, you already have a leg up—that is, you're already motivated and willing to put in the effort and commitment it takes to become more grateful. How exactly you accomplish this is up to you; what's needed is simply to select at least *one* activity from the array of possibilities below.

**Gratitude journal.** If you enjoy writing, if you are good at it, or it feels natural to you, then a promising way to practice this strategy is with a gratitude journal, much like that used by my gratitude intervention participants. Choose a time of day when you have several minutes to step outside your life and to reflect. It may be first thing in the morning, or during lunch, or while commuting, or before bedtime. Ponder the three to five things for which you are currently grateful, from the mundane (your dryer is fixed, your flowers are finally in bloom, your husband remembered to stop by the store) to the magnificent (your child's first steps, the beauty of the sky at night). One way to do this is to focus on all the things that you know to be true—for example, something you're good at, what you like about where you live, goals you have achieved, and your advantages and opportunities.[16] Don't forget specific individuals who care for you, have made contributions to or sacrifices for you, or somehow touch your life. The results of my laboratory's gratitude intervention suggested that on average, doing this once a week is most likely to boost happiness, and that's my recommendation to the majority of people. However, *on average* means that some individuals—and those may include you—may benefit most from doing this strategy on an entirely different timetable, perhaps even daily or three times a week or twice a month. You need to determine the ideal timing tailored to your lifestyle and disposition. (See Chapter 10 for more about timing.)

**Paths to gratitude.** The particular means by which you go about counting your blessings will depend on your individual personality, goals, and needs. Instead of writing, some of you may choose a fixed time simply to contemplate each of your objects of gratitude and perhaps also to reflect on why you are grateful and how your life has been enriched. Others may choose to identify just one thing each day that they usually take for granted and that ordinarily goes unappreciated. Alternatively, some may want to acknowledge one ungrateful thought per day (e.g., "my sister forgot my birthday") and substitute a grateful one (e.g., "she's always been there for me").[17]

Friends and family can also help foster your appreciation. One idea is to procure a gratitude partner with whom you can share your blessings list and who prompts and encourages you if you lose motivation or simply forget. Chapter 10 describes the power and potential of social (buddy) support in greater detail. Another idea is to introduce a visitor to the things, people, and places that you love. Show off your comic book collection, your favorite park, or your favorite niece. Doing this will help you see the ordinary details of your life through another person's eyes, affording you a fresh perspective and making you appreciate them as though you were experiencing them for the very first time.

**Keep the strategy fresh.** Another important recommendation is to keep the gratitude strategy fresh by *varying* it and not overpracticing it. My research suggests that variety—the spice of life—is extremely important.[18] (Again, consult Chapter 10 to find out more.) For example, if you count your blessings every single day—in the exact same way, in a nonvarying routine—you may become bored with the routine and may cease to extract much meaning from it. You might instead pause to express gratitude only after particular triggers—for example, after enduring a hardship or when you are most needful of a boost. Or you may choose to write in a journal some weeks, talk to a friend other weeks, and express gratitude through art (photography, collage, watercolor) during other weeks. On the other hand, you may purposefully want to vary the domains of your life on which to focus—for example, alternately counting your blessings with respect to your supportive relationships or work life or past events or your physical surroundings or even to life itself. These techniques will help make the expression of gratitude a meaningful practice, such that it continues to bolster happiness instead of hitting a plateau.

**Express gratitude directly to another.** Finally, the expression of gratitude may be particularly effective when done directly—by phone, letter, or face-to-face—to another person. If there's someone in particular whom you owe a debt of gratitude, express your appreciation in concrete terms. Perhaps it's your mom, favorite uncle, or old friend; perhaps it's an old coach, teacher, or supervisor. Write him or her a letter now, and if possible, visit and read the letter out loud in person, on either a special day (birthday, anniversary, or holiday) or a random one. Describe in detail what he or she did for you and exactly how it affected your life; mention how you often remember his or her efforts. Some people find it uplifting to write gratitude letters to individuals whom they don't know personally but who have influenced their lives (such as authors or politicians) or made their lives easier (such as their postal carriers or bus drivers).

A person close to me shared this letter that he had sent to his high school English teacher, more than thirty years after being in her class. I'd like to think that this chapter on gratitude (which he had freshly read) inspired him to write it:

> The main thing I want to tell you is that you were, without question, the most influential teacher I encountered at Deer Park High School, and that I am extremely grateful for the interest you took in me. You seemed to think I had something on the ball, and trust me on this, that was a minority opinion among the school faculty. Your estimation of my abilities, inflated as it may have been, translated into a certain degree of self-confidence that served me well, I think, in the years that followed.
>
> Perhaps more importantly, you treated me—a pretty unsophisticated 17–18 year old—as an adult, and there is nothing on earth more empowering, to a teenager, than that. Even allowing for the fact that the 1970s were very different times than these, I sometimes find myself thinking "What was she thinking?"

Martin Seligman and his colleagues tested the well-being benefits of expressing gratitude in this way.[19] They investigated a gratitude visit exercise that was completed over the course of just one week. People from all walks of life logged on to the researchers' Web site and received their instructions there. In the gratitude visit condition, participants were given one week to write and then hand deliver a letter of gratitude to someone who had been especially kind and caring to them but whom they had never properly thanked. In other conditions, participants were offered alternative self-guided happiness exercises. Those participants who did gratitude visits showed the largest boosts in the entire study—that is, straightaway they were much happier and much less depressed—and these boosts were maintained one week after the visit and even one month after. These findings reveal just how powerful it is to express your gratitude directly to an important person in your life. It's an activity that you can assign yourself to do on a regular basis, perhaps mixing the writing of gratitude letters (directed at the same or different individuals) with keeping a weekly gratitude journal.

There will be times, however, when you will choose to write the letter but not to send it. Indeed, in a recent study from my laboratory, we found that simply writing a gratitude letter and not sending or otherwise delivering it was enough to produce substantial boosts in happiness.[20] Participants were asked to identify several individuals who had been especially kind to them over the past several years. Those who spent fifteen minutes once a week (over eight weeks) writing letters of gratitude to these individuals became much happier during and after the study. The happiness boost was especially pronounced if the study participants were particularly motivated to become happier, if the gratitude letter activity fitted their goals and preferences, and if they put extra effort into the writing task.

For one of the homework assignments in my psychology of happiness class, I regularly ask my undergraduate students to compose a gratitude letter. Every year it's been one of the most potent and moving exercises that they do. Last year Nicole, one of the best students in the class, described for me the experience of writing a gratitude letter to her mom:

> I felt overwhelmed with a sense of happiness. I noticed I was typing very quickly, probably because it was very easy for me to express gratitude that was long overdue. As I was typing, I could feel my heart beating faster and faster. . . . Towards the end of the letter, as I reread what I had already

written, I began to get teary eyed and even a little bit choked up. I think my expressing my gratitude to my mom overwhelmed me to such a point that tears streamed down my face.

Nicole then recalled the effects the letter had on her:

Later that week (three days after I initially wrote the gratitude letter), I was sitting in front of my computer writing a paper and I was extremely frustrated. Since I was not having much success with my paper, I felt compelled to open up my gratitude letter. I reread it and even made a few changes. Instantly, I noticed that I had a smile on my face. It was almost strange how fast my mood had shifted. I had not even looked at the letter with the intention of elevating my mood, but rather I was merely bored of my research paper, so I thought I'd just do something else. Similar to my reactions the day I actually wrote the letter, after reading it, I felt much happier and less stressed for the rest of the evening. Overall, I found that the effects of writing such a letter to be quite amazing in that the letter not only elevated my mood, but the changes were lasting.

In sum, there are multiple ways to practice the strategy of gratitude and it would be wise to choose what works best for you. *Select at least one option from this section and give it a go.* When the strategy loses its freshness or meaningfulness, don't hesitate to make a change in how, when, and how often you express yourself.

## Spontaneous Gratitude: A Postscript

I am reluctant to reveal this, but although I wholeheartedly recognize its many rewards, expressing gratitude turns out to be one of the strategies that suit me least. It's no big deal; each of us will wind up with a list of happiness activities that fit and, unavoidably, with a longer list of activities that don't fit. The important fact is that as much of a platitude as counting blessings is sometimes, it is also incredibly effective, as the scientific evidence shows persuasively. The anecdotal evidence is also hard to disregard;

I know many (now happy) individuals who report that becoming grateful changed their lives.

So, this having been said, something that happened during the writing of this chapter took me by surprise. One day, after spending long hours reading through the research on gratitude, I spontaneously wrote an e-mail to all my colleagues publicly thanking our department chair for something he had done. He wrote me back immediately saying how much he appreciated my note. It felt great. And it only hit me later what had occurred: Reading about gratitude must have rubbed off, and I had unwittingly written a gratitude letter that day!

---

## Reading Guide

If you benefit from this activity, you may also want to try:

1. Practicing acts of kindness (Happiness Activity No. 4, p. 125)
2. Learning to forgive (Happiness Activity No. 7, p. 169)

---

# Happiness Activity No. 2: Cultivating Optimism

Looking at the bright side, finding the silver lining in a cloud, noticing what's right (rather than what's wrong), giving yourself the benefit of the doubt, feeling good about your future and the future of the world, or simply trusting that you can get through the day all are optimism strategies. Cultivating optimism has a lot in common with cultivating gratitude. Both strategies involve the habit of striving to make out the positive side of your situation. Building optimism, however, is about not only celebrating the present and the past but anticipating a bright future.

Before continuing, I want to dispel some myths about optimism. Learning to be optimistic doesn't mean coming to believe that you live in the "best of all possible worlds" (as Candide would have it) or that your past, present, and future are pristine and without complications. Indeed, consider the distinction between "big optimism" and "little optimism."[21] The difference involves how specific or small are one's positive expectations—for example, "My flight tomorrow will arrive on time" (little optimism) versus "We are on the threshold of a glorious age" (big optimism). Both are adaptive, but in different ways. Little optimism predisposes people to behave in constructive, healthy ways in specific situations (e.g., completing the next project at the office), whereas big optimism produces an overall feeling of vigor; it makes you feel resilient, strong, and energetic. I shall add another form of optimism, which you could call very small optimism. This is just the feeling that you will make it through this day, this month, this year, that there may be ups and downs, but everything will turn out all right in the end. Although for some of you, practicing optimistic thinking may mean posting optimistic quotes on your Web site or your walls or chanting daily affirmations of the order of "I'm good enough, I'm smart enough, and doggone it, people like me!,"[22] for others, the exercise of optimism may look very different. If optimism befits your lifestyle and personality, it can be practiced with maturity, levelheadedness, grace, and even humor.

Like gratitude, optimism means different things to different people. For example, optimism is most widely assumed to mean expecting a desirable future, that good things will be abundant and bad things scarce.[23] Obviously, what one person perceives as desirable or good (e.g., marrying Peter or enrolling in med school or following the Grateful Dead) is another person's nightmare. In addition, a person can be optimistic in one context (e.g., about recovering from knee surgery), but pessimistic in another (e.g., about reconciling with an old friend).

Psychologists who study optimism have offered somewhat different definitions. Some researchers characterize it as a global expectation about a positive future—that is, a belief that one's goals can be accomplished (somehow).[24] Others diagnose optimism (versus pessimism) in the ways that people tend to explain their outcomes.[25] When faced with a negative or unpleasant event, we invariably ask why. For example, a person who has tried and failed to sell her car would be called optimistic if she attributed her failure to causes that were external, transient, and specific ("Wintertime is a buyers' market"), as opposed to causes that were internal, long-lasting, and pervasive ("I'm terrible at persuading people"). It turns out that such explanations are important; they influence our reactions to our circumstances and make it more or less likely that we'll succeed, fall prey to depression, or succumb to illness. Finally, other researchers focus not on the target of our optimism (e.g., "I will secure that job") but on how we believe we'll get there. This approach is concerned with people's determination to attain a particular goal, and their beliefs regarding specific steps needed to reach that goal.[26] So, optimism is not only thoughts like "I will get there" but about exactly how it will be accomplished.

## YOUR BEST POSSIBLE SELVES

My friend Laura King, a professor at the University of Missouri–Columbia, pioneered the first ever systematic intervention (or experimental study) of optimism.[27] It's quite simple. She asked participants to visit her laboratory for four consecutive days. On each day they were instructed to spend twenty minutes writing a narrative description of their "best possible future selves." Basically, this is a mental exercise in which you visualize the best possible future for yourself in multiple domains of life. For example, a twenty-nine-year-old woman might imagine that in ten years, she'll be married to her soul mate, have two healthy children, be working in the field of advertising, and be playing the violin in an amateur chamber music ensemble. This is essentially her fantasy of what her life might be like if all her dreams were realized. Then again, perhaps the term *fantasy* is poorly chosen, inasmuch as it implies that this vision of her life is only a fanciful, farfetched daydream. To the contrary, this exercise involves considering your most important, deeply held goals and picturing that they will be achieved. Laura King found that people who wrote about their visions for twenty minutes per day over several days, relative to those who wrote about other topics, were more likely to show immediate increases in positive moods, to be happier several weeks later, and even to report fewer physical ailments several months thence.

The Best Possible Selves exercise turned out to be a potent intervention, and we decided to apply it in our laboratory. Ken Sheldon and I instructed participants to do the same exercise, except we had them complete just one writing session in the lab, and then urged them to continue the writing sessions at home, as often and for as long as they wished, over four weeks. The participants were told: "You have been randomly assigned to think about your best possible self now and during the next few weeks. 'Think about your best possible self' means that you imagine yourself in the future, after everything has gone as well as it possibly could. You have worked hard and succeeded at accomplishing all your life goals. Think of this as the realization of your life dreams, and of your own best potentials."[28]

As we expected, participants who engaged in the Best Possible Selves exercise caught a significant lift in mood compared with a control group that wrote simply about the details of their daily lives. Additionally, as described in Chapter 3, the biggest boosts in happy mood were observed among those participants who believed that the exercise "fitted" them best (i.e., who found it interesting, challenging, and meaningful) and practiced it with sustained effort. This constitutes yet more direct empirical evidence that if you want to reap long-term emotional benefits from a happiness activity, you need to devote persistent effort. Of course, if you identify with and enjoy what you are doing, you'll be more energized and committed. Our participants were clearly willing to adopt our recommendation to continue carrying out the Best Possible Selves activity at home and seemed to have turned it into personal goals of their own. That should be your aim as well when it's time for you to select a happiness-enhancing activity to pursue.

Why did the Best Possible Selves strategy work so well? Our participants who tried it apparently found it motivating, relevant to their current lives, and easy to relate to. They appeared to enjoy visualizing reaching their future goals. But the exercise wasn't just about imagining a model future for them; it was also about building a best possible self *today* that can make that future come true. Committing their Best Possible Selves to writing enabled them to recognize that it was in their power to transform themselves and to work toward valued goals, that their dreams today and tomorrow didn't hinge on their spouses or on money or on some stroke of luck.

Another advantage of the Best Possible Selves exercise is the fact that it's conducted through writing.[29] Because writing is highly structured, systematic, and rule-bound, it prompts you to organize, integrate, and analyze your thoughts in a way that would be difficult, if not impossible, to do if you were just fantasizing. Writing about your goals helps you put your thoughts together in a coherent manner, allowing you to find meaning in your life experiences. Writing about your dreams also gives you an opportunity to learn about yourself—that is, to understand better your priorities, your emotions, and your motives, your identity, who you really are and what's in your heart. In other words, the Best Possible Selves exercise can help you see the "big picture" of your life anew and where you're going. This new understanding may provide you with a feeling of control (e.g., "I now see a way to make my dream come true") and help you recognize and reduce conflict among your goals and the obstacles that might stand in your way (e.g., "How can I honor my family's wishes but also strike out on my own?"). All those things will ultimately make you happier.

One young woman, Molly, did this exercise and wrote to me how it made her understand *what* her goals really were and realize that they were not unattainable:

> Before beginning the exercise, I felt nervous since I'm not certain as to exactly what I want to do or where I want to be in the future. I was nervous that I wouldn't have anything to write about. During the [writing] sessions . . . the time went by as though it was nothing, it felt very relaxing

to allow myself to express my goals. After the writing sessions I felt really good, really happy with myself. The more I thought about the goals, the more I realized that they weren't unattainable and far out of my reach, in actuality they were within my reach—they didn't seem so far away. . . . [The exercise] made me realize that I could be doing more to reach these goals, and with a little effort now I could achieve this best possible life. I had never really contemplated them seriously, so now I feel like I have more of an idea of what is important to me, what I can achieve, and how far I have to go to get these things. I had never realized so much that what I want is a stable life (love, family, friends, occupation, living situation). I hope to be with a complementary partner, successful in my work, continue to maintain the relationships I have today with my friends and family, and to try my hardest to live in a city that makes me happy, with lots of things to do and close to the ocean. I think that would make me ultimately happy, and I do not think that these goals are unreachable.

Molly demonstrates several benefits of the Best Possible Selves strategy. She gained insight into her goals and needs, recognized what might make her happy, and became more confident in how to get what she wants. She is now more likely to strive effortfully to achieve her dreams and, I hope, to be a happier person.

## WHY DOES OPTIMISTIC THINKING BOOST HAPPINESS?

The Best Possible Selves strategy is one of several effective ways to tap into optimistic thinking. All such strategies share the benefits of an optimistic outlook. Let's now consider the many advantages of becoming more optimistic. After all, if you are willing to put a great deal of energy into something, you should be assured that it will work.

First, if you're optimistic about the future—for example, you're confident that you'll be able to achieve your lifelong goals—you will invest effort in reaching those goals. For this reason, optimistic thoughts can be self-fulfilling. If you perceive an outcome as attainable, if you see a possible future for yourself (say, as a nurse) and the possibility of realizing it, you will persist in the plan even when you hit inevitable obstacles (e.g., failing the math prerequisite or having to drop out for a time) or when progress is slow. Indeed, researchers have shown that optimists are more likely to persevere and to engage fully even in the face of difficulty.[30] They also set a greater number of goals—and more difficult goals—for themselves.[31] Optimism motivates us and leads us to take initiative. Optimists don't easily give up. This is likely one major reason that optimists are more successful across a wide variety of arenas—professional, academic, athletic, social, and even health. And of course, persistence, social skill, vigor, health, and career success all are things that contribute to our happiness.

Another important way that optimistic thinking enhances happiness is that it prompts us to engage in active and effective coping.[32] There's a great deal of evidence that optimists routinely maintain relatively high levels of well-being and mental health during times of stress.[33] For example, optimistic women are less likely to become depressed following childbirth than women who are less optimistic, and optimistic college freshmen are less likely to experience distress three months after entering college. Furthermore, optimists are more likely to make plans and take direct action when faced with adversity. They are good copers. Even at the worst of times, such as after receiving grave health diagnoses, they don't deny the situation but instead are likely to accept the reality of their condition and make efforts to make the best of it and even grow from it. This seems almost too good to be true (are they for real?), but research bears it out. Perhaps because of these strengths, research has found that people who have frequent optimistic thoughts are physically healthier.

Finally, you may not be surprised to learn that optimistic thinking promotes positive moods, vitality, and high morale. Studies also show that optimists are relatively more likely to report a sense of mastery and high self-regard and less likely to show depression and anxiety. It feels good to believe that your prospects are bright. If you have something to look forward to, you will feel energized, motivated, and enthusiastic. You will feel good about yourself and feel able to control your destiny. You will even be better liked by others.[34] In short, you will reap the benefits of an excellent happiness-enhancing strategy.

## How to Practice Optimism

If cultivating optimism is a well-fitting strategy for you, you can begin to practice it today with one of the ideas below.

**Best Possible Selves diary.** There are many ways to practice optimism, but the one that has been empirically shown to enhance well-being is the original Best Possible Selves diary method. To try it out, sit in a quiet place, and take twenty to thirty minutes to think about what you expect your life to be one, five, or ten years from now. Visualize a future for yourself in which everything has turned out the way you've wanted. You have tried your best, worked hard, and achieved all your goals. Now write down what you imagine.

This writing exercise in a sense puts your optimistic "muscles" into practice. Even if thinking about the brightest future for yourself doesn't come naturally at first, it may get there with time and training. Amazing things can come about as a result of writing. William Faulkner reportedly once said, "I never know what I think about something until I read what I've written on it." You may discover new insights into yourself as you write about your future and your goals. Keeping a journal may even be a way of cultivating patience and persistence.

**Goals and subgoals diary.** A twist on the Best Possible Selves diary is that as part of developing hopeful thinking, you identify your long-range goals and break them up into subgoals.[35] For example, during the first session of your journal writing you could describe how five years from now you'll be the owner of your own business. In future sessions you could write about the steps you'll take to reach that point. (Remember that there may be many such steps or paths, not just one.) If a discouraging or pessimistic thought comes to mind ("How could I ever get the money?"), pinpoint it and try to generate alternative scenarios or possible resolutions. One technique is to recall times in the past when you've been successful at something, to recognize the strengths and resources that you already have (and will continue to develop), allowing that to motivate and invigorate you.

**Identify barrier thoughts.** Another strategy to increase optimistic thinking involves identifying automatic pessimistic thoughts. For example, you might put a penny in a jar every time you have a pessimistic thought. Then try to replace that thought with a more charitable or favorable point of view. For example, such spontaneous thoughts as "I feel so stupid for giving the wrong advice to my officemate; he'll never ask me again to collaborate on a project" and "Ever since my relationship ended, I feel unlovable and unappealing" are called barrier thoughts because they serve as barriers to optimism. Write down your barrier thoughts, and then consider ways to reinterpret the situation. In the process, ask yourself questions like . . .

- What else could this situation or experience mean?
- Can anything good come from it?
- Does it present any opportunities for me?
- What lessons can I learn and apply to the future?
- Did I develop any strengths as a result?[36]

Be sure to practice this exercise when you're in a neutral or positive mood, and consider writing down your answers. This approach should prevent your reflections from devolving into circular, negatively biased ruminations (see Happiness Activity No. 3).

A successful twelve-week optimism training program for fifth and sixth graders has already used a very similar technique.[37] The children were taught to be more optimistic by learning to identify pessimistic explanations (e.g., "My friend didn't call me today; he must hate me"), to dispute them ("What evidence do I have that this is really true?"), and then to generate more optimistic alternatives (e.g., "Maybe he's too busy").[38] Notably, the children who participated in this program were less depressed than a control group for an entire two years after the program ended, and their reduction in depression turned out in some measure to be due to their learned optimism.

## Making Optimism a Habit

Essentially, all optimism strategies involve the exercise of construing the world with a more positive and charitable perspective, and many entail considering the silver lining in the cloud, identifying the door that opens as a result of one that has closed. It takes hard work and a great deal of practice to accomplish effectively, but if you can persist at these strategies until they become habitual, the benefits could be immense. Some optimists may be born that way, but scores of optimists are made with practice.

So although it might seem that your naturally optimistic peers are in a far-flung category from you, there's really no trick to their way of thinking. All that is required to become an optimist is to have the goal and to practice it. The more you rehearse optimistic thoughts, the more "natural" and "ingrained" they will become. With time they will be part of you, and you will have made yourself into an altogether different person. The positive spins and the silver linings will come about automatically and habitually, such that you would need to "practice" optimistic thinking effortfully and intentionally only during times of stress, insecurity, or heartbreak.

## A Recipe for Self-deception?

Some of you may still be skeptical. Making oneself "think positive" or "look on the bright side" sometimes smacks of naiveté or, worse, of foolishness. Perhaps you're a person who values "seeing things as they really are" above all else—that is, your primary motivation is to perceive yourself, people around you, and your world in a realistic manner. According to this view, reframing negative events in a positive and optimistic way or anticipating a sunny future would actually be wrong or at the very least unrealistic. To this reaction, I prefer the rejoinder by my graduate school adviser Lee Ross: "[Optimism] is not about providing a recipe for self-deception. The world can be a horrible, cruel place, and at the same time it can be wonderful and abundant. These are both truths. There is not a halfway point; there is only choosing which truth to put in your personal foreground."

Being optimistic involves a choice about how you see the world. It doesn't mean denying the negative or avoiding all unfavorable information. It also doesn't mean constantly trying to control situations that cannot be controlled. Indeed, research shows that optimists are *more*, not less, vigilant of risks and threats[39] (they don't have their blinders on), and optimists are very much aware that positive outcomes are dependent on their efforts (they don't wait around for good things to happen). As with anything in life, however, you should aim for moderation in optimistic thinking. Optimism expert Martin Seligman recommends a "flexible optimism," to be marshaled when the situation calls for it, but not when "clear sight or owning up is called for."[40]

## Reading Guide

If you benefit from this activity, you may also want to try:

1. Savoring life's joys (Happiness Activity No. 9, p. 190)
2. Learning to forgive (Happiness Activity No. 7, p. 169)

# Happiness Activity No. 3: Avoiding Overthinking and Social Comparison

Finish each day and be done with it. You have done what you could;
some blunders and absurdities have crept in; forget them as soon as you can.
Tomorrow is a new day; you shall begin it serenely and with too high
a spirit to be encumbered with your old nonsense.

—*Ralph Waldo Emerson*

During all the years that I've been studying happiness, I've also been keenly interested in a phenomenon that psychologists call self-focused rumination. My friend and collaborator Susan Nolen-Hoeksema has spent two decades investigating this phenomenon, which she calls overthinking, exactly what it is. Overthinking is thinking too much, needlessly, passively, endlessly, and excessively pondering the meanings, causes, and consequences of your character, your feelings, and your problems: "Why am I so unhappy?," "What will happen to me if I continue to procrastinate at work?," "I'm so dismayed by how thin my hair has gotten," "What did he really mean by that remark?," and so on.

Many of us believe that when we feel down, we should try to focus inwardly and evaluate our feelings and our situation in order to attain self-insight and find solutions that might ultimately resolve our problems and relieve unhappiness. Susan Nolen-Hoeksema, I, and others have compiled a great deal of evidence challenging this assumption. Numerous studies over the past two decades have shown that to the contrary, overthinking ushers in a host of adverse consequences: It sustains or worsens sadness, fosters negatively biased thinking, impairs a person's ability to solve problems, saps motivation, and interferes with concentration and initiative.[41] Moreover, although people have a strong sense that they are gaining insight into themselves and their problems during their ruminations, this is rarely the case. What they do gain is a distorted, pessimistic perspective on their lives.

I received recently an e-mail from one of three sisters, Theresa, who described herself as a chronic overthinker: "I'm the youngest of three girls and the most likely to ruminate, [making] myself unhappy by pondering and yearning and wondering and just feeling stuck." If Theresa is feeling unhappy about her situation—say, she is having trouble drumming up clients for her tax preparation business—obsessing over the whys, hows, and what ifs of her problems not only will fail to deliver any insight or make her feel better but might make things even worse. The combination of rumination and negative mood is toxic. Research shows that people who ruminate while sad or distraught are likely to feel besieged, powerless, self-critical, pessimistic, and generally negatively biased. The more she over-thinks her problems, the more likely that Theresa will have thoughts like "I'm not assertive enough for this business," "I'll never get another client," "This is just like that summer I couldn't find a job," "Maybe I should just quit," or "My finances will be in ruins." She may also have trouble concen-trating at work and be less able to resolve minor dilemmas or obstacles that might come her way, or she may perceive making calls or even doing rou-tine tasks as an unbearable hurdle. Ultimately, Theresa's distorted predic-tions and beliefs could create a self-fulfilling prophecy; she really *will* now have even more trouble attracting new clients. Ruminators can make less than appealing social partners, so her friends and coworkers might start avoiding her. All these factors together could lead Theresa to lose confi-dence in herself and even to spiral into clinical anxiety or depression.

The evidence that overthinking is bad for you is now vast and over-whelming. If you are someone plagued by ruminations, you are unlikely to become happier before you can break that habit. I will go so far as to say that if you are an overthinker, one of the secrets to your happiness is the ability to allay obsessive overthinking, to reinterpret and redirect your negative thoughts into more neutral or optimistic ones. I have found that truly happy people have the capacity to distract and absorb themselves in activities that divert their energies and attention away from dark or anxious rumina-tions.[42] Daily life is replete with minor upsets, hassles, and reversals. In most people's experience, other unavoidables include illness, rejection, failure, and sometimes devastating trauma. However, those who react strongly to life's ups and downs, who have great difficulty shaking off unfavorable information, are the unhappiest people in my studies. Even slightly difficult, unpleasant, or disagreeable events can make such people feel bad about themselves. Becoming happier means learning how to disengage from overthinking about both major and minor negative experiences, learning to stop searching for all the leaks and cracks—at least for a time—and not let them affect how you feel about yourself and your life as a whole.

My friend Leda was going through a very tough time taking care of her mother, who was terminally ill. Leda once described to me taking a daily break from the endless nursing by paying a visit to the local farmers' market. She loves outdoor markets, and this one was especially lively, thronged, and brimming with beautiful produce, warm breads, fresh fish, and many other goods. Leda said she was absolutely joyful during her free hour and a half. She could have easily slid into worry and despair, grieving the imminent loss of the dearest person in the world to her, feeling sorry for herself, obsessing over medical bills, or feeling depressed that she didn't have a social life. Of course she had bad moments. Of course there were times when scrutinizing the medical bills was necessary. But even during a trying time she was able to absorb herself in an attention-grabbing activity, stay busy, and feel joy.

## Overthinking in the Laboratory

A notable feature of overthinking is that it draws on a person's mental resources. Have you ever tried to read an article or a book immediately after an unpleasant encounter or after hearing bad news? You may notice yourself reading the same sentence over and over again. You may have trouble concentrating—at school, during work, in the midst of conversations, and even when trying to have fun. My students and I decided to conduct a series of studies to test this phenomenon in the laboratory. We found, indeed, that some of our participants tend to ruminate about bad experiences and that this overthinking harms their concentration, and ultimately their performance, at demanding everyday activities like reading and writing.[43] Not surprisingly, those who show this pattern are the ones who report being the most unhappy.

We also found evidence that in the face of an unpleasant event (e.g., a teacher's criticism, a social snub, an ambiguous health symptom), some people, but not all, find themselves pondering negative aspects of themselves. They may be distressed or anxious, chewing over what's happened and wondering about its implications. For example, in some studies, we expose our participants to negative feedback—for example, informing them that they've done very poorly on a test of verbal ability. Immediately afterward we offer them a sort of puzzle task, in which they are asked to complete words. For example, how would you fill in the missing letters to complete the following words? Don't spend more than fifteen seconds thinking about each word.

- D U __ __
- __ __ S E R
- I __ __ __ T
- E M __ __ __ __ __ __ __

Interestingly, relative to individuals who had learned they had "succeeded," those participants told earlier in the day that they had presumably "failed" (an experience likely to trigger ruminative thoughts) were likely to complete the words above as DUMB, LOSER, IDIOT, and EMBARRASS, revealing what was on their minds—namely, negative, self-evaluative thoughts (e.g., "I'm a loser," "I'm dumb," "I'm a failure"). However, it was only the participants who identified themselves as fairly unhappy who did this. Our happiest participants, by contrast, were able to shake off the ruminations. If you are the type of person who is "jolted by every pebble in the road," the persistent rumination is likely to take a significant toll on you. You need to imitate the behavior of the happy person and work to break free of overthinking.

## SOCIAL COMPARISON

Social comparisons are ubiquitous. In our daily lives we can't help noticing whether our friends, coworkers, family members, and even fictional characters in the movies are brighter, richer, healthier, wittier, or more attractive than we are. Every time we ask, "How was your day, honey?"; every time we flip through a magazine; every time we chat about our relationships with others, we are inviting social comparisons. Researchers have shown that such comparisons can be useful.[44] Sometimes they inspire us to strive for ambitious goals or to improve weaknesses. Watching a piano prodigy play a beautiful sonata can motivate the amateur to work harder. At other times social comparisons can make us feel better about our own plight. In the neonatal intensive care unit the parent of a low birthweight infant may be comforted by noticing that other parents' babies are even more fragile.

Much of the time, however, observations of how other people are doing or about what they have can be pernicious. "Upward" comparisons (e.g., "He's paid a higher salary," "She's thinner") may lead to feelings of inferiority, distress, and loss of self-esteem, while "downward" comparisons (e.g., "He got laid off," "Her cancer's spread") may lead to feelings of guilt, the need to cope with others' envy and resentment, and fears of suffering the same (equally bad) fate. The more social comparisons you make, the more likely you are to encounter unfavorable comparisons, and the more sensitive you are to social comparisons, the more likely you are to suffer their negative consequences. Indeed, social comparisons are particularly invidious because no matter how successful, wealthy, or fortunate we become, there's always someone who can best us. I once heard an anecdote on the radio that brought this home to me. A woman was recounting her father's sage advice in response to her complaints that other people had more than she did: "My father used to say to me, 'Look at these two mansions on Mission Street. They're both stunning multimillion-dollar homes. But the mansion on the left side of the street has an ocean view, and the one across from it does not. Do you think that the people who live in the second mansion are envious?' "

You can't be envious and happy at the same time. People who pay too much attention to social comparisons find themselves chronically vulnerable, threatened, and insecure. Interestingly, the phenomenon of comparing ourselves with others was the first topic I ever investigated as a research scientist. During my very first year in graduate school at Stanford, my adviser, Lee Ross, and I decided to seek out people who had been singled out by their acquaintances and friends to be "exceptionally happy" or "exceptionally unhappy" and to interview both groups at length. Our initial hypothesis (quite naive in hindsight) was that the happy people would be more likely to compare themselves with others who were inferior (thus making themselves feel better off), whereas unhappy people would be inclined to compare themselves with others who were superior (thus rendering themselves unhappy). However, when we asked the participants our carefully prepared questions about social comparison, the happy folks didn't know what we were talking about! Of course they understood what it meant to compare themselves with others—everyday observations, social interactions, and the media inundate us with information about others' successes and failures, opinions, personalities, lifestyles, and relationships— yet faced with such readily available and inescapable opportunities for social comparison, the happy people we interviewed didn't seem to care. Instead, they appeared to use their own internal standards to judge themselves (e.g., how good they sensed they were at math or cooking or conversation), rather than let others' performances influence their feelings about themselves (e.g., not falling prey to thoughts like "Ella is so much more knowledgeable than I am; therefore I must be mediocre"). Intrigued by these preliminary findings, Lee and I resolved to confirm them in more controlled laboratory studies. Over the next few years we found that the happiest people take pleasure in other people's successes and show concern in the face of others' failures. A completely different portrait, however, has emerged of a typical unhappy person—namely, as someone who is deflated rather than delighted about his peers' accomplishments and triumphs and who is relieved rather than sympathetic in the face of his peers' failures and undoings.

## SOCIAL COMPARISON UNDER THE MICROSCOPE

The social comparison studies were fun to do. On one occasion we brought happy and unhappy people into the lab and told them they'd be

solving "anagram puzzles" alongside a peer.[45] If you had been the participant in this study, you and your peer would have been asked to take seats
side by side, with the experimenter (often me) sitting by a table in front.
At the beginning of the session I would have handed each of you a card
with three anagrams on it, and your task would have been to unscramble
them (e.g., A-S-S-B-I, Y-O-N-S-W, and N-O-X-T-I).[46]

Every time you or your peer would have finished a card, you would
have handed it back to me, and I would have given you a new one. The
setup was created to make it very apparent to you at what rate the *other*
person was going because you couldn't help noticing the exchange of
cards. In addition, the cards were numbered consecutively, so if you had
been handed Card 1 followed by Card 5, you would have grasped immediately that while you had been frantically working on Card 1, the other
participant had already solved Cards 2, 3, and 4. You would have known
you were behind. In addition, we asked that participants use blue books as
scratch paper; this required turning the page every time a new anagram
was begun. The swooshing of pages again would have highlighted the dis-
crepancy between your speed and that of the other participant, an effect
familiar to anyone who's ever taken a test.

Here's the clincher. Your supposed "peer," unbeknownst to you, would
not actually have been another participant, but a confederate (or stooge)
working for me, whom I'd have instructed to solve the anagrams (or pre-
tend to solve them) either a great deal faster or a great deal slower than you.
How would that experience have made you feel?

The results of this study were dramatic. After the anagram-solving task
was over, happy participants felt more upbeat than they had been earlier
and thought better of their ability, regardless of whether they had witnessed someone perform much better or much worse than they. The self-
assessments of unhappy people, by contrast, were keenly sensitive to the
experience of witnessing another person's superior performance. Unhappy
people thought less of themselves—for example, judging their anagram-
solving ability as quite a bit worse—and reported feeling more sad, frustrated, and anxious after sitting next to someone who outperformed them.

Since then my students and I have conducted many more studies showing essentially the same result: that the happier the person, the less attention she pays to how others around her are doing. Once again the research tenders an example of what we can learn from the habits of a happy person. Indeed, the practice of incessantly comparing ourselves with others is part of the wider-ranging habit of overthinking.

## How to Shake Off Ruminations and Social Comparisons

Rumination can be very compelling. When you're in its tangle, it pulls and pushes you. You feel that you absolutely need to continue, that you need to figure things out. But as we have learned, when a person is distraught or stressed or nervous or insecure, no insight is gained from overthinking. To the contrary, rumination makes things only worse. Susan Nolen-Hoeksema advises chronic overthinkers to try the following three-step approach to battle their persistent ruminations: break free, move to higher ground, and avoid future traps.[47] These steps are described below. *If this is a well-fitting activity for you, choose at least one strategy to try from each of the sections that follow.*

**Cut loose.** First, you need to free yourself from the clutch of your ruminations—in other words, immediately stop overthinking and stop focusing on comparisons with others. There are no fewer than five effective strategies to accomplish this, and as always, you should pick the ones that feel most natural and most meaningful to you. The first strategy to arrest overthinking is simple and underrated yet incredibly powerful: distract, distract, distract. The distracting activity you select must be engrossing enough so that you don't have the opportunity to lapse back into ruminations. Good bets are activities that make you feel happy, curious, peaceful, amused, or proud. When you catch yourself thinking, "Why did I get so few lines in the community play?," or "I'll never get a promotion if Howard doesn't give me more responsibilities," or "She has so much more free time than I do," you should redirect your full attention somewhere else: Read or watch something that's funny or suspenseful; listen to a song that's transporting; meet a friend for tea; do a physical activity that gets your heart rate up. It doesn't matter what you do, as long as it absorbs you, compels you, and isn't potentially harmful. Sometimes all it takes to stop ruminating is to get up and leave the scene of the crime.

It's worth noting that although distraction seems like an almost too simple short-term solution or quick fix, the positive emotions that it begets can "debias" your thinking (opening up a new, more objective, and more positive perspective on your troubles) and hone resources and skills (like creativity, sociability, and problem-solving skills) that will be useful in the future.[48] Even a transient lift in mood can make you feel energized, more motivated to interact with people, and more creative in how you approach your problems.

The second strategy is the "Stop!" technique, in which you think, say, or even shout to yourself, "Stop!" or "No!" when you find yourself resuming overthinking. (A hairdresser once told me she imagines a red stop sign as she's doing this.) Use your intellectual powers to think about something else—like your shopping list or what you will say when you call the plumber on the phone or the steps you need to take in planning your next vacation. This technique is valuable in many situations, including moments when your thoughts wander even during a distracting pastime. I remember once finding myself ruminating whenever I went running. I would force myself to stop and redirect my attention to something else. This feat involved what seemed at the time like terrific powers of mental control, but it worked.

The third is a strategy I learned from Dear Abby a long time ago. She advised an obsessive reader to set aside thirty minutes every day to do nothing but ruminate. Accordingly, if you find the negative thoughts pushing and pulling, you can truthfully tell yourself, "I can stop now, because I'll have the opportunity to think about this later." Ideally, that thirty-minute period should be at a time of the day when you're not anxious or sad. More often than not, when the appointed time arrives, you'll find it difficult and unnatural to force yourself to overthink, and the issues you had set aside to contemplate will seem less consequential than before.

The fourth strategy is to talk to a sympathetic and trusted person about your thoughts and troubles. Much of the time, a simple tête-à-tête will bring an immediate reprieve to your feelings of negativity. You may find yourself feeling that your problems aren't as overwhelming as you initially thought they were. Or you might recognize the futility of being envious of a fellow mom's apparent parenting virtuosity and realize that in fact she is just as flawed as you are. However, a couple of caveats are in order. One is to choose carefully your confidant(e); he or she must be able to think objectively, not make you feel even worse *or* end up ruminating out loud with you. The other is not to abuse your opportunity. If you bring up your negative thoughts and worries ad infinitum, you may wear people out so much that they avoid you.

The final strategy involves writing. Whether in a handsome journal, in a computer file, or on a scrap of paper, writing out your ruminations can help you organize them, make sense of them, and observe patterns that you haven't perceived before. Writing is also a way to unburden yourself of your negative thoughts—to spill them on the page, so to speak— allowing you to move past them.

**Act to solve problems.** Second, you need to gain a new perspective on yourself and on your life in general. Essentially, this step jump-starts you into trying to solve the very real, concrete problems that might inspire your overthinking. For example, even if you're feeling weighed down by your problems and responsibilities and are indecisive about what to do, take a small step now. Perhaps this entails making an appointment with a marriage counselor (even if you're pessimistic about the outcome), or starting the first day of a financial planning program, or doing research on the Internet about possible new jobs, or writing an e-mail to someone who's slighted you. It could be writing a list of every possible solution to a particular problem—for example, ways to improve your relationship with your boss, to help your daughter's sleeping problems, to make extra money during the summer—and then implementing one of those solutions. If you're hesitant, think of a person whom you highly respect and admire and ask yourself which solution he or she would choose. Don't wait for something to happen or for someone else to step in and help you. Act right away. Even small steps will improve your mood and self-regard.

**Dodge overthinking triggers.** Third, you need to learn how to avoid future overthinking traps. For example, write a list of situations (places, times, and people) that appear to trigger your overthinking. If at all possible, avoid those situations or modify them just enough to thwart their ability to trigger an episode of overthinking. This is not that different from what a smoker must do when quitting, avoiding locations, times of the day, and specific people that set off his desire to smoke. Another technique is to strengthen your identity and work toward building your sense of self-worth. This is a biggie, but you can begin by taking small active steps, like learning or undertaking something new, such as cooking, hiking, gardening, painting, dog training. (Don't take on anything too grand.) This will enhance your self-confidence (e.g., "I'm much better at taking photos than I thought") and provide an alternative source of self-esteem by expanding your identity (e.g., "I've always thought of myself as a bookworm, but now I feel so good when I go to dance class. It brightens the days when my teaching job isn't going well").

Finally, if this is up your alley, learn how to meditate. The skills involved in this relaxation technique can help you distance yourself from your worries and ruminations and impart a positive sense of well-being. See Chapter 9 for detailed instructions or read one of the many books on the topic. Many people who meditate habitually claim that they find themselves feeling less burdened, worried, and stressed for the rest of the day.

**Take in the big picture.** To add to these recommendations, I challenge those of you who have chosen to commit to avoiding overthinking and social comparisons to try a couple of techniques proposed in *Don't Sweat the Small Stuff.*[49] Whenever a rumination or social comparison prevails upon you (e.g., "How will I ever get through this week?," "Teddy has been so distant and short-tempered lately," "Once again our manager took more notice of Cecilia's presentation than of mine," "Could that light-headed feeling be another flu coming on?," "Was I the only one not invited to the party?") ask yourself: Will this matter in a year? Your answer will afford you a big picture view of your troubles and diminish your worries. It's remarkable how quickly things that seem so momentous and pressing this very moment emerge as fairly trivial and insignificant. Sometimes when I'm facing a horrendous week or am upset over a perceived slight, I remind myself that I won't remember it (much less care about it) one month, six months, or a year from now. (The more extreme version of this strategy is to use the deathbed criterion: Will it matter when you're on your deathbed?)

Another valuable approach is to distance yourself from rumination even further by contemplating your particular problem in the context of space and time. If you're an astronomy enthusiast, visualize yourself (and the strains, worries, and tribulations facing you) as a microscopic dot on earth, which is a tiny part of the Milky Way, which makes up a infinitesimal speck of the universe. This may seem like a silly exercise, but in doing it you will undoubtedly recognize that your problems are trifling. When my son went through an astronomy phase, I was taken aback about how serene and unruffled I felt every time I read him a book about galaxies, stars, or planets. How can I stress over my carpooling situation when the farthest galaxy is thirteen billion light-years away? When the universe is expanding! It seemed magical that this knowledge would have this impact, but it did. An alternative exercise is to reflect on how 150 years from now, no one who is alive today will still be living. This also sharply brings home the point that few things in life are so significant that they are worth overthinking.

Finally, if you resolve that the trouble you're enduring now is indeed significant and *will* matter in a year, then consider what the experience can teach you. Focusing on the lessons you can learn from a stress, irritant, or ordeal will help soften its blow. The lessons that those realities impart could be patience, perseverance, loyalty, or courage. Or perhaps you're learning open-mindedness, forgiveness, generosity, or self-control. Psychologists call this posttraumatic growth,[50] and it's one of the vital tools used by happy, resilient people in facing the inevitable perils and hardships of life.

## Reading Guide

If you benefit from this activity, you may also want to try:

1. Developing strategies for coping (Happiness Activity No. 6, p. 151)
2. Committing to your goals (Happiness Activity No. 10, p. 205)

# 5.

# Investing in Social Connections

*If I am not for myself, who will be for me? If I am only for
myself, what am I? And if not now, when?*

*—Talmud*

The centrality of social connections to our health and well-being cannot be overstressed. "Relationships constitute the single most important factor responsible for the survival of homo sapiens," writes one social
psychologist.[1] I don't think this is an overstatement. One of the strongest
findings in the literature on happiness is that happy people have better relationships than do their less happy peers.[2] It's no surprise, then, that investing
in social relationships is a potent strategy on the path to becoming happier.
This chapter describes two happiness activities that have social connections
in common: practicing kindness and nurturing relationships.

## Happiness Activity No. 4:
## Practicing Acts of Kindness

The moral dimension of being kind, generous, and giving is undisputed.
The Bible exhorts us "to be generous and willing to share" (1 Timothy

6:18), and a principled, moral person helps those who are in need and, when necessary, sacrifices his own well-being for another. Indeed, the German philosopher Arthur Schopenhauer wrote: "Compassion is the basis of all morality." From a very early age we are inculcated with the idea that kindness and compassion are important virtues. Of course we are taught to develop and apply these virtues for their own sakes, because by definition, it is the right, good, and ethical thing to do. What scientific research has recently contributed to this agelong principle is evidence that practicing acts of kindness is not only good for the recipient but also good for the doer. It may be ironic, but being kind and good, even when it's unpleasant or when one expects or receives nothing in return, may also be in the doer's self-interest. This is because being generous and willing to share makes people happy.

## THE MILK OF HUMAN KINDNESS IS . . . HAPPINESS

To be sure, the notion that doing acts of kindness can make a person feel good is not exactly novel. Writers, philosophers, and religious thinkers have appreciated this truth for centuries. "If you want to be happy, practice compassion" is a common refrain of the spiritual leader of Tibetan Buddhism, the fourteenth Dalai Lama. "True happiness consists in making others happy," according to a Hindu proverb. And Scottish-born essayist Thomas Carlyle quipped that "without kindness, there can be no true joy." Nice thoughts, but their veracity had until recently not been tested systematically, using the scientific method. My laboratory was the first, to my knowledge, to accomplish this. Previous research had only reported correlations (but not causation) between happiness and helping. For example, we know that happier people are more likely to describe themselves as doing frequent altruistic acts (e.g., shopping for sick friends or stopping to help strangers), to spend a greater percentage of their time helping others, and to perform behaviors at the office that go beyond the call of duty (e.g., helping colleagues with work problems despite their own heavy workloads).[3] These findings are illuminating, but they have little to say about whether doing all those things (helping strangers or colleagues) actually *makes* people happy.

To address this very question, my collaborators and I conducted a happiness intervention (or experiment) in which we recruited participants into two groups and asked them to perform five acts of kindness per week over the course of six weeks.[4] The first group was instructed to do these acts anytime throughout the week, but the second group was instructed to do the five acts on one single day each week (e.g., all on a Monday). These were our exact instructions:

> In our daily lives, we all perform acts of kindness for others. These acts may be large or small and the person for whom the act is performed may or may not be aware of the act. Examples include feeding a stranger's parking meter, donating blood, helping a friend with homework, visiting an elderly relative, or writing a thank-you letter. Over the next week, you are to perform *five* acts of kindness. The acts do not need to be for the same person, the person may or may not be aware of the act, and the act may or may not be similar to the acts listed above. Do not perform any acts that may place yourself or others in danger.

Every Sunday night our participants turned in their "kindness reports," in which they described the acts of kindness they had done each week, to whom, and when. Examples of the types of kind acts that they performed ranged widely, from very small, simple helpful behaviors to fairly big ones—e.g., "bought a friend a sundae," "washed someone else's dishes," "donated blood," "stayed with a friend on her first night at a new place," "visited a nursing home," "helped a stranger with computer problems," "let my sister borrow my car for the weekend," "gave a homeless man $20," and (my personal favorite) "told a professor thank you for his hard work."

The results were a bit surprising. As expected, being generous and considerate made people happy—that is, the participants who committed acts of kindness over the course of the study experienced a significant elevation in their happiness. But interestingly, this boost was reported only by those who showed their weekly generosity all in one single day. So, although both groups who committed kind acts described themselves as being much more helpful after the intervention than before, the group that was instructed to distribute its five weekly acts of kindness over the course of the week didn't become any happier. Why did this happen? My hunch is that because many of the kind acts that the participants performed were small ones, spreading them over seven days each week might have diminished their conspicuousness, their prominence, and their power or made them less distinguishable from the participants' habitual kind behavior. After all, most of us do minor thoughtful and helpful things on a regular basis, and we may not even be aware of it.

So we see evidence in this study for the notion that optimal *timing* is critical for a happiness activity to be effective. In the section on gratitude (in Chapter 4), I noted that when we asked people to count their blessings on a regular basis, only those who did it once a week (versus three times a week) were rewarded with an increase in well-being. So you need to determine precisely how, when, and how often to commit to a happiness-enhancing practice in order to maximize its success. The results of our kindness intervention suggest that doing more than is your custom (at least when it comes to kindness) is ideal.

Our study was the first to show that a strategy to increase kind behaviors is an effective way to elevate happiness. Since then we have been conducting longer and more intensive investigations, working out how and why this and other strategies work. For example, we did another study in which we asked people to commit acts of kindness, though this time we checked in on them a month after the intervention had ended, to determine whether their happiness levels were preserved.[5] Furthermore, some of our participants had the opportunity to *vary* the kindnesses that they performed, whereas others did not. At the beginning of the study everyone was asked to make a list of acts of kindness that they would "like to do more in the future" and that are "easily repeatable on a daily basis." For example, they might choose to do an extra household chore, send e-cards to family members, help someone carry or pick up something, give their pet a special treat, or make breakfast for their boyfriend. Those in the "high variety" condition could mix and match any three acts they wanted to do each week, but those in the "low variety" condition had to perform the same three acts every week for ten weeks in a row.[6]

This second kindness study confirmed for us, once again, that doing acts of kindness on a regular basis makes people happy for an extended period. But the extent to which people vary what they do makes an enormous difference. Indeed, those participants who had to repeat their three kind acts over and over again actually dropped in happiness by the middle of the study before bouncing back to their original levels. These individuals probably found their exercise to be just another item on their to-do list—that is, a tedious experience that detracts rather than adds to happiness. If an activity is meant to enhance well-being, it needs to remain fresh and meaningful. Of course, when you embark on your own happiness-increasing program, you will do so by your own free will, not because an experimenter in a white lab coat is prompting you. Indeed, when you select an activity that fits you, you are choosing, by definition, to do something that you value and that you believe you will enjoy. This is empowering in and of itself. The singular act of choosing an activity can make you feel brighter and gladder even before you commit your first act of kindness (or gratitude or whatever else). Nevertheless, this study alerts us to be mindful of not falling into a rut when practicing our chosen strategy. Spicing up your happiness strategies will be worth the effort. (See Chapter 10 to hear more.)

## WHY DOES DOING KIND DEEDS MAKE PEOPLE HAPPY? LET US COUNT THE WAYS

Plentiful evidence for the reasons (or mechanisms) for why helping brings happiness comes from psychological theory and research. Being kind and generous leads you to perceive others more positively and more charitably (e.g., "the homeless veteran may be too ill to work" or "my brother really tries at math, but it doesn't come easily to him") and fosters a heightened sense of interdependence and cooperation in your social community (e.g., "it takes a village to raise a child" or "we must all pitch in to improve the environment"). Doing kindness often relieves guilt, distress, or discomfort over others' difficulties and suffering and encourages a sense of awareness and appreciation for your own good fortune. In other words, helping others makes you feel advantaged (and thankful) by comparison (e.g., "I'm grateful that I have my health"). Indeed, providing assistance or comfort to other people can deliver a welcome distraction from your own troubles and ruminations, as it shifts the focus from you to somebody else.

A considerable benefit of kindness is its impact on self-perception. When you commit acts of kindness, you may begin to view yourself as an altruistic and compassionate person. This new identity can promote a sense of confidence, optimism, and usefulness. Helping others or volunteering for a worthy cause highlights your abilities, resources, and expertise and gives you a feeling of control over your life.[7] You may learn new skills or discover hidden talents—for example, by honing your teaching aptitude or social skills, through uncovering a flair with children, or by learning the workings of a hospital. This in itself can confer a sense of efficacy and accomplishment. Some researchers argue that acts of kindness can even promote a sense of meaningfulness and value in one's life.[8]

Finally, and this is probably the most important factor, kindness can jump-start a cascade of positive social consequences. Helping others leads people to like you, to appreciate you, to offer gratitude. It also may lead people to reciprocate in *your* times of need.[9] Helping others can satisfy a basic human need for connecting with others, winning you smiles, thankfulness, and valued friendship. My laboratory actually obtained evidence for this dynamic in our second kindness intervention. We measured not only how helpful our participants were and how much their happiness increased over ten weeks but also the extent to which they perceived gratitude in those they helped. Indeed, we found that a chief reason that being kind to others made our participants happier is that it led them to recognize how much the recipients appreciated their kind acts.

So there are multiple ways that kindness can make us happier. Surveys of volunteers, for example, show that volunteering is associated with diminished depressive symptoms and enhanced feelings of happiness, self-worth, mastery, and personal control—a "helper's high."[10] Although these studies can't disentangle causal direction (i.e., "Does volunteering make people feel good about themselves, or are people who feel good about themselves more likely to volunteer in the first place?"), studies that follow volunteers over time strongly suggest that it's the munificent behavior of the volunteers that enhances happiness and not the other way around.

Consider an unusual study that followed five women volunteers over a three-year period.[11] These five women, all of whom had multiple sclerosis (MS), were chosen to act as peer supporters for sixty-seven other MS patients. They were trained in active and compassionate listening techniques and instructed to call each patient for fifteen minutes once a month. The results showed that, over the three years, the peer supporters experienced increased satisfaction, self-efficacy, and feelings of mastery. They reported engaging in more social activities and enduring less depression. Indeed, when interviewed, these five women described having undergone dramatic changes in their lives as a result of their volunteering experience. For example, their role as peer supporters appeared to shift their focus away from themselves and their problems and toward others. They recounted acquiring improved, nonjudgmental listening skills and becoming more open and tolerant of other people. They also reported a stronger sense of self-esteem and self-acceptance—for example, confidence in their ability to cope with life's ups and downs and in managing their own disease. One woman stated. "There's no cure for MS, but I really feel that I'm able to handle whatever comes my way."

Remarkably, the positive changes experienced by the five women peer supporters were larger than the benefits shown by the patients they supported. For example, the volunteers witnessed a boost in their global life satisfaction that was seven times greater than that shown by the patients! Furthermore, the benefits experienced by the peer supporters grew as time went on—an incredible finding, given that the benefits incurred by most happiness interventions (no matter how powerful) tend to diminish over time.

This was a small study, with only five participants,[12] but it nicely illustrates the multiple rewards of helping. Although volunteering (or community service) is a unique type of helping activity, involving sustained commitment within an institutional framework, it shares many of the same features, and benefits, as other, more spontaneous or mundane types of helping behavior.

## How to Practice Kindness

I have some very altruistic friends. One who especially comes to mind is always there for other people, always saying yes, forever sensitive to a situation when he's needed. I don't know how he does it, how kindness has become so habitual to this man, but many of us need to practice consciously and intentionally what comes so easily to him. Then again, the advantage for the rest of us is that doing something over and above what we are used to will give us an extra lift, a special boost in positive well-being.

I have come across numerous books, magazine articles, and Web sites advocating doing acts of kindness,[13] and I always get the sense, perhaps unfounded, that they patronize the reader a bit. If you decide to become a more generous, compassionate, and giving person, you will know what you should do. Ever babysat for a harried parent when you weren't asked? Ever traveled to see a friend in need? Donated your money or your time? Smiled at someone who needed a smile even when it was the hardest thing to do at that very moment? Needless to say, the options for helping are unlimited. You only have to open your mind to the possibilities for kindness; if you look with fresh eyes, they are all around you.

Furthermore, no particular talent, measure of time, or amount of money is required. The deed need not be grand or complicated. Moreover, if you're ever at a loss about *what* act of kindness, generosity, or charity to carry out, you need to look no farther than your home, your workplace, or your community. Sometimes people go to great lengths seeking special causes to which to dedicate themselves when those special causes could be their spouses, children, coworkers, or old friends. An acquaintance with a baby at home related to me a story about her husband. He was a cello player and had learned about a community service music program that involved visiting nursing homes once a month and entertaining the residents there. Despite a grueling work schedule that left him with little time to see his wife and baby daughter, he started taking out several hours per month to do this. He was very earnest and well-meaning about the new endeavor. But his wife was beside herself. "How can he play for strangers when he doesn't have time to entertain his own little girl?" she complained to me. Choose your acts of kindness with care, as any change in your behavior can have unintended consequences, good or bad. Above all, you don't have to be a Mother Teresa or the Dalai Lama; the acts can be small and brief.

**Timing is everything.** The first step in practicing the kindness strategy is to select which acts you intend to do, how often, and how much. The results of my intervention studies suggest that this is an important decision point. If you do too little, you won't obtain much benefit in happiness. If you do too much, you may end up feeling overburdened, angry, or fatigued. My suggestion is to follow the model of the one group in my first kindness intervention that was rewarded with the biggest increases in happiness—namely, pick one day per week (say, a Monday), and on that day (and on no others) commit one new and special large act of kindness or, alternatively, three to five little ones. I say "new and special" because you likely already dole out numerous small and large kindnesses every day, and the kindness strategy calls for doing something extra, something that pulls you out of your usual routine. If you always let cars ahead of you in line or you already volunteer at a hospital once a week, then, of course, don't make those your new and special acts of kindness. Resolve to do something else.

**Variety is the spice of life.** A second implication stemming from my kindness studies is to mix up, spice up, *vary*, what you do. Putting change into a parking meter or doing an extra chore gives you a lift the first few times you do it, but after a time you will adapt to the new habit, and it will no longer grant the same amount of happiness. (This doesn't mean that you should necessarily stop doing it, only that you'll be obliged to add another act of kindness to your routine.) Major commitments that involve regular contact with other people—e.g., tutoring a middle school student, visiting a sick neighbor, fund-raising for a cause—may not lend themselves to the same degree of adaptation and may continue delivering benefits to you (and others!) in terms of happiness, self-esteem, and other resources and skills.

Continually varying your acts of kindness takes effort and creativity. Here are some ideas. First, if you're short of money or other resources, give the gift of time: Offer to make a needed repair, weed a garden, take a child to the playground, or look over someone's taxes. Second, surprise someone—with a home-cooked meal, an outing, a gift, a letter, or a phone call. Third, each week try to do more of something that doesn't come naturally. For me, it's being courteous to telemarketers. For another person, it may be offering a sincere smile and hello (or thank you) to a passerby or the cashier at the grocery or fully listening (with eye contact) to a friend's concerns. Fourth, work to develop your compassion—that is, the willingness and ability to sympathize with others' plights and points of view. It may be a cliché, but it's really very difficult to put yourself in another person's shoes, to see the world from his perspective. Imagine what it would be like to be unable to pay your bills, to be laid off, to care for a disabled child, to be illiterate, or to be too weak to change a lightbulb. Offering assistance each week to such a person can help enhance your gratitude and develop and reinforce your compassion. Fifth, at least once a week do a kind deed about which you tell no one and for which you don't expect anything in return. Resolve not to sit around and wonder why other people aren't as considerate as you. This resolution will fortify your conviction that you are not being generous solely for approval and admiration, and this will deepen your sense of value, meaning, and self-worth.[14]

**Chain of kindness.** Standing at the cash register at Whole Foods recently, I overheard a twenty-something guy in front of me tell the cashier, with great embarrassment, that he was $1.15 short of his grocery charge. I don't remember ever doing this before, but I immediately offered him the $1.15. He was at first a bit taken aback and then incredibly and genuinely grateful. He thanked me earnestly and at length. The experience was unexpectedly exhilarating and wonderful (even to me, who does research on kindness!). A dollar is so trivial, I thought, and here was someone who indisputably appreciated and valued what I did. He had a wide and self-conscious smile on his face, yet as he hurried out, I saw him helping a woman in a wheelchair to lift her groceries.

In designing your unique kindness strategy, remember that acts of kindness often have such ripple (or "pay it forward") effects. The recipient may be cheered, surprised, or comforted, and your thoughtful act may trigger him or her to return the favor to other individuals, who may in turn be more generous the next day, and so on. In other words, one benevolent act can set in motion a series of kind acts. Another way that acts of kindness can have positive social consequences is that, as recent research shows, simply witnessing or hearing about a kindness leads people to feel "elevated" (warm in the chest, being "moved" and awed) and increases their desire to perform good deeds.[15] After observing the heroic acts of kindness by New York City firefighters, emergency personnel, and others in the aftermath of 9/11, TV viewers left their couches and went on to donate blood at two to five times the normal rate.[16]

**A final caveat.** All the recommendations outlined here are aimed to maximize how much happiness you receive as a result of committing to a kindness strategy. Sometimes this involves doing less or stopping what you're doing. I want to underscore that most people act compassionately and generously not primarily for their own benefit, but for that of others. Thus they may continue volunteering or repairing or teaching or listening or cleaning or donating because it's their moral duty. So, take my suggestions with a grain of salt. At times you'll be called to help others at the expense of your own well-being. As long as this is not a persistent pattern in your life and a key cause underlying your unhappiness, you should consider saying yes.

## WHEN KINDNESS IS PERNICIOUS

The platitude that being kind to others can bring you happiness has several important qualifications. The first is that certain categories of helping behavior are actually detrimental to physical and mental health. The one researchers know the most about is full-time caregiving for a chronically ill or disabled loved one. Studies show, for instance, that caregivers of spouses with Alzheimer's disease show depression levels *three times* greater than the average person.[17] Caregivers of spouses with spinal cord injuries report severe physical and emotional stress, burnout, fatigue, anger, and resentment. Furthermore, these caregivers are even more depressed than their disabled partners.[18] The caregiving job is relentless and often accompanied by grieving for the loss of companionship or the impending loss of life. Of course, this doesn't mean that caregiving should be forsaken, but benefactors need to recognize the detriments, so that they can prepare for them and cope as best they can. Indeed, any helping behavior that is burdensome, interferes with your daily goals and functioning, or causes bitterness would surely backfire as a path to happiness, though it may remain the appropriate, honorable, or right thing to do.

Another caveat is that a kind act needs to be done freely and autonomously to bring the maximum improvement in well-being. If you are forced to help someone, you may still believe that you are a generous and decent person, and you may still garner the appreciation and gratitude of the one you helped, but these benefits could be outweighed by the resentment you might feel or the sense of being taken advantage.

Finally, other people may not always welcome your kindness. Helping someone can put him in an uncomfortable position, making him feel needy, disadvantaged, and beholden. Consequently, instead of gratitude and appreciation, the response from the recipient may be something closer to hostility and resentment. Your attitude and approach can diffuse or minimize such potential feelings. When you undertake your weekly acts of kindness, don't behave self-righteously or condescendingly. Don't puff up your abilities and resources or talk down to the person you are helping. And unless the situation is critical, don't help those who don't want your help.

## POSTSCRIPT: KINDNESS VERSUS WEALTH

As I recounted in Chapter 2, there is now overwhelming evidence that money doesn't make people happy—or, more precisely, that it doesn't make people as happy (and for as long) as they suppose. What if I told you that becoming a more generous, compassionate, and charitable person would make you happier than earning a higher income? Would you believe me? I actually won't allege this because there are no data that directly compare kindness and wealth. But there is plenty of anecdotal evidence. The most persuasive, in my mind, comes from the example of Bill Gates, who announced that he would give up his day-to-day duties as chairman of Microsoft in 2008 to devote more energy to philanthropy. He is the richest man in the world, according to Forbes, yet he spends a great deal of time and effort *giving his money away*—more than half of his fortune, to be exact. Since 2000, for example, the Bill and Melinda Gates Foundation has donated $6 billion—more than most nations—to improve health in developing countries, including hundreds of millions of dollars for vaccinations for children and for medical research, and $2.5 billion for education for the poor. It is entirely possible that one of his donations will make more of a difference in the world than anything he has ever done as Microsoft chairman. Why does he do it? I can't say, except to speculate that it makes him as happy to give money away as to make it. "It's fun, and it is also an enormous responsibility," is how Gates explains his philanthropy. "But having my job at Microsoft is also fun and a huge responsibility. That is true for being a parent. Many of the most important things in life are like that. Why else would you want to get up in the morning?"[19]

Another fascinating example is that of Sherry Lansing, the first woman to run a major Hollywood studio. She gave up power, fame, and riches (as head of Paramount Pictures) to pursue philanthropy full-time. According to news reports, her associates and friends were stunned. But it appears that she may be far wiser than they are in appreciating what truly makes for lasting happiness. She's been busy starting a nonprofit foundation that targets cancer research and education, advocating on behalf of stem cell research, and fund-raising for human rights causes. Presumably, Lansing finds this more gratifying than a seven-figure salary.

*Reading Guide*

⌒

If you benefit from this activity, you may also want to try:

1. Savoring life's joys (Happiness Activity No. 9, p. 190)
2. Increasing flow experiences (Happiness Activity No. 8, p. 181)

# Happiness Activity No. 5:
# Nurturing Social Relationships

One of the themes of this book is that in order to become happier, we must learn to imitate the habits of very happy people. Happy people are exceptionally good at their friendships, families, and intimate relationships. The happier a person is, the more likely he or she is to have a large circle of friends or companions, a romantic partner, and ample social support. The happier the person, the more likely she is to be married and to have a fulfilling and long-lasting marriage. The happier the person, the more likely she is to be satisfied with her family life and social activities, to consider her partner her "great love," and to receive emotional and tangible support from friends, supervisors, and coworkers.[20]

The causal relationship between social relationships and happiness is clearly bidirectional. This means that romantic partners and friends make people happy, but it also means that happy people are more likely to acquire lovers and friends. This conclusion, which my colleagues and I have put forth on the basis of numerous studies, is actually rather optimistic. It implies that if you begin today to improve and cultivate your relationships, you will reap the gift of positive emotions. In turn, the enhanced feelings of happiness will help you attract more and higher-quality relationships, which will make you even happier, and so on, in a continuous positive feedback loop. In other words, by applying this happiness-increasing strategy, you will embark on what psychologists call an upward spiral.

## WHAT'S GREAT ABOUT RELATIONSHIPS?

Why are social connections so important to well-being? Because good social relationships serve many vital needs.

**Lessons from Darwin.** An article titled "The Need to Belong"[21] has become a classic in social psychology, and I can now appreciate why. Its authors lay out a persuasive case that humans are powerfully motivated by a pervasive drive to seek out and maintain strong, stable, and positive interpersonal relationships. We strongly resist the breakup or dissolution of relationships and friendships, and without a sense of belongingness, we suffer numerous negative consequences for our physical and mental health. This is not surprising; most scientists would agree that a desire to form and preserve social bonds has an evolutionary basis. Human beings would not have been able to survive or reproduce without such a motivation. Social groups hunted together, shared food, and fought off common enemies. Adults who pair-bonded bore children, protected them from predators and from the elements, and raised them to maturity. "No man [or woman] is an island," proclaimed John Donne, and "The Need to Belong" has shown us the reasons why.

**Social support.** One of the most important functions of a social bond is the provision of social support in times of stress, distress, and trauma. I know firsthand (and the research confirms) that there may be no better coping mechanism than confiding or sharing a problem with a friend or intimate. Social support can be tangible (e.g., driving us to the hospital), emotional (e.g., listening, reassuring, and helping us generate solutions or alternate perspectives on problems), and informational (e.g., providing financial advice). Indeed, people with strong social support are healthier and live longer.[22] An intriguing analysis of three communities of very long-living people—Sardinians in Italy, Okinawans in Japan, and

Seventh-Day Adventists in Loma Linda, California—revealed that they all had five things in common. At the top of that list were "Put family first" and "Keep socially engaged."[23]

**All you need is love.** My four-year-old used to insist that we teach him a new word at bedtime. One night I tried something new. "Your word tonight is 'love,' " I said. "I knoooow what looove means! I love *you*, Mommy." "But what does it mean that you love me?" He thought about this. "It means I want to kiss you a lot. And I want to live with you forever." In ten years he might regret having said that, but I think that definition of *love* is perfect. From the time of their conception to the moment of their death, human beings are embedded in relationships with others. It is within interpersonal relationships that most of us experience for the first time the emotion of love—the most wildly happiness-inducing emotion there is—and find meaning and purpose in our lives. Of course, as everybody knows, love has its ups and downs; nonetheless, most identify it as one of the chief things that makes them happy.[24]

**Less hedonic adaptation.** As the pie chart theory vividly portrays, all our life circumstances combined (health, wealth, age, job title, ethnicity, residence, life events, etc.) have only a small influence on our happiness. This is primarily because we so rapidly adapt to any circumstantial life change. For example, as we acquire income and consumer goods that we desire (e.g., gadgets, computers, cars, homes, or swimming pools), our aspirations simply rise to the same degree, thereby trapping us in a hedonic treadmill. In one study that surveyed people over a thirty-six-year period, respondents were asked how much income was needed by a family of four to "get along."[25] The higher the person's income, the more they estimated was required for a family of four. Remarkably, the estimate for "get along" income increased almost exactly to the same degree as did actual income, suggesting that the more you have, the more you think you "need."

But what about our friendships, family, and intimate relationships? Do we adapt to them as easily and quickly as we adapt to material goods? The answer turns out to be no. One economist has shown, for example, that people's desires for happy marriages, for children, and for "quality" children (as bizarre as that term sounds) do not change as they successfully attain those things.[26] In other words, there is something special and unique about relationships, and we would do well to strengthen, nourish, and enjoy them.

## STRATEGIES FOR INVESTING IN RELATIONSHIPS

Because at least 90 percent of adults eventually marry, most of my recommendations in this section refer to strengthening intimate (or "romantic") relationships, such as marriages. However, you'll recognize that many of the suggestions apply to other kinds of close relationships, such as with close friends and family members. *Pick one strategy from the array below, and start doing it* today.

John Gottman is a marriage researcher who has psychologically dissected hundreds of married couples. His book *The Seven Principles for Making Marriage Work* is, in my opinion, the best marital advice manual on the market by far.[27] I have talked it up to dozens of acquaintances and friends—indeed, to anyone who currently is, has been, or wishes to be in a committed romantic relationship. Even if your relationship is already solid, there is always room to strengthen and enjoy it even more. In his research, Gottman videotapes married couples and systematically observes how they behave and talk with each other. He then follows them over time to see what happens in their relationship. Based on these observations, he is able to predict with 91 percent accuracy which couples will stay together and which will divorce. This level of predictive accuracy, I should add, is unprecedented in the field of psychology.

**Make time.** So, what are the secrets of the successful marriages? The first is that the partners talk . . . a lot. The successful couples spend five hours more per week being together and talking.[28] The first recommendation, therefore, is to commit to extra time each week with your partner, perhaps starting with one hour and working your way up toward more. Spend five minutes every day expressing appreciation or gratitude for particular behaviors (even if it's simply to say, "Thank you for taking care of the bills this month"). Furthermore, before you part in the morning, find out *one thing* that each of you is going to do that day. When you meet again in the evening, have a "reunion conversation" in a low-stress setting, and *listen*. Coming from a household with two full-time jobs and two small kids, I fully appreciate that this is easier said than done. Be creative. If you're in a situation similar to mine, then return from work fifteen minutes before your kids do (or your babysitter leaves), or allow them to watch a fifteen-minute video or play a video game immediately when you come home. (The potential adverse effects of the media are far outweighed, in my expert opinion, by the benefits of a better marriage.) If children aren't the issue, then create a routine to reunite, taking a walk together, sitting on the couch, having a drink in the kitchen—whatever works. It doesn't have to be the moment you step in the door. My husband used to be notorious for his—dare I say it?—rigidity in needing time to put his stuff away, putter around, and glance at the paper before he could even think about saying, "How was your day?" The immediacy of babies' demands changed that.

There are several other ways to reserve time together. First, make every effort (including creatively reshuffling work or hiring a sitter or carpooling) to schedule several hours together once a week, and make it a dedicated ritual. It could be Thursday night or Friday lunch or Sunday morning. During this time you can talk or do something side by side in silence, take a hike, enjoy each other's company. Ideally, share an experience together, like taking a drive somewhere (to look at a view or a historic building), cooking together, reading poetry out loud, going out to dinner or to a sporting event.

Second, create a media-free zone in your home and reserve it for conversations only. If you're the kind of couple who truly shares listening to music or watching television (laughing, discussing, mocking), then by all means continue. But for most, television watching and Web surfing rob us of our intimacy and time together. It's remarkable how many couples insist that their harried lives leave them with utterly no time to spend with each other, yet if you ask them how many hours a week they watch TV, you'll be surprised.

Regarding whether it's right to take time away from work (if it's even possible) or children (if you have them) to dedicate to your relationship, this is a no-brainer. A massive literature shows that people who are lonely or in unhappy relationships suffer severe ill effects, including depression, anxiety, jealousy, stress, and impaired health. Needless to say, your job and your children will suffer if your marriage or partnership is tense, hostile, or unhappy.

**Express admiration, appreciation, and affection.** One of the key conclusions of two decades of research on marriages is that happy relationships are characterized by a ratio of positive to negative affect of five to one.[29] This means that for every negative statement or behavior—criticizing, nagging, lecturing—there are five positive ones. Make your weekly goal to raise your positive affect ratio. You can do this, first, by increasing the number of times you show affection to your partner—verbally (e.g., saying or e-mailing, "I love you," more often), physically (no need to explain this), or through other behaviors (like kindness). I once heard a family expert say, "A spontaneous kiss while doing household chores can do wonders."

Second, communicate your admiration and gratitude directly. This is something that most of us don't do often enough. Recall the large German study that showed that it takes an average of two years to adapt to the wonderfulness of marriage; after that, we start taking each other and the relationship for granted. Giving genuine praise (e.g., "I'm so proud of what you did") not only makes your significant other happy but inspires her to strive for greater heights. Indeed, in the most flourishing relationships partners evoke the best in each other, helping them come closer in reaching their ideal selves. This has been termed the Michelangelo effect.[30] Just as Michelangelo unearthed an ideal form by sculpting a block of marble, so romantic partners can support and facilitate each other to do the same. Because satisfied and stable couples are relatively more likely to idealize each other,[31] they may be more likely to reinforce each other's positively biased perceptions, helping make them come true.

Third, to increase respect, value, and admiration for your partner, there are some exercises that can be accomplished on your own on a weekly basis. Here's a sample four-week plan. During Week 1, you could write a list of attributes that initially attracted you to your partner or that you appreciate right now, and for each characteristic you generate (be it honesty, sense of humor, intelligence, punctuality, or charm), come up with at least one episode that illustrates it well. One couple told me that the secret of their relationship—she's an intelligent, sweet-tempered former model, and he's an outgoing, funny, self-described geeky journalist—is that each of them thinks he or she has the better deal. Contemplate how you might have the better deal.

During Week 2, try to remember and write about a good time in your marriage: when you first met or fell in love; when your partner showed support; when you successfully endured a difficult time together. The flip side of this exercise—try this in Week 3—is to consider a recent or memorable thing your partner did that angered or disappointed you. Then (and this is hard) write down two or three charitable explanations for his or her behavior—that is, explanations that attribute the behavior to forces other than your partner's bad character or motives (e.g., stress, misunderstanding, well-meaning intentions, etc.). A final exercise, for Week 4, is to sit down and write about particular goals, values, or beliefs that you and your partner share.

**Capitalize on good fortune.** This strategy involves taking delight in your friends', family members', and partner's windfalls and successes. Social psychologists have shown that what distinguishes good and poor relationships is not how the partners respond to each other's disappointments and reversals but how they respond to *good* news.[32] Recall the last time something really good happened in your life. Perhaps you earned a promotion, received a commendation or award, were invited to a special trip, or won tickets to a sold-out show. How did your partner react when you broke the news to him? Was he thrilled and enthusiastic on your behalf, or did he ignore, criticize, or scoff at your good fortune? How did *you* last respond to your partner's sharing of good news? Personal triumphs and strokes of luck can be threatening or intimidating to close others, evoking envy (e.g., "How come he gets to go to Europe when I've wanted to go all my life?"), jealousy ("She cares more about what her boss thinks now than about me"), or anxiety ("Does this mean we'll have to move again?"). As a result, the fact that your partner appreciates and validates your good news means not only that he is pleased for you but that he respects your dreams and values your relationship. Thus how people respond to things going right for others may be diagnostic of the sense of connection between them. If your close friend or romantic partner shows genuine pleasure, support, and understanding, the relationship receives a boost in intimacy and closeness.

Starting today, resolve to respond "actively and constructively"—that is, with interest and enthusiasm—to your friend's or loved one's good news, however small. One study showed that people who tried to do this three times per day over the course of just a week became happier and less depressed.[33] If your partner is excited to tell you something, pay close attention, ask lots of questions, and relive the experience with him. If you're happy for him, express it, and, if appropriate, insist on celebrating and tell others about it. Researchers find that people who are only "silently supportive," as well as those who seem uninterested or who point out the downsides of the good news, have relationships that are less close, less intimate, and less trusting.

**Manage conflict.** Observations of hundreds of couples have revealed that unhappy marriages are characterized by a particular style of handling conflict: a harsh start-up in disagreement (e.g., immediately launching into accusation or sarcasm), criticism (impugning the partner's entire character, like "What's wrong with you?"), contempt (expressing disgust with the partner by sneering, eye rolling, name calling, or demeaning), defensiveness ("I'm not the problem; it's *you*"), and stonewalling (eventually tuning out, disengaging, or even leaving the room).[34] Happy couples don't necessarily fight any less or any less loudly; they just fight differently (see below).

If any of these behaviors characterize your relationship, it may seem daunting to face up to them. But I believe that most people instinctively know how *not* to do these things; it may take thirty seconds (and a lot of self-control) to look up (rather than look down) when your spouse is sending a signal to make up, to voice a complaint ("Why didn't you call?")

instead of a criticism ("You never remember anything"), or to make a tiny gesture to stay connected while fighting (as simple as eye contact or touch or a "got it"). One of the secrets of the happiest couples has been found to be something very powerful but actually simple. It involves doing a little thing in the middle of a row that deescalates tension and negativity, an attempt at patching up. One of the most common such behaviors is friendly (as opposed to hostile) humor (e.g., screwing up your face like your two-year-old). Another is expressing affection or saying something directly (e.g., "I see your point"). You've heard it before: The happiest partnerships are also strong friendships.

However, a caveat is in order here. Sometimes, no matter what you do, your primary relationship will not improve, in which case it's time to make some hard decisions. If your relationship is damaging to your self-esteem, degrading, or abusive, it's imperative to see a counselor without delay or to consider leaving.

**Share an inner life.** Even if you and your partner excel at doing all the other things on this list, it won't necessarily mean that you are happy and fulfilled together. In truth, a deep sense of shared rituals, dreams, and goals underlies thriving relationships. These all are elements that connect you to each other and create a singular inner life shared by just the two of you. You grow together, explore new directions and take risks together, challenge your assumptions together, and take responsibility together.

Every week try to do at least one thing that supports your partner's roles (e.g., as parent, skier, manager, chef) and dreams (to travel abroad, to climb the corporate ladder, to go back to school, and so on). The goal should be to honor and respect each other and each other's life dreams and interests, even if you don't share them all.

## WHAT IF YOU DON'T HAVE OR DON'T WANT A ROMANTIC PARTNER?

Scientific research leaves no question that relationships are exceedingly important to well-being. But I don't believe that those relationships have to be romantic ones. Although in almost every study, married people have been found to be happier than their divorced, separated, widowed, or single peers, this doesn't mean that happiness is reserved only for them. Deep, long-term friendships are also important for happiness, as are other critical relationships, including those with pets.[35] Indeed, people who are single (and, in particular, women who have always been single) often have close, positive, and lasting interpersonal relationships—particularly with siblings, friends, and nieces and nephews. Studies have found, for example, that relative to married people, singles are closer to their friends and have more frequent contact with them and that lifelong single older women tend to have close to a dozen devoted decades-long friends. This evidence for the flourishing of many single people has led some psychologists to challenge the assumption that "the sexual partnership is the only truly important peer relationship."[36] Other partnerships matter too. Take note, then, that a strategy to invest in relationships can bring happiness when directed not only at lovers and spouses but at almost any significant relationship in your life.

## STRATEGIES FOR MAKING FRIENDS

Friendships don't just happen; they are made. One prominent psychologist suggests that the magic number is to have three friends or companions you can really count on. Here are some suggestions for how to get your friendship number up to three and to make them thrive.[37] Select *one* strategy for now and take it upon yourself to implement it as soon as possible.

**Make time (again).** Show interest in other people and offer them encouragement. Once a friendship forms, create rituals that allow you to get together and be in touch on a regular basis—a weekly date to go to the gym, a book club, a monthly dinner out, a joint vacation, or a daily e-mail. In this way, friends become as much a priority as all the other areas of your life. However, don't control all your interactions (let your friends decide which movie to attend at least half the time), and don't overdo it; give them space when they require it.

**Communicate.** Self-disclosure, revealing intimate thoughts and feel-ings, is difficult for some individuals, but it's critical to friendships, espe-cially women's friendships. This is because honest self-disclosure, when it occurs unhurriedly and appropriately, breeds more self-disclosure and cultivates intimacy. The flip side is to listen to your friends' disclosures and problems: Make eye contact, give your full attention, and acknowledge his or her statements. Hold off giving unsolicited advice or turning atten-tion back to yourself by recounting your own story (e.g., "I know just how you feel"). Sometimes this is appreciated and welcomed, sometimes not. Finally, just as with a romantic partner, convey feelings of affection and admiration from time to time in whatever way feels comfortable to you—e.g., "I missed you over break," "We always have a good time get-ting together," "I'm so happy for you that you're expecting," "Thanks for being there." It may appear sentimental, but people are amazingly grati-fied to hear such words. "A kind word is like a spring day."[38]

**Be supportive and loyal.** Be helpful and supportive when your friends need it, and affirm their successes. As I mentioned earlier, we often feel threatened by our friends' triumphs. Instead of feeling envious, try to bask in their reflected glory. Other universal rules of friendship include standing up for your friends when they're not there, keeping secrets, not putting down their *other* friends, and reciprocating favors.[39] In the words of William Shakespeare, "Keep thy friend under thy own life's key."

**Finally, hug.** Frequent hugging is enthusiastically endorsed by popu-lar magazines and Web sites as a means to increase happiness, health, and connectedness to others. If this is your cup of tea, the science is there to prove it. In a one-of-a-kind study, students at Pennsylvania State Univer-sity were assigned to two groups.[40] The first group was instructed to give or receive a minimum of five hugs per day over the course of four weeks and to record the details. The hugs had to be front-to-front (nonsexual) hugs, using both arms of both participants; however, the length and strength of the hug, as well as the placement of hands, were left to the their discretion. Furthermore, these students couldn't simply hug their boyfriends or girlfriends half a dozen times; they had to aim to hug as many different individuals as possible. The second group, the controls, was instructed simply to record the number of hours they read each day over the same four weeks.

The hugging group (which partook in an average of forty-nine hugs over the course of the study) became much happier. Not surprisingly, the students who merely recorded their reading activity (which averaged a not-too-shabby 1.6 hours per day) showed no changes. So, hugging is an excellent intimacy and friendship booster. The author of the study told me that some of the students—the guys, in particular—were a bit uncomfortable and embarrassed at first but ended up generating creative ways to hug (such as embracing teammates after successes on the field).[41] Try it. You may find that a hug can relieve stress, make you feel closer to someone, and even diminish pain.[42]

## Reading Guide

⁓

If you benefit from this activity, you may also want to try:

1. Practicing acts of kindness (Happiness Activity No. 4, p. 125)
2. Taking care of your body (Happiness Activity No. 12, pp. 240, 244, 250)

# 6.

# Managing Stress, Hardship, and Trauma

But we also boast in our sufferings, knowing that suffering produces
endurance, and endurance produces character, and character
produces hope, and hope does not disappoint us.

*—Romans 5:5*

N o life—if we live long enough—is without stress, adversity, or crisis. The possibilities are endless: the death of a loved one, a grave
illness, an accident, victimization, a natural disaster, a terrorist attack,
domestic violence, poverty, stigmatization, divorce, and job loss. Close to
half of U.S. adults will experience one severe traumatic event during their
lifetimes.[1] In the wake of acute challenges like these, many people
become depressed, fearful, or confused. They may find it difficult to concentrate on the daily tasks of living, and they may not be able to sleep or
eat well. Some have such intense and long-lasting reactions to a trauma
that they are unable to return to their previous ("normal") selves for many
months or even years.

Some people ask me: "How can I even *begin* to think about how to
become happier before I am able to tackle the many problems in my life?"
There isn't a simple answer. Becoming a happier person means rising
above your happiness baseline or set point. If a terrible event or chronic
problem has undermined that happiness baseline and is absorbing all your
resources and attention, then your priority is to cope. Fortunately, most, if

not all, of the strategies that help you be happier—counting your bless-ings, cultivating optimism, practicing religion, nurturing relationships, savoring life's joys, and so on—are also strategies that help you manage life's lowest ebbs. Furthermore, the two strategies described in this chap-ter, coping and forgiveness, are valuable not only in response to severe traumas but also as a way of dealing with the normal and expected daily challenges of life. For this reason, coping and forgiveness are foundational strategies that embody the potency of the 40 percent solution, the fact that how you behave and how you think has a great deal to do with how happy you ultimately become, no matter what hurts, stresses, and tribula-tions life doles out to you.

# Happiness Activity No. 6: Developing Strategies for Coping

We deem those happy who from the experience of life have learned
to bear its ills, without being overcome by them.

—*Juvenal*

Coping is what people do to alleviate the hurt, stress, or suffering caused by a negative event or situation. Psychologists call this managing stressful demands, and everyone has done it. When faced with a difficult or painful circumstance, how do you generally contend with it or sort it out?

## THE VARIETIES OF COPING

Your beloved pet has died. You're under terrific pressure at work. Your baby has a heart problem and has to have surgery immediately. Your car is totaled, and you don't have insurance. A close friend isn't returning your calls. These all are situations that can range from stressful to traumatic. How do you cope? A long-standing convention in psychology has been to divide coping into two types: problem-focused and emotion-focused. Some people tend to be problem-focused copers; they try to take the situation into their own hands, to act on it, resolve it somehow, and make a bad thing go away. This isn't always possible, of course. When a loved one has died, you cannot "fix" the problem. The only coping you can really do is to manage your emotional reactions to the event. If you are overwhelmed by grief, you can take steps to alleviate it or work through it—perhaps with psychotherapy, by spending more time with family, or by absorbing yourself in a meaningful project. It's not surprising then that people are more likely to use problem-focused coping when they believe that something constructive can be done about their situation and to use emotion-focused coping when they think that the negative event is something that simply must be endured.

**Problem-focused coping.** As its name implies, problem-focused coping basically involves solving problems. Suppose that you are having great trouble meeting deadlines at your job and are feeling overwhelmed. You need to generate solutions, weigh the costs and benefits of each, then choose one and act on it. Your solutions to your problem might be to confer with your supervisor about a change in duties, to create a new, feasible work schedule for yourself, or even to look for a new line of work. People who use problem-focused coping experience less depression during and after stressful situations.[2]

Below are some examples of how people describe themselves when using problem-focused coping strategies. They come from a popular scale that measures the ways that people cope.[3]

- I concentrate my efforts on doing something about it.
- I do what has to be done, one step at a time.
- I try to come up with a strategy about what to do.
- I make a plan of action.
- I put aside other activities in order to concentrate on this.
- I try to get advice from someone about what to do.

- I talk to someone who could do something concrete about the situation.

That's problem-focused coping, in a nutshell.

**Emotion-focused coping.** The items on this list all sound very well and good, but if the event or situation that you're facing is uncontrollable, or if you are so overwhelmed by negative emotions that you're unable to begin to take action, then emotion-focused coping is the appropriate and oftentimes the only available approach.

There are many emotion-focused strategies, some behavioral and others cognitive (or involving different ways of thinking). Behavioral strategies, for example, might entail distraction or physical exercise (e.g., a hike to lift your spirits) or seeking emotional support from people close to you (e.g., getting sympathy and understanding from a friend). Basically, people who involve themselves in pleasant activities, like going to the movies or picnics with friends, give themselves a breather from their sadness, anxiety, or distress and are thus more ready and better equipped to act on their problems.[4] Cognitive strategies, in contrast, may include positively reinterpreting the situation (e.g., trying to learn from the experience or looking for something good in what is happening), acceptance (e.g., learning to live with it or accepting the reality of what has happened), or turning to religion (e.g., finding solace in beliefs about the afterlife). With the exception of social support, researchers have overwhelmingly focused on studying the effectiveness of—take a breath—cognitive emotion-focused coping strategies. The rest of this chapter reflects that history, but for a good reason: The coping techniques I introduce are the most malleable and learnable—and potent.

**Teaching problem-focused and emotion-focused coping.** It's clear that both types of coping are valuable, depending on the situation and the person. Some researchers have actually attempted to teach people how to use both strategies. In one study, highly distressed widows and widowers were offered seven sessions of counseling to learn how to cope with their losses. They all reported some relief from their distress, but men benefited more from emotion-focused strategies and women from the problem-focused ones.[5] Presumably these widows and widowers obtained the greatest advantages when they learned something that they didn't already habitually do. This means focusing more on emotions among men and focusing less on emotions (and trying to problem solve) in women.

Other research shows that *both* problem-focused and emotion-focused coping is essential when you cope with a chronic problem. For example, women experiencing long-term infertility attended six weeks of training sessions to learn how to use the two kinds of coping.[6] Learning emotion-focused strategies led these women to become less distressed about their situation (e.g., they were found to be relatively less depressed in the follow-up after the study ended), and learning problem-focused strategies led them to resolve their problems (e.g., the majority who learned such strategies ultimately become mothers).

## CONSTRUING BENEFIT IN TRAUMA

Imagine being the mother of four and watching your husband die of Lou Gehrig's disease, as he slowly and painfully loses his ability to play with his children, dress and feed himself, talk, nod, and smile. Lynn was confronted with this heartbreaking situation.[7] As the end was nearing, she told a doctor that she "felt that there was a freight train coming." "There *is* a freight train coming," he replied.

Lynn's response was to cherish the remaining moments with her husband:

> I don't mean to be a Pollyanna, but I had 20 wonderful years with that man. There are people who don't have one day as happy as I had. It took me six months after Charley died to realize that that feeling will never go away. It's like the Grand Canyon. There's this big hole, and it hurts like hell, but it's beautiful.

A colleague I know lost his dearest friend and closest collaborator, a brilliant scientist, abruptly and cruelly, to cancer, cutting short a twenty-seven-year-long magical partnership. "I am the luckiest man I know, " he said recently at an event honoring his friend. "I wish on each of you the marvelous collaboration that I had."

Construing benefit in trauma involves seeing some value or gain (a silver lining, if you must) in your loss or negative life event—for example, a change in life perspective, a feeling that one's life has greater value, or a sense of personal growth. Although at first glance it would seem extremely difficult, if not impossible, to come to believe that your life has improved in many positive ways after a major trauma, psychologists have observed such benefit finding in numerous studies and populations—in bereaved individuals, cancer patients, stroke victims, and HIV-positive men, among others.[8] Indeed, 70 to 80 percent of people who've lost loved ones report finding some benefit in their experience.[9]

For example, a groundbreaking, now classic study found that female breast cancer survivors reported that their lives had been altered—often for the better—after developing the disease.[10] Indeed, two-thirds of the women interviewed (many with poor diagnoses) claimed this. What precisely were the supposed "benefits" of having breast cancer? The women spoke of a wake-up call, prompting them to reorder their priorities and to realize what was truly important in life (a common one was family over work), of deciding to devote more time to their most significant relationships and to spend less time on things like housework and yard work.

Interestingly, many of these same women seemed to have biased perceptions of themselves and their illness—for example, claiming that they could control the course of their cancer (e.g., by preventing a recurrence through nutrition or exercise) when the medical evidence clearly revealed that they couldn't or feeling extremely optimistic about their prognoses (e.g., reporting that they had "beat" the cancer) when the reality was that they were dying. Furthermore, fully seventy out of the seventy-two cancer survivors who were interviewed alleged that they were coping better than the average person in their situation (of course, statistically impossible). Could these views be possibly adaptive? The empirical evidence shows that they were. Women who held such optimistic beliefs were described by their oncologists and expert clinical psychologists, as well as by themselves, as being perfectly mentally healthy and well adjusted. Furthermore, these women's overly positive views did not seem to hurt them even when their beliefs were flagrantly disconfirmed (e.g., when the cancers returned). Interestingly, these women's remarkable ability to perceive benefits in their ordeal have been observed in individuals who are coping effectively with a variety of illnesses, including HIV, AIDS, and heart disease.[11]

In sum, construing benefit in negative life events is a tremendously effective coping strategy, which involves seeing some value in a loss or trauma. Some people claim that their relationships have benefited, that they are more profound, significant, and meaningful after the trauma than before. In a study of caregivers of hospice patients in the San Francisco Bay area, recently bereaved individuals reported that "there was a rallying of support, and a camaraderie that I think only shows itself . . . when something like this happens" and "I have learned and seen a lot of positive things in people—they just glowed." Other caregivers find guilt-free solace in the ending of the unrelenting caregiving that a death naturally provides.

Still others assert that they have grown enormously as a result of their traumatic experience, discovering a maturity and strength of character that they didn't know they had—for example, reporting having found "a growth and a freedom to . . . give fuller expression to my feelings or to assert myself." A new and more positive perspective is a common theme among those enduring traumas or loss, a renewed appreciation of the preciousness of life and a sense that one must live more fully in the present. For example, one bereaved person rediscovered that "having your health and living life to the fullest is a real blessing. I appreciate my family, friends, nature, life in general. I see a goodness in people."[12] A woman survivor of a traumatic plane crash described her experience afterward: "When I got home, the sky was brighter. I paid attention to the texture of sidewalks. It was like being in a movie."[13]

Construing benefit in negative events can influence your physical health as well as your happiness, a remarkable demonstration of the power of mind over body. For example, in one study researchers interviewed men who had

had heart attacks between the ages of thirty and sixty.[14] Those who perceived benefits in the event seven weeks after it happened—for example,
believing that they had grown and matured as a result, or revalued home
life, or resolved to create less hectic schedules for themselves—were less
likely to have recurrences and more likely to be healthy eight years later. In
contrast, those who blamed their heart attacks on other people or on their
own emotions (e.g., having been too stressed) were now in poorer health.

## POSTTRAUMATIC GROWTH

Friedrich Nietzsche's exhortation "That which does not kill me makes me
stronger" is familiar to many of us. The experience of pain, loss, and trauma
can indeed make us stronger or, at least, lead us to *perceive* that we are
stronger and more resourceful than we had thought. A woman who cared
for her eighty-three-year-old father before he died of cancer described her
realization this way:

> I saw myself acting in a role of competence where I had to pull on all my
> resources just to get through sometimes. I would have to be directing the
> medical people about what I wanted to do. A person like me who hates
> showing anger and can't stand conflict. I would have to stand and demand
> care from the nursing home, and it was necessary and I did it. So I came
> away with a feeling of competence and strength and gratitude. . . . I was
> forced to grow.[15]

Some psychologists believe that finding benefit in a trauma represents a
true personal *transformation*.[16] When you think about it, a major loss can
catapult a person into new roles and novel situations. A new widow, who
has always thought of herself as a "wife" and has been greatly dependent
on her husband—financially, emotionally, and socially—may be abruptly
propelled to learn numerous assorted skills. She may be surprised to find
herself rising to the occasion and accomplishing things that she never
judged herself capable of doing: selling a used car, playing catch with her
son, calculating her taxes, or attending a party solo. This can certainly lead

to new self-perceptions, enhanced self-esteem, and possibly even growth. But is it a transformation?

The available data say yes. When a challenge or trauma is profound, unsettling a person's foundations and forcing him to confront his personal priorities, sense of meaning, and identity, a subset of individuals report personal growth, strengthening, and even thriving. Researchers have studied people's responses to a variety of traumas: terminal illness, loss of a home in a natural disaster, divorce, military captivity, sexual assault, and having a low birth weight child. Some of the common transformative experiences reported by such trauma survivors are as follows:[17]

- Renewed belief in their ability to endure and prevail.
- Improved relationships—in particular, discovering who one's true friends are and whom one can really count on. Some relationships pass the test, while others fail.
- Feeling more comfortable with intimacy and a greater sense of compassion for others who suffer.
- Developing a deeper, more sophisticated, and more satisfying philosophy of life.

This last item is likely to be triggered by traumas that force people to face mortality, their own or others'. It's not uncommon to become absorbed in life-and-death existential questions: What is the meaning of my life? Why did this trauma happen? What reason is there to go on? Of course people rarely find simple and satisfying answers, but the very process of grappling with such philosophical or spiritual questions leads some to report experiencing life at a heightened level of awareness.

The research on posttraumatic growth offers much-needed good news to those of you facing hardships and crises. Not only can you survive, not only can you recover, but you can flourish. I've seen hundreds, if not thousands, of graphs throughout my career, but there was one that has always stayed with me, and I was recently thrilled to rediscover it. Reproduced below, it illustrates three potential paths that an individual can take in the face of a major challenge: survival, recovery, or thriving.[18] Survival involves a permanent impairment of functioning. This path shows a person who is merely surviving following a trauma, someone who may have lost much happiness and motivation to enjoy love, work, or leisure. Recovery describes a person who suffers in the aftermath of a trauma, perhaps unable to work productively or have satisfying relationships for a period of time, but who eventually returns to his original state. Finally, thriving involves someone who also suffers in the aftermath but who ultimately not only returns to her original state but rises above it! This person has experienced a transformation.

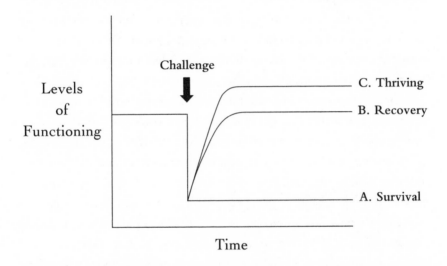

How do you pull this off? Psychologists point to real-life examples, like this one of a woman professor diagnosed with metastatic cancer.[19] Throughout her many treatments—surgeries, radiation, bone marrow transplant, chemotherapy—she continued her life at a brisk pace, teaching, doing research, sitting on committees, and traveling for business as well as to ski and scuba dive. "When her oncologist expressed puzzlement over the fact that her tumor neither grew nor shrank, noting that 'cancer does not act like that; it never sits still for so long,' she replied with a laugh. 'I am living my life so fast that it can't catch up.'" Although she seems superhuman, she acknowledges experiencing pain, fear, and uncertainty, but reports that her postcancer life has become more meaningful and that many other women in her cancer support group share a similar view. She reports having more self-confidence and being more easygoing and happier, explaining that her spirituality accounts for some of her posttraumatic growth. She now believes that everything she faces, whether positive or negative, affords an occasion for redemption.

Sometimes, however, the barriers to thriving are massive, calling for demanding and creative strategies. A woman concentration camp survivor was asked how she could possibly carry on and prevail in the aftermath of her calamitous experience. She replied that in order to function, she makes a "sort of schizophrenic division . . . a compartmentalization between her memories of the camp and what she describes as her so-called normal life."[20] Compartmentalization is a strategy that people facing a variety of woes, big and small, have found effective, including most publicly, a recent U.S. president confronting a sordid scandal.

I hope these portraits of flourishing individuals are inspiring and not discouraging. The higher you aim in terms of how you cope with trauma, the more you will achieve. Recovery is good. Indeed, it is excellent. Thriving and flourishing are even better. But remember that posttraumatic growth—and happiness, for that matter—are not the same as always being joyful and carefree. Indeed, most survivors experience a great deal of distress *at the same time* as they report strengthening and progress. The uphill road that leads to a more fulfilling and more meaningful life may be laid with stones and punctuated by troughs. There's absolutely nothing good about tragedy and loss, but something of value can come from the struggle in their aftermath.

## SOCIAL SUPPORT

When twenty-three-year-old Sylvia lost her daughter Sierra to an unexpected, accidental death, she turned to her companions for consolation and support. Bereavement has been found to be associated with an elevation in stress hormones called glutocorticoids, and friendly social contact can lower these hormones.[21] This phenomenon has been observed in both baboons—like Sylvia—and humans.

Turning to social support—the comfort and contact offered by other people (or monkeys) in times of strain, distress, and trauma—is one of the most effective coping strategies that exist. Social support not only makes us happier and less anxious and depressed but even affects our bodies. In one study, researchers located men and women who'd lost their spouses about a year earlier either to accidental death (like a motor vehicle crash) or to suicide.[22] Perhaps not surprisingly, they found that the sudden death of spouses was related to an abrupt decline in their physical health. However, those widows and widowers who had confided in others close to them had fewer health problems and were less likely to ruminate about their situation.

Another study focused on women facing a very different kind of stressor, life-threatening cancer.[23] Those who actively sought social support as a coping strategy immediately after surgery showed greater natural killer cell activity. Remarkably, this finding indicates that using social support may have triggered these women's immune systems to fight their cancer more aggressively. Women cancer patients who attend weekly support groups have been found to live an average of eighteen months longer.[24]

In sum, social support is pretty incredible, a strategy of almost magical proportions. Except that it's not magic at all. Friends, partners, companions, confidants: All give you a place to belong, room to share feelings, opportunities to discover that you're not alone in your troubles. Talking to others about a traumatic experience not only helps you cope and see the event with a new perspective but ultimately reinforces and strengthens your relationship. How many times have you been plagued by intrusive worries and ruminations about a recent problem and then observed those worries almost palpably lift from your shoulders after talking to an understanding friend? Women especially tend to rely on social relationships as a key to their resilience in the face of stress and trauma. From childhood on, girls are encouraged to value and even define themselves in terms of connections with others.[25] As we grow up, those connections bring us many benefits.

Is all social support beneficial? Of course not. Not every person from whom you seek sympathy or in whom you confide will be responsive in a helpful way, and some may do downright damage. If your confidant is hostile, puts you down, makes you even more miserable and anxious, or obsesses right along with you, find a more helpful partner. Studies show that the *quality* of social support is just as important as whether you have it. People who endure problematic, conflictual relationships or abrasive interactions with others close to them suffer in terms of their emotional and physical well-being.[26]

## FINDING MEANING

A traumatic event, like a serious illness, a death in the family, an unexpected loss of status or employment, or being the victim of a crime, can shake your assumptions to their foundations. "Why me?" you might ask, or "How could God let this happen?" Psychologists call this a threat to your assumptive world. It's critical, they say, that in its aftermath you gain an understanding of the trauma and of its implications.[27] In Western cultures, people tend to believe that their world is generally a controllable and predictable place, that bad things don't happen to good people, that people get what they deserve and deserve what they get.[28] This belief in a just world, where things don't happen at random, is implicit but very potent. When a bad thing does happen to a good person, her assumptions about the justice, control, and benevolence of the world is exposed as an illusion. What's more, a traumatic event can threaten a person's self-worth (e.g., a victim of random violence might blame herself) and her dreams (e.g., a mother who has lost a child has to reenvision an entire new childless future).

As a result, coping with a terrible event may require you to rethink your assumptions and beliefs, to find some meaning in the loss or trauma. This can be a difficult and painful process. How does one make sense of an event that can seem senseless? Studies have found that people make sense of loss in many ways—for example, by acknowledging that life is short and fragile (one bereaved person said, "My basic attitude to life was that there's a beginning and an end, and it's going to happen to one or the other of us sooner or later"), by attributing the tragedy to God's will ("I think that my father's illness was meant to be, and that was God's plan"), or by explaining a death in terms of the deceased's behavior ("It always made sense to me. I mean, he smoked for years").[29] Other ways that people have been able to find meaning in a tragedy is to accept the fact that sometimes things happen for no reason or to construe benefits in the negative event—for example, that it put an end to a loved one's suffering, or that they've learned a great deal about life and about themselves, or that the event has spurred them to do good in their community. Finally, some people may interpret a loss or trauma as sending them an important signal (e.g., "She would have wanted me to turn my life around" or "The accident was a sign that I should stop drinking").

In sum, it is undoubtedly terrifically hard to find meaning in a traumatic—and often seemingly meaningless and arbitrary—occurrence. Those who do, however, are better able to cope. One study followed individuals who had recently lost their loved ones from before the loss to a year after.[30] Those who reported finding some meaning in their loss (it didn't matter how) showed less depression and fewer symptoms of posttraumatic stress disorder twelve months later. The benefit of finding meaning in a loss extends to physical health as well. In another study, HIV-seropositive men who had lost friends or partners to AIDS and had found some meaning in the death showed healthier immune systems and themselves lived longer over a two- to three-year period.[31] The "meaning" included gaining a new perspective on themselves and their own lives (e.g., that they should spend more time with friends and family, that they should live life to the fullest, that they should take more risks), as well as growth in their spirituality or faith.

## SPECIFIC STRATEGIES FOR COPING

If coping is a strategy that you wish to develop, then choose one of the following three recommendations.

**Finding meaning through expressive writing.** About twenty years ago James Pennebaker embarked on research to explore whether writing about a traumatic or upsetting experience could affect people's health and well-being.[32] The procedure he developed has now been adopted by scores of other researchers, including me. If you were to participate in one of Pennebaker's typical studies, you would be invited to a laboratory, presented with a sheaf of paper (or, in more recent years, a computer screen), and, with assurances of confidentiality, asked to write about one of your most distressing or painful life experiences. You would be urged to describe the experience in detail and to explore your personal reactions and deepest emotions fully. The writing would go on for fifteen to thirty minutes, and you would be asked to come back and continue writing about the experience for a total of three to five consecutive days. Participants in a control condition usually would be asked to do the same amount of writing but on neutral topics, like their daily schedules, their shoes, or the layouts of their living rooms.

The growing body of results in this area reveals that such expressive writing about past traumatic events has many beneficial consequences. Compared with control groups, people who spend three days exploring their deepest thoughts and feelings about ordeals or traumas in a journal make fewer visits to a doctor in the months following the writing sessions, show enhanced immune function, report less depression and distress, obtain higher grades, and are more likely to find new jobs after unemployment.[33] These effects have been found among a wide variety of individuals, healthy and sick, young and old, poor and rich, and those residing in Europe, East Asia, and North America.

Initially, researchers believed that the benefits of expressive journal writing about trauma were due to emotional catharsis—that is, because the act of writing allows us to overcome our inhibitions over the trauma by venting and letting go of our emotions. This hypothesis has now been widely challenged. The critical mechanism appears to be the nature of the writing process itself, which helps us understand, come to terms with, and make sense of our trauma. Finding meaning in the trauma through writing also seems to reduce how often and how intensely we experience intrusive thoughts about it.

I've wondered quite a bit about what makes journal writing so special and effective. What is it about converting our emotions, thoughts, and images about a highly distressing event into words and sentences that alters the way we think about it? Suppose that you have had your heart broken, or you have experienced a harrowing physical assault, or your healthy and active mother has been diagnosed with Alzheimer's. You might find yourself ruminating about the experience, even when you're supposed to be focused on something else, and you might be troubled with intrusive images and thoughts. Writing about the experience in a journal forces you to organize and integrate those thoughts and images into a coherent narrative. Language by its nature is highly structured; indeed, the very act of writing sentences may prompt you to think in causal terms (e.g., A may have led to B, which may have led to C), thereby triggering an analysis that could help you find meaning, enhanced understanding, and, ultimately, a sense of control. When an experience has structure and meaning, it seems much more manageable and controllable than when it's represented by a chaotic and painful jumble of thoughts and images. For example, Pennebaker and his colleagues found that the more people used causal words (e.g., *because, infer, cause*) and insight words (e.g., *understand, realize, see*) over the course of their writing sessions about a distressing topic, the bigger the improvements they experienced in their health.[34]

It makes sense that if writing helps people find meaning and resolution in their trauma, they might find their emotional reactions to it more manageable and might be less disturbed by unwanted ruminations. The process of creating a narrative about your experience, telling a story, can lead you to accept it. Furthermore, writing involves recording your thoughts externally, whether on a page in your diary or a Word document. This may allow you to unburden yourself by chronicling your emotions, thoughts, and memories outside yourself and thus allowing yourself to move past your troubles.

So, for your first exercise in coping, get out a notebook, PowerBook, diary, or a sheet of paper, and follow the directions given to Pennebaker's participants:

> For the next four days, I would like for you to write about your very deepest thoughts and feelings about the most traumatic experience of your entire life. In your writing, I'd like you to really let go and explore your very deepest emotions and thoughts. You might tie your topic to your relationships with others, including parents, lovers, friends, or relatives, to your past, your present, or your future, or to who you have been, who you

would like to be, or who you are now. You may write about the same general issues or experiences on all days of writing or on different traumas each day.[35]

At minimum, you should spend fifteen minutes writing each day, and you should write for several days in a row, for as long as needed. You could even start a blog. Be patient and persistent, and watch the benefits unfold.

**Construing benefit in trauma through writing or conversing.** As you can tell, expressive writing is fairly open-ended. You can write whatever you want about your loss or trauma, as long as you strive to express your emotions honestly and fully. The second coping exercise I'd like to introduce also involves journal writing, but in a more guided form. Alternatively, it can be done in conversation with a supportive confidant. A sequence of three general steps is taken, with the ultimate goal of finding benefit in pain.

First, whether through writing or talking, acknowledge that your loss or trauma has caused you a great deal of pain and suffering. Then consider what you have done during your loss or in response to it that you are proud of. If a family member has died, perhaps you worked extremely hard to make his or her last days comfortable. If your marriage fell apart and you sank into a depression, perhaps you bravely slogged through your workdays and kept it together, at least in front of people who depended on you.

Next, consider how much you have grown as a result of your loss. Do you think that you have a new perspective on life (even if it's a negative one)? Do you believe that you are more compassionate now, or more grateful, or sensitive, or patient, or tolerant, or open-minded?

Finally, think about how the trauma has positively affected your relationships. Have any of them been strengthened in any way? Have any of them become closer, more intimate, or more supportive?

**Coping via thought disputation.** This last strategy, derived from cognitive therapy for depression, involves disputing or challenging your own pessimistic thoughts. When bad things happen, we are often overwhelmed with negative emotions and negative beliefs, which exacerbate and feed back into each other: "I'll never get a boyfriend," "I'm so unattractive," "My son doesn't respect me," "It was my fault that our night out was a disaster," "My job is going to be eliminated any day now." These are often automatic thoughts that are overly pessimistic, distorted, and negatively biased. A valuable exercise is to follow—in writing—the five elements of the ABCDE disputation technique: A for adversity, B for belief, C for consequence, D for disputation, and E for energize.[36] Here are the steps, in order:

1. Write down the nature of the *adversity,* the bad event or problem you are facing—e.g., "My best friend hasn't called me in three weeks."

2. Identify any negative *beliefs* triggered by this problem—e.g., "She must hate me" or "I'm terrified that she thinks that I'm too boring."

3. Record the *consequence* of the problem, how you are feeling and acting as a result—e.g., "I feel miserable and lonely" or "I've never been good at keeping friends" or "I'll skip the dinner party this weekend."

4. *Dispute* the negative belief, challenging it, thinking of other possible reasons for the problem—e.g., "Perhaps my friend has been extremely busy (I remember her mentioning a big contract at work)," or "Maybe she's feeling down herself and wants *me* to call."

5. Considering the more optimistic explanations for your problem can *energize* you and lift your spirits, so that you become less anxious and more hopeful.

ABCDE disputation basically involves arguing with your own overly pessimistic thoughts rather than let those thoughts control you. You may have noticed how the different parts (A through E) are related. Our reactions (the *consequence*) to the bad event (the *adversity*) are in great part determined by our *beliefs* and interpretations about why the bad event has happened and what it means to us. A more optimistic, more encouraging, more charitable interpretation changes our reaction and our outlook (the *consequences*), by *energizing* us.

The hardest part, of course, is the *disputation*. To challenge your automatic negative thoughts, you need to take the role of a detective, hunting for evidence that might disconfirm your initial hunches. Say that your bad event is "My husband has been distant lately" and your belief is "He's not attracted to me anymore." Below are questions you should ask yourself and answer, preferably in writing and preferably when you're in a neutral mood.

- What specific evidence do I have for this belief?
- What alternative explanations are there for his recent behavior?
- Even if my belief is true, what are the implications? Put another way, what is the worst possible thing that could happen? How likely is it?
- What is the best possible thing that could happen, and what is the likelihood of that?
- What do I *honestly* think is the most likely outcome?
- Is this belief useful to me? What do I get out of having it?
- Finally, what do I plan to do to address the problem?

## Reading Guide

If you benefit from this activity, you may also want to try:

1. Committing to your goals (Happiness Activity No. 10, p. 205)
2. Learning to forgive (Happiness Activity No. 7, p. 169)

# Happiness Activity No. 7:
# Learning to Forgive

When I was a doctoral student at Stanford, a twenty-six-year-old woman, Amy Biehl, who had graduated with a BA in international relations and had taken a Fulbright scholarship to research women's rights and fight segregation in South Africa, was pulled from her car and stabbed to death by a mob in Guguletu township, near Cape Town. It happened two days before she was coming home to be reunited with her family and her long-time boyfriend in California. She didn't know that he was planning to ask her to marry him. It was a tragedy, one that unnerved several people close to me, especially parents of children just about her age. They tried to put themselves in the heads of her parents, an effort that was agonizing. Two years later Amy's parents returned to the township where she was killed and met with some of the killers' families to console them.

To *console* them?

Four young men had been sentenced for eighteen years for Amy's murder. The Biehls came to witness their testimony in front of the Truth and Reconciliation Commission, during which the four men expressed remorse and pleaded for amnesty. The Biehls supported their release. They were able to bury their anger, hurt, and hatred.

Amy's father died shortly after that trip, but Amy's mother returned to South Africa yet again, this time to forgive one of the four killers, a man named Ntobeko Peni. He saw himself as a young freedom fighter, growing up poor and segregated in South Africa's townships, taught from child-hood that whites were the enemy. But she didn't just forgive him. She gave him a job and, with the job, a future. He works as a guide and peer educa-tor for HIV/AIDS awareness at the Amy Biehl Foundation, which has programs in townships outside Cape Town. He also travels the world with Amy's mother to tell their story of forgiveness and reconciliation. Amy's mother says that Ntobeko is part of her family now.

This might appear at first glance as an extreme example, and few of us would aspire to hold the reservoir of forgiveness that Amy's mother seems to have. But research suggests that we can learn from her.

## WHAT IS FORGIVENESS?

I've been describing in this chapter how to respond to a variety of adverse life experiences. One particular kind of painful ordeal comes when you are wronged, hurt, or attacked by another person. The injury or abuse could be physical, sexual, or emotional. It may involve an insult, an offense, a betrayal, or a desertion. It appears that the natural first inclination of human beings to such injuries is to respond negatively, to reciprocate with an equal harm.[37] The two other typical responses are a desire to avoid the person or to seek revenge. It would seem obvious that such responses breed negative consequences. Trying to distance yourself from the transgressor—and especially trying to retaliate—ultimately makes you unhappy, damages or destroys relationships, and may even harm society at large. Throughout history and continuing through today, the drive for revenge has motivated numerous ills and horrors of our world, including murder, rape, and pillage, and also war, terrorism, and genocide.

The focus of this book, however, is on the individual, on you. What does forgiveness mean, and is it worthwhile to learn and practice it? Forgiveness may be the one factor that can disrupt the cycle of avoidance and vengeance in which we often find ourselves. Advocated by many, if not most, of the world's religions (a common notion is that people should be forgiving in their life on earth because they have been forgiven by God), forgiveness involves suppressing or mitigating one's motivations for avoidance and revenge (which often bring with them accompanying emotions of anger, disappointment, and hostility), and, ideally, replacing them with more positive or benevolent attitudes, feelings, and behaviors.[38] It's worth noting that we forgive another individual; the term *forgiving ourselves* refers to a separate process of bolstering self-worth, *not* to reducing drives for avoidance and revenge.

Psychologists who study forgiveness use a definition that differs a bit from that of the average person on the street. It's important to under-stand what they mean by it and what they don't mean by it. Forgiveness is *not* reconciliation—that is, it does not necessarily involve the reestablish-ment of the relationship with the transgressor. Nor is it equivalent to par-don, which is a legal term and is something usually accomplished within the justice system, or condoning, which implies justifying, minimizing, or tolerating the victimization or hurt, thus eliminating the need for forgive-ness entirely. Forgiveness does not mean excusing, which offers extenu-ating circumstances or a "good reason" (i.e., "He did it when he was high on drugs") or denial of harm, which connotes the Freudian concept of repression, or an unwillingness to accept what had occurred. Finally, "for-give and forget" is a misnomer, inasmuch as forgiving does not involve a decaying of memory for the hurt. Indeed, truly forgiving someone involves contemplating the injury at some length while forgetting the injury would make that process rather difficult.

How, then, do you know if you've forgiven someone? It's when you have experienced a shift in thinking, such that your desire to harm that person has decreased and your desire to do him good (or to benefit your relationship) has increased. Consider how much you agree with the fol-lowing statements, borrowed from a forgiveness scale:[39]

- I'll make him/her pay.
- I want to see him/her hurt and miserable.
- I live as if he/she doesn't exist, isn't around.
- I keep as much distance between us as possible.

The more you agree with any of these items—the first two tapping revenge and the second two measuring avoidance—the more work you still need to do in order to forgive.

## WHY FORGIVE?

Both research evidence and anecdotal observations suggest plenty of good reasons that we should forgive those who hurt, offend, or victimize us. Before I go on to depict this very powerful evidence, I want to underscore that forgiving is something that you do for *yourself* and not for the person who has wronged you. Wise people surely disagree about when forgiveness is or is not appropriate, about tough questions of justice and morality, and about which acts are unforgivable. If you have strong reasons not to forgive, those reasons must be respected. However, many of you are reading this section precisely because you have already ascertained that forgiveness would be a successful or necessary and fitting strategy for you. Just remember that forgiving does not mean that you should necessarily restore the relationship with the transgressor, nor does it mean excusing or condoning. Some acts may indeed be inexcusable.

There are a number of folk sayings all of which carry something like the following message: Clinging to bitterness or hate harms *you* more than the object of your hatred. (Buddha said, "Holding on to anger is like grasping a hot coal with the intent of throwing it at someone else; you are the one getting burned.") Empirical research confirms this insight:[40] Forgiving people are less likely to be hateful, depressed, hostile, anxious, angry, and neurotic. They are more likely to be happier, healthier, more agreeable, and more serene. They are better able to empathize with others and to be spiritual or religious. People who forgive hurts in relationships are more capable of reestablishing closeness. Finally, the inability to forgive is associated with persistent rumination or dwelling on revenge, while forgiving allows a person to move on.

None of these findings is surprising, but they don't tell us if forgiveness is the causal agent behind all these good things. Fortunately, a number of interventions have been done to test whether training in forgiveness brings about improvements in well-being and mental health. In one such study, women over sixty-five who felt considerably hurt by a particular interpersonal experience were randomly assigned to either a forgiveness group or a discussion (or control) group.[41] The groups met for eight weeks. Women in the forgiveness group reported learning to forgive more than did the controls and had lower anxiety and higher self-esteem. Other such interventions have been done with individuals experiencing a variety of injuries and offenses—for example, men who were hurt over their partners' decisions to have abortions, women survivors of incest, people experiencing romantic infidelity, and adolescents who perceived their parents as neglectful. In each of these studies, whether forgiveness was taught as part of group workshops or one-on-one, those in the forgiveness conditions were generally more successful in forgiving and showed diminished negative emotions and higher self-esteem and hope after the interventions, even months later. Not surprisingly, the longer that people are given to think about and learn forgiveness in these studies, the more they benefit. Also, interestingly, women appear to benefit more than men, with men holding on to hurts and grudges longer.[42]

So, the answer to why people bother to forgive is pretty straightforward. In the long run, the preoccupation, hostility, and resentment that we harbor serve only to hurt us, both emotionally and physically. Furthermore, forgiveness can be regarded in the larger context of community and society; it can deepen our sense of shared humanity (that we are not alone in experiencing hurts) and strengthen our personal relationships and our wider connections with others. Indeed, studies show that simply remembering someone you forgave compels you into a "we" frame of mind, to feel closer to others and to desire to help them.[43]

## How to Practice Forgiveness

Of all the happiness-promoting strategies described in this book, I believe that forgiveness is one of the most challenging to carry out. But, as is said, "no pain, no gain." What you reap may be enormous. The following techniques can be carried out in a journal, letter, or conversation or by using your own imagination. If forgiveness fits your personality, goals, or needs, select just one activity from those below for the time being, and give it your best shot.

**Appreciate being forgiven.** Before you are able to forgive another person, a good first exercise is to appreciate an instance of when you yourself have been forgiven.[44] Recall a time that you did harm to another person. Perhaps it was being hateful to your parents, betraying a lover, or avoiding a friend. If those individuals forgave you, how did they communicate it to you, and what was your response? Why do you believe they did it? Do you think they benefited from forgiving you? Did you and your relationship with the person benefit as well? Did the experience teach you anything or change you in any way? Finally, what insight do you have about the experience right now? This exercise will help you see the benefits of forgiveness and perhaps provide a model for your own forgiving.

Another way to appreciate being forgiven is to *seek* forgiveness for yourself. Whether it's for a past or present wrong, write a letter of apology. Recognizing and accepting that sometimes *you* are the transgressor may give you empathy and insight into people who are the transgressors in your own life. In this letter, describe what you have done (or *not* done, when action was called for), and acknowledge that it was wrong. Describe the harm it has done to the other person or to your relationship with that person. Apologize for the behavior—either directly (by saying "I'm sorry . . .") or by affirming the value of the relationship and your desire to restore it. You may wish to pledge to change your behavior, to offer some way to "repay" the person, or to inquire what it would take to reestablish the relationship.

Whether you send the letter of apology is up to you. Sometimes this may not be possible, if you are no longer in contact with the person; sometimes it may be risky or unwise.

**Imagine forgiveness.** In this exercise, try to imitate the participants from an intriguing study on the role of imagination in forgiveness.[45] First, identify a particular person whom you blame for mistreating or offending you. Second, engage in an imagination exercise, during which you imagine empathizing with the offender and granting him or her forgiveness. Trying to feel empathy involves viewing the situation through the offender's eyes and ears, seeing him as a whole person rather than defining him solely by the offending behavior. Granting forgiveness does not necessarily imply excusing or tolerating the offender's behavior, but it does entail trying to let go of your hurt, anger, and hostility and adopting a more charitable and benevolent perspective. While doing the imagining, make an effort to consider your thoughts, feelings, and behaviors in detail. For example, when you imagine forgiving your father for abandoning you, what would you say to him? What emotions would you feel, and how intensely and in what order? What would your facial expression look like? Which physical sensations would be triggered in your body?

If you do this successfully, you might experience what the participants in this study experienced. The practice of empathic and forgiving thoughts (compared with the practice of nursing grudges and painful memories) led them to feel a greater sense of control over their thoughts, less sadness and anger, and less reactivity in terms of their physiological stress responses (such as lower heart rate, lower blood pressure, and less furrowed brows). In other words, the bodies of participants who practiced empathy and forgiveness experienced less stress, and yours could too.

**Write a letter of forgiveness.** This exercise involves letting go of your anger, bitterness, and blame by writing, but not sending, a letter of forgiveness to a person who has hurt or wronged you. Sit down and consider the people throughout your life who have injured you or abused you and whom you have never forgiven. (These individuals may or may not still be part of your life; they may even no longer be alive.) Does this experience, and the lack of forgiveness, lead you to persist in dwelling on the person or the circumstances of the hurt or offense? Does it keep you from feeling happy, tranquil, and free of intrusive images and thoughts? If the answer is yes, you would do well on working to forgive this person.

One of the best strategies is to write a forgiveness letter. In it describe in detail the injury or offense that was done to you. Illustrate how you were affected by it at the time and how you continue to be hurt by it. State what you wish the other person had done instead. End with an explicit statement of forgiveness and understanding (e.g., "I realize now that what you did was the best you could at the time, and I forgive you"). Below are some real-life examples I have come across from a variety of people who have successfully forgiven:

- I forgive my father for his alcoholism.
- I forgive my freshman writing teacher for telling me that I couldn't write.

- I forgive my boyfriend for not being there for me when I got depressed.
- I forgive the guy who rear-ended my car.
- I forgive my wife for having an affair.
- I forgive my brother for humiliating me in public.
- I forgive my friend for using me.

The second one is mine.

You may have a hard time writing the forgiveness letter. You may believe that the act is unforgivable or that the person doesn't deserve to be forgiven or that you are too overwhelmed by negative emotions about the event even to begin to think about letting it go. If this is the case, put the letter aside, and try again in a few days or weeks. Another approach is to choose another person (or act) to forgive, one that is a bit less painful. Forgiveness is a strategy that takes a great deal of effort, willpower, and motivation. It must be practiced. Starting with an "easy" forgiveness exercise might be best for some of you. You can move on to more and more difficult cases with time.

Another strategy to help you overcome a block in writing the forgiveness letter is to learn about other people who have successfully forgiven. Perhaps you know people in your life for whom forgiveness is a strength. Write or phone them and ask them about their experiences of forgiveness and how they do it. Alternatively, read about public figures who are famous for practicing forgiveness, like Mahatma Gandhi, Nelson Mandela, Bishop Desmond Tutu, and Martin Luther King, Jr.[46]

**Practice empathy.** Empathy is the vicarious experience and understanding of another person's emotions and thoughts. It often, but not always, involves feeling sympathy, concern, compassion, or even warmth for that individual. The importance of learning and practicing empathy for the person who has hurt you is underscored by findings that empathy correlates highly with forgiveness.[47] The more successful you are at achieving understanding, concern, and consideration of the other person's perspective, the more likely you are eventually to forgive him or her.

One way to practice empathy in your daily life is to notice every time someone does something that you do not understand. Try to work out such a person's thoughts, feelings, and intentions. Why did he behave the way he did? What factors might explain it? If possible, ask him yourself and (assuming that he is self-insightful), you might learn something.

**Consider charitable attributions.** Besides empathy, one of the key factors that facilitates forgiveness is positive or charitable attributions about the transgressor.[48] An effective way to generate generous attributions is to write the letter that you'd *like* to receive from the transgressor in response to your forgiveness of her—her apology letter, if you will. What explanation (or explanations) might she offer for her conduct? (One technique is to imagine that *you* were the transgressor in this exact situation and consider what might have driven you to do harm and whether you expect to be forgiven.) Do you buy this explanation? Do you find it reasonable and adequate? Would you believe her? Would you give her the "benefit of the doubt"? As you write down her response to you, you may sense your perception of her and the situation shifting. The circumstances that caused you so much anguish may be seen from a new perspective.

Why are apologies so helpful in fostering forgiveness? Because they produce empathy.[49] They humanize. When the person who has caused you pain, suffering, or harm apologizes, he is showing you a side of him that is vulnerable and imperfect. An apology often includes an explanation of what he was thinking when he hurt you: Perhaps he made a huge mistake, perhaps he underestimated the harm, perhaps he was motivated by good intentions, and so on. No matter what, you end up seeing the situation a little more from his perspective. This makes forgiving easier.

**Ruminate less.** In Chapter 4, I discussed the pernicious nature of rumination. Dwelling on how bad you're feeling, or on a worry, or on how much better a tennis player your friend is makes you unhappy, anxious, pessimistic, and insecure. It turns out that rumination is also a considerable barrier to forgiveness. People who brood on or obsess over a transgression are more likely to hold on to their hurt and anger and less motivated to forgive.[50] Many of you are probably well aware what form these ruminations take. You go over the event (or series of events) in your mind; you feel angrier and angrier, more and more resentful, humiliated, put upon. You imagine what you want to say or do to the person who has hurt you.

Some people believe that this kind of imagination exercise—an exercise in vicarious aggression, if you will—will make them feel better, much the way hitting a punching bag or knocking around foam bats might defuse anger or blow off steam. A long tradition of research has now shown that this notion, which psychologists call catharsis theory, is dead wrong. Fantasizing about how you might physically or verbally cause pain to someone may make you immediately feel better or release some tension, but it actually increases rather than decreases hostility. This is because each time you remember the offense, you trigger all over again the old feelings of hurt, blame, antagonism, or rage.

When thoughts and images of the injury or offense become intrusive and even interfere with your daily life, it's time to do something about them. You may borrow the techniques described at the end of Chapter 4— like distraction (immediately diverting your attention to another thought, or absorbing yourself in an engrossing activity) or just say, "Stop!" Although putting a stop to the ruminations will not automatically lead to forgiveness, it is a necessary first step.

**Make contact.** I mentioned earlier that you shouldn't actually send your forgiveness letter. Here is where I get to change my mind. Sometimes it is appropriate and healthy and happiness-promoting to send the letter. The act of forgiveness (writing the letter *and* believing in it) is something you do for yourself. It will make you happier in the long run. Communicating that act (if it's even possible) is something that you do to benefit the other person and your relationship with him or her. Prepare for it to backfire (maybe even very badly), but also know that communicating forgiveness might end up restoring your relationship and ultimately bring more joy than you had possibly imagined. Only you will know whether to send the letter or make that call. Finally, remember that there's an alternative, even if you don't send the letter: Simply be kind to the person you've privately forgiven.

**Remind yourself.** An instructive story about forgiveness was told about former President Bill Clinton. Apparently Clinton once asked Nelson Mandela how he was able to bring himself to forgive his jailers. "And Mandela said, 'When I walked out of the gate I knew that if I continued to hate these people I was still in prison.' Clinton believes it, but he has to keep reminding himself. That story [for him] is a little bit of a prayer."[51] If you have chosen forgiveness as your happiness activity, you have chosen a difficult but ultimately meaningful and rewarding path. When you find yourself slipping into the old furies and bitternesses, remind yourself on a daily basis. Make forgiveness a habit, as you would a prayer.

---

## *Reading Guide*

If you benefit from this activity, you may also want to try:

1. Developing strategies for coping (Happiness Activity No. 6, p. 151)
2. Cultivating optimism (Happiness Activity No. 2, p. 101)

---

# 7.

# Living in the Present

There's a clever cartoon from the *New Yorker* that has three panels. In the first, a man is sitting at his desk and daydreaming about playing golf. In the second panel, the same man is playing golf while fantasizing about sex. In the third, he is in bed with a woman while thinking about work.[1] Like the man in the cartoon, we habitually fail to enjoy, savor, and live in the present, as our minds are often someplace else.

However, when you think about it, the present moment is all we are really guaranteed. In this chapter, I describe two strategies that promote living in the present, flow and savoring. Both are states of mind associated with positive emotions and well-being. Putting them into practice is one way that you can overcome your genes and life circumstances and take a step toward transforming yourself into a happier person by making the most of the 40 percent solution.

# Happiness Activity No. 8:
# Increasing Flow Experiences

Have you ever been so absorbed in what you were doing—painting, writing, conversing, playing chess, woodworking, fishing, praying, Web surfing—that you completely lost track of time? Perhaps you even failed to notice that you were very hungry or that your back ached from sitting for so long or that you needed to use the bathroom? Did nothing else seem to matter? If the answer is yes, then you have experienced a state called flow. Coined by Mihaly Csikszentmihalyi (chick-SENT-me-hi), flow is a state of intense absorption and involvement with the present moment.[2] You're totally immersed in what you're doing, fully concentrating, and unaware of yourself. The activity you're performing is challenging and engrossing, stretching your skills and expertise. When in flow, people report feeling strong and efficacious, at the peak of their abilities, alert, in control, and completely unselfconscious. They do the activity for the sheer sake of doing it.

The concept of flow came to Csikszentmihalyi in the 1960s, when he was researching the creative process. During his interviews and observations of dedicated artists, he was struck by how they often ignored hunger, discomfort, and fatigue while working on paintings, yet lost interest in the work as soon as they were finished. These artists clearly found the process of painting intrinsically rewarding. In describing their subjective experience of painting, they used the metaphor of a current gamely carrying them along. This is flow.

Csikszentmihalyi argues that the good life, a happy life, is characterized by flow, by "complete absorption in what one does."[3] The key to creating flow is to establish a balance between skills and challenges. Whether you are rock climbing, performing surgery, doing your taxes, or driving on the freeway, if the challenges of the situation overwhelm your level of skill or expertise, you will feel anxious or frustrated. On the other hand, if the activity is not challenging enough, you will become bored. Flow is a way of describing an experience that falls in just the right space between bore-dom and anxiety. Your happiness depends on your ability to find that per-fect space, to extract flow from what you are doing.

Indeed, we can experience flow in almost anything we do, however monotonous or tedious it might appear: waiting for the bus; changing a diaper; working on an assembly line, listening to a lecture; even standing at baggage claim. I often experience flow while analyzing data. Sometimes five hours will go by, and they feel like five minutes. On the other hand, some of us fail to experience flow (feeling bored or anxious instead) even during apparently exciting or captivating events—a sailing adventure, an action movie, or a dance recital. If we train ourselves to obtain flow in as many circumstances as possible, we will have happier lives.

## THE BENEFITS OF FLOW

Why is flow good for you? The first reason is obvious: because it is inher-ently pleasurable and fulfilling, and the enjoyment you obtain is generally of the type that is lasting and reinforcing. Flow provides a natural high that, unlike artificial highs or pure hedonistic pleasures, is a positive, pro-ductive, and controllable experience that does not cause guilt, shame, or other damage to the self or the society at large.

Second, because flow states are intrinsically rewarding, we naturally want to repeat them. However, therein lies a seeming paradox. As we mas-ter new skills (e.g., skiing, writing, speech making, gardening, etc.), our experience of flow diminishes because the task at hand is no longer as stimulating and demanding. Thus, to maintain flow, we continually have to test ourselves in ever more challenging activities. We have to apply focused mental discipline or strenuous physical exertion. We have to stretch our skills or find novel opportunities to use them. This is wonder-ful, because it means that we are constantly striving, growing, learning, and becoming more competent, expert, and complex. One study fol-lowed talented teenagers over four years. Those who, at age thirteen, had identified their talent area (whether music, mathematics or soccer) as a source of flow, and who experienced relatively more flow and less anxiety during school activities, were more likely to stay committed to their talent through the teen years than to disengage from it.[4] Presumably, these teenagers continued to develop their talents and to expand their abilities and interests.

One of the primary themes of this book is that we cannot allow our happiness to depend on our external circumstances, for every positive event and accomplishment we experience are accompanied by rapid adaptation and escalating expectations. Even as we attain greater heights, we begin to want even more. Here is Csikszentmihalyi's solution to this dilemma: "There is no inherent problem in our desire to escalate our goals, as long as we enjoy the struggle along the way."[5] However, when we are preoccupied with the goal (the graduate degree earned, the children grown up, the kitchen remodeled), we will no longer derive pleasure and contentment from the process of achieving it—that is, from the present moment.

The experience of flow leads us to be involved in life (rather than be alienated from it), to enjoy activities (rather than to find them dreary), to have a sense of control (rather than helplessness), and to feel a strong sense of self (rather than unworthiness). All these factors imbue life with meaning and lend it a richness and intensity. And happiness.

## How to Increase Flow Experiences

I discovered the concept of flow in 1990, in my second year of graduate school. I remember reading Csikszentmihalyi's classic work and my roommate and best friend, who was working on a master's in international relations, asking me one day what had possessed me to read a whole book about menstrual flow. Needless to say, Csikszentmihalyi's *Flow* opened up to me a world of a very different kind of flow, a world of a thousand possibilities and opportunities. Finding flow involves the ability to expand your mind and body to its limits, to strive to accomplish something difficult, novel, or worthwhile, and to discover rewards in the process of each moment, indeed in life itself. Choose at least one recommendation, below, and adopt it in your day-to-day life.

**Control attention.** To increase the frequency and length of flow experiences in your daily life, you need to become fully engaged and involved. Whether it's writing a letter, making phone calls on behalf of a client, or playing Candy Land or a round of golf, seek work, home, and leisure activities that engage your skills and expertise. How exactly do you accomplish this? The secret is *attention*. William James, the "father" of psychology (and brother to Henry James), once wrote, "My experience is what I agree to attend to." This is a revolutionary thought. What you notice and what you pay attention to *is* your experience; it *is* your life. There's only so much attention that you have to go around, so how and where you choose to invest it is critical. To enter the state of flow, attention needs to be directed fully to the task at hand. When you're intensely concentrating on doing something, you're essentially directing your attention to the task (e.g., drawing) as opposed to other things (i.e., thoughts like "What time is it?," "What will I have for dinner?," and "This is not going as smoothly as last time").

Maintaining the state of flow also involves the control of your attention. If the challenge is too low and you become bored or apathetic, your attention drifts elsewhere. If the challenge is too high and you become tense or stressed, your attention shifts to yourself and your limitations, making you self-conscious. Your aim is to gain control over what you pay attention to—in a sense, to gain control over the contents of your consciousness moment by moment. Controlling your consciousness means controlling the quality of your experience. Although this may be difficult or even painful, in the long term it can provide a sense of mastery and participation in life. As with all the other strategies described in this section, you will need to exert effort and creativity.

**Adopt new values.** Happy people have the capacity to enjoy their lives even when their material conditions are lacking and even when many of their goals have not been reached. How do they do it? By using the following values as their guide: (1) Be open to new and different experiences (cooking for ten, joining a softball team, hiking to a remote location, learning to play squash) and (2) Learn until the day you die—be it barbecuing, Spanish, knitting, the history of World War II, a more effective way to maintain friendships, a new word game, etc. Try to imitate the rapt concentration on the face of a small child, who is learning wonderful new things every day—walking, jumping, doing a jigsaw puzzle, and the meanings of words—or understanding for the first time how things work (traffic, eyes, school, mail). The state of flow comes naturally to the child, but you may have to work at it.

**Learn what flows.** In one study, adult workers were given pagers that beeped them at preprogrammed intervals as they went about their days.[6] Each page was a signal to the participants to consider their behaviors at that very moment and to complete several rating scales—that is, how much were they concentrating, did they want to continue what they were doing, and how happy, strong, and creative they were feeling. Interestingly, though perhaps not surprisingly, the study found that *while at work* (relative to home/leisure), these individuals spent a great deal more time in high-challenge, high-skill situations (that is, those situations that foster flow) and less time in low-skill, low-challenge situations. Indeed, they were inclined to experience a sense of efficacy and self-confidence during work hours but to experience apathy at home. However, when probed about what they'd *rather* be doing, these participants uniformly stated that they'd rather be doing something else when working and that they preferred to continue what they were doing when at leisure.

The workers in this study clearly showed a disconnect between their beliefs about work and leisure (e.g., the former as a duty that one is forced to do, the latter as a chosen—and thus valued—activity) and their actual experiences, which were powerfully more positive during work hours. Similarly, many of us may not even recognize when we experience flow. Thus one of your first steps in applying this strategy is to establish the precise time periods and activities during which you find yourself in flow . . . and then multiply them.

**Transform routine tasks.** Even seemingly boring and tedious activities—waiting for the bus, listening to a dull presentation, getting one's teeth cleaned, or vacuuming—can be transformed into something more mean-ingful and stimulating. What you need to do is to create microflow activities with specific goals and rules.[7] For example, you could solve puzzles in your head, draw cartoon characters, tap melodies to favorite songs, or compose funny limericks. So, while you sit in a doctor's waiting room, your goal might be to draw an intricate design, and a rule might be that all lines must be symmetrical. German-born Philipp recounted to me his microflow strategy while driving in heavy traffic:

> I listen to a lot of music while I am driving . . . trance/techno and Japanese video game and anime sound tracks, sometimes called J-pop. [Most of these] have very good and methodical bass lines, melody lines, and even some drum or bass guitar lines. . . . I picked a particular beat, whether it was a bass of a trance song (it's the "thump" of a trance song if you have ever heard one) or a bass guitar riff of an anime rock song and did my best to tap my finger or foot with the exact rhythm in synchrony of the particular riff or beat I was con-centrating on. . . . I was able to alternate songs and then the different parts of the same songs to really explore and keep up with. . . . I did this while driving for long periods of time on the freeway. . . . When I was running short errands, I found myself getting equally frustrated, so I did it every time I was stopped at a red light or stop sign or even if the lane was just moving a bit too slow for my liking. I was able to take this microactivity of keeping in perfect tapping synchronicity of a song to wherever I went with my car, whenever I felt like I was beginning to feel too many negative emotions. . . .
> I found that with this microflow activity I was able to drive perfectly but at the same time be able to concentrate on the song and my tapping.

Philipp came up with a fairly idiosyncratic and rarefied microflow activity. Whether yours is unique or mundane doesn't matter, as long as it's somewhat challenging and interesting, and yields a richer, and less bor-ing and stressful, experience of daily life.

**Flow in conversation.** Depending on your job and lifestyle, a sig-nificant percentage of your days may be spent in conversations with others. Do you usually experience flow when you are talking with another person? Are you frequently so interested in the conversation that you almost feel yourself step into a different reality, not noticing time passing or the sights and sounds around you? If the answer is no, you may benefit from implementing the following exercise designed to promote flow during conversations.[8] During your next tête-à-tête—whether by phone or face-to-face—focus your attention as intensely as possible on what the other person is saying and your reactions to her words. Don't be too quick to respond; rather, give her the space to expand on her thoughts, and prompt her with brief follow-up questions (e.g., "And then what happened?" or "Why did you think that?"). One way to smooth this process is to give yourself the goal of learning more about the speaker. What is on her mind? What emotions is she experiencing right now? Have you learned something about her that you didn't know? If you're more of a talker than a listener, this exercise might be difficult and awkward at first and might inhibit flow by making you self-conscious, but the strategy should get easier with time.

**Smart leisure.** Many of us believe that our free or leisure time is precious. There is much too little of it, so we save it for something really special, something that gives us joy. Or do we? Consider the hours of the day during which you are free of obligations and have freedom to choose what to do. Do you watch TV? Read an entertainment magazine? Chat on your cell phone? Send text messages? During what percentage of your leisure activities are you truly concentrating, using your mind, or exercising your skills? If the percentage is low, this means that you're unlikely to be in flow during much of your leisure time.

Of course, after a long and stressful day, vegging out in front of the evening news, *Seinfeld* reruns, or ESPN might be your idea of heaven. I agree. That decompression time is sorely needed. But be honest with yourself about how long it truly takes to decompress. I would bet forty-five minutes are enough. After that, you're not vegging but vegetating and might end up emerging from the couch hours later, in time for bed, and wondering where the evening has gone and why you're in such a rut.

**Smart work.** "We're playing work," my kindergartner announced to me one night right before dinner. She and her three-year-old brother were having a blast. He was sitting at his Barney laptop ("I have to check my e-mails," he announced), and she was writing and talking earnestly into the phone ("Let me call you right back"). Work can be rewarding, gratifying, and enjoyable if you're lucky and if you make it be.

One fascinating study of workers found that people tend to see their work in one of three ways, as a job, as a career, or as a calling.[9] Those who place their work in the job category essentially perceive it as a necessary evil, a means to an end—the job is needed to support them—and not as something positive or rewarding. Accordingly, they labor in order to have the money to enjoy their time away from work. By contrast, the career category is essentially a job with advancement. People who report having careers may not see their work as a major positive part of their lives, but they have opportunities or ambitions for promotion. They invest more time and energy in their work because the opportunities they create for themselves may bring the rewards of higher social status, power, and self-esteem. Finally, those who see their work as a calling report enjoying working and find what they do to be fulfilling and socially useful. They work not for the financial rewards or for advancement but because they want to; it is inseparable from the rest of their lives.

You might wonder whether certain kinds of occupations are more conducive to callings versus careers or jobs. This is probably true. Artists, teachers, scientists, and neurosurgeons might be relatively more likely to enjoy their work and to believe that it makes the world a better place. However, by no means do these occupations have a monopoly on callings. Indeed, researchers have found that people are remarkably adept at crafting their jobs to derive maximum engagement and meaning. For example, interviews with twenty-eight members of a hospital cleaning crew revealed that some of them disliked cleaning, felt that it entailed low-level skills, and did the minimum amount of work required; others, in contrast, transformed the job into something grander and more significant.[10] This second group of hospital cleaners described their work as bettering the daily lives of patients, visitors, and nurses. They engaged in a great deal of social interaction (e.g., showing a visitor around, brightening a patient's day), reported liking cleaning, and judged the work as highly skilled. It's not surprising that these hospital cleaners found flow in their work. They set forth challenges for themselves—for example, how to get the job accomplished in a maximally efficient way or how to help patients heal faster by making them more comfortable. They added tasks outside their formal duties, such as rearranging the paintings on the walls or fetching wildflowers. They saw themselves as part of a larger, integrated whole, not just mopping floors and emptying trash cans but serving as part of a system that improved people's lives. People in other occupations—from hairdressers and engineers to computer techs and kitchen workers—have also been observed crafting their jobs in ways to maximize flow and meaning. It's worth considering how your own job could benefit from a new perspective.

**Strive for superflow.** At times you may experience flow by fully immersing yourself in music, becoming one with nature, or losing track of time during a phone call. At other times you may experience something even more magnificent. Let me propose a related state, which I'll call superflow. This is when you are not only completely absorbed and unselfconscious but absolutely transcendent. This happened to me one Saturday morning when my son learned how to do a new kind of math problem and we worked on math computations, both of us exhilarated, energized, suspended in time, for an hour or maybe two hours; I don't know, because the experience rushed by in an instant. Another time I remember chatting with a colleague at a conference. We were sitting in a busy, crowded, noisy bar area, and we talked and talked, oblivious of the presentations and meetings we were missing, not noticing a single passerby. I was utterly and joyfully unaware of my surroundings or worries or any thoughts other than our conversation during the entire time. Both these experiences left me feeling happier, more creative, more amiable. They bolstered my sense of belonging, vigor, and self-confidence. Strive to achieve the state of superflow whenever you possibly can.

**Caveat.** If you discover particular activities that reliably deliver for you the experience of flow, you are fortunate. But be aware that such activities—even those viewed as constructive by the wider culture (like volunteering for a charity, playing with your child, or working on a contract at the office)—can become addictive. When you notice yourself consistently ignoring the needs of people close to you, that should be a warning signal. We all are aware that hobbies such as playing video games can prompt people to avoid or disregard their responsibilities, not to mention other sources of satisfaction.[11] But this can happen with socially desirable behavior as well. I learned this lesson when my husband pointed out to me that I had become so absorbed in my daily reading of the *Harry Potter* books with my daughter that I was ignoring other pressing responsibilities.

---

*Reading Guide*

⌒

If you benefit from this activity, you may also want to try:

1. Savoring life's joys (Happiness Activity No. 9, below)
2. Committing to your goals (Happiness Activity No. 10, p. 205)

---

# Happiness Activity No. 9: Savoring Life's Joys

My advice to you is not to inquire why or whither, but just
enjoy your ice cream while it's on your plate.

—*Thornton Wilder*

Parents tell their children to be good, so that they can grow up to be moral adults and responsible citizens. Teachers tell their pupils to study hard, so that they can earn high grades, get into good colleges, and find decent jobs. Supervisors tell their employees to work hard and aim high, so that they can win pay raises and promotions. Senior citizen friends tell their still-working chums that the golden years of retirement are near. And if you're a little like me, even when the present *is* wonderful, you can't take full pleasure in it, as you're already imagining being nostalgic for it in the future.[12] We rarely seem to live in and savor the present moment, believing that what counts most will happen in the future. We postpone our happiness, convincing ourselves that tomorrow will be better than today.

Yet the ability to savor the positive experiences in your life is one of the most important ingredients of happiness. Most people truly understand what it means to savor after overcoming uncomfortable or painful symptoms or following a brush with mortality or a major scare. When you have a toothache and it's gone, you suddenly delight in its absence. When you're overwhelmed with terrific allergies that abruptly dissipate, you truly relish breathing freely. After a near-death experience or an alarming diagnosis, you may also feel able (at least temporarily) to appreciate and enjoy the good things in your life, to live each day as if it were your first day and your last day.

You can think of savoring as having a past, present, and future component. You savor the past by reminiscing about the good old days—your first love, your wedding, the acceptance letter, the phone call when you learned you got the job, your summer road trip, and so on. You savor the present by wholly living in, being mindful of, and relishing the present moment, whether it's having lunch with a colleague, listening to Grandma's stories, shooting hoops, or immersing yourself in a book, song, or project at work. This type of savoring overlaps a great deal with flow and with gratitude. Finally, you savor the future by anticipating and fantasizing about upcoming positive events. This is an element of optimistic thinking. Notably, although it may appear that the past and future components of savoring don't belong in a chapter titled "Living in the Present," both involve ways of heightening and preserving pleasure—that is, bringing the pleasure of the past and future into the present moment.

Researchers define *savoring* as any thoughts or behaviors capable of "generating, intensifying, and prolonging enjoyment."[13] When you "stop and smell the roses" instead of walking by obliviously, you are savoring. When you bask and take pride in your own or your friends' accomplishments, you are savoring. When you suddenly emerge out of a frazzled or distracted state (e.g., while talking on the phone or running errands) and become fully aware of how much there is to enjoy of life, you are savoring. This is the slight difference between savoring and flow: Savoring requires a stepping outside of experience and reviewing it (e.g., "How redolent are the roses!"), whereas flow involves a complete immersion in the experience. Of course, ideally you need not step outside experience too much or too often in order to savor the moment, for after all, frequently asking yourself, "Am I savoring yet?" or "Am I appreciative enough?" will ultimately detract from your enjoyment.

Whether it involves a focus on the long ago, the present moment, or future times, the habit of savoring has been shown in empirical research to be related to intense and frequent happiness. Moreover, savoring is associated with many other positive characteristics. For example, in several studies people who are inclined to savor were found to be more self-confident, extraverted, and gratified and less hopeless and neurotic.[14] Interestingly, those adept at savoring the present versus the future versus the past experience different benefits. Those skilled at capturing the joy of the present moment—hanging on to good feelings, appreciating good things—are less likely to experience depression, stress, guilt, and shame. People prone to joyful anticipation, skilled at obtaining pleasure from looking forward and imagining future happy events, are especially likely to be optimistic and to experience intense emotions. In contrast, those proficient at reminiscing about the past—looking back on happy times, rekindling joy from happy memories—are best able to buffer stress. Although these studies do not speak to whether savoring causes these good things versus the reverse, the investigator was confident enough to provide the following recommendations to individuals who are sad or unfulfilled: "Rather than merely reacting [sic] to positive events when they happen to occur, [people] can learn to savour proactively—to consciously anticipate positive experiences, to mindfully accentuate and sustain pleasurable moments, and to deliberately remember these experiences in ways that rekindle enjoyment after they end." (p. 195).[15]

Of course, this is easier said than done. First, like all happiness-enhancing strategies, effort and motivation are necessary for true savoring. Our attention is often brimming with intrusive and persistent thoughts about the past and present (conversations, tasks undone, problems unsolved) and the future (to-do lists, plans), and committed effort is required to redirect our minds to positive experiences in the here and now. Second, as we already know, the process of hedonic adaptation leads us to obtain less and less pleasure from initially thrilling experiences, be it the view of the snowcapped mountains on the way to work, the song of bagpipes in the town square, or the smell of our new leather jackets. With time, such sights, sounds, and aromas simply fade into the background. It takes dedicated willpower to reappreciate those things and stop taking them for granted. The next section describes a number of specific suggestions for accomplishing just that.

## STRATEGIES TO FOSTER SAVORING AND THE RESEARCH BEHIND THEM

If savoring life's joys is one of the happiness activities that fit you best, don't be daunted by the many ways to realize it. For now, select just one of the options in this section, and get started right away.

**Relish ordinary experiences.** The first challenge in using the strategy of savoring is to learn how to appreciate and take pleasure in mundane, everyday experiences. Consider as a model what participants were asked to do in recent research aimed at exploring the extent to which making savoring a habit can produce tangible benefits. In one set of studies, depressed participants were invited to take a few minutes once a day to relish something that they usually hurry through (e.g., eating a meal, taking a shower, finishing the workday, or walking to the subway). When it was over, they were instructed to write down in what ways they had experienced the event differently as well as how that felt compared with the times when they rushed through it.[16] In another study, healthy students and community members were instructed to savor two pleasurable experiences per day, by reflecting on each for two or three minutes and trying to make the pleasure last as long and as intensely as possible.[17] In all these studies those participants prompted to practice savoring regularly showed significant increases in happiness and reductions in depression.

Starting tomorrow, consider your daily routine activities and rituals. Do you notice and savor the pleasures of the day, or do you dash through them? If the latter, then resolve to seize those pleasures when they happen and take full advantage of them. Linger over your morning pastry or your afternoon snack, absorbing the aroma, the sweetness, or the crunchiness (rather than mindlessly consuming). Strive to bask in the feeling of accomplishment when you've finished a task at home or work, rather than distractedly moving on to the next item on your to-do list. Luxuriate in a long, hot shower after a brisk walk in the cold. That perfect moment can last a few seconds or a weekend. "Enjoy the little things, for one day you may look back and realize they were the big things."[18]

**Savor and reminisce with family and friends.** Often it's easier to savor when you share a positive experience with another. Whether you're visiting a Japanese garden together, hiking to the top of a mountain, or listening to jazz in front of a fire, the pleasure of the moment can be heightened in the company of others who similarly value the experience. Marvel at the present moment with the other person. Set aside an hour, an afternoon, or an entire day to this activity.

Another person can also bolster the power of positive reminiscence. For example, you might reminisce together about a party you both attended or a vacation or job or friend you shared. You might make a pilgrimage together to a meaningful place from your past or flip through a scrapbook or yearbook together. You might listen (or sing along) to a piece of music associated with a particular memory. Researchers suggest that using a specific technique to trigger or intensify one's recall of the past may be successful at producing vivid, engaging reminiscence. For instance, you might use guided imagery to vividly re-create the details of a pleasant memory in your mind. This strategy allows you and a close other to revisit pleasant times.

The advantages of savoring and reminiscing with others have empirical support. Researchers have found that mutual reminiscence—sharing memories with other people—is accompanied by abundant positive emotions, such as joy, accomplishment, amusement, contentment, and pride.[19] This appears to be particularly true for older individuals. Indeed, the more time older adults spend reminiscing, the more positive affect and higher morale they report.[20] These studies suggest that everyone—but especially older people, who have a wealth of life experiences—is able to extract positive feelings from reminiscence.

**Transport yourself.** The ability to engage in positive reminiscence—to transport yourself at will to a different time or place—can provide both pleasure and solace when you need it most. I know someone who conjures up the mental image of herself on her mountain bike whenever she is under stress or feeling down or bored. It's an imagination skill that can be honed with practice. Consider one study that successfully taught people how to travel to a mental destination through recall of positive images and memories.[21] Participants were first asked to make lists of happy memories and personal mementos (such as photographs, gifts, and souvenirs) and then instructed to engage in positive reminiscing twice daily for a week. Specifically, they were told:

> First, turn to your list of positive memories and choose one to reflect upon.
> Then sit down, take a deep breath, relax, close your eyes, and begin to think
> about the memory. Allow images related to the memory to come to mind.
> Try to picture the events associated with this memory in your mind. Use
> your mind to imagine the memory. Let your mind wander freely through
> the details of the memory, while you are imagining the memory.

As the researchers predicted, those participants who reminisced on a regular basis showed considerable increases in happiness, and the more vivid the memories conjured, the greater the gain in happy feelings.

Positive reminiscence boosts happiness in several ways. Focusing on positive aspects of past experiences may prompt you to feel that you are attaining your ideals or dreams and help reinforce your sense of identity. For example, as you recall past experiences and life transitions, you may come to recognize continuity with the past, gain insight into yourself, and appreciate your uniqueness. Furthermore, retelling experiences in positive ways can boost self-esteem and compel you to present a positive self-image. Positive reminiscence can also produce pleasure and enjoyment for its own sake, by laughing at funny moments, reveling in the memory of the wind in your hair, or reliving a beautiful day. Doing this can also provide comfort and respite from stress during difficult or painful times.

Supporting some of these arguments, a recent study found that after positive reminiscence, 29 percent of people reported a new perspective and self-insight toward current problems, 19 percent reported positive affect, 18 percent reported "escape from the present," and only 2 percent claimed that it did nothing for them.[22] Most important, the more time that these respondents reported reminiscing about happy events or images from their past, the more they felt able to enjoy their *present* lives. Here's what a female participant observed about her experience reminiscing:

> Thinking of good times from the past makes me feel better about the present. It helps me appreciate things more. It gives me an idea of where I was then, where I am now, and where I ultimately want to be. It helps me understand the present and deal with it. . . . These memories also give me a sense of confidence, kind of a "you did it before, you can do it again" type of thing. If things are bad, I use my memories to start thinking of ways to make it better rather than thinking about how bad it is.[23]

Best of all, if you master this strategy, you "will always have Paris" even when you haven't been back for decades.[24]

**Replay happy days.** In a recent study, my graduate students and I showed that the practice of repetitively replaying your happiest life events serves to prolong and reinforce positive emotions and make you happier.[25] So think about one of your happiest days—commencement day (yours or your child's), the first time you heard, "I love you," the first day of your European vacation, the day you brought home a puppy—and replay it in your mind as though you were rewinding a videotape and playing it back. Think about the events of the day, and remember what happened in as much detail as you can. What exactly did you (or other people involved) say or do? What were the thoughts and emotions running through your head at the time? Don't analyze this day; just replay and revel in it. We found that people who performed this exercise for eight minutes per day on three consecutive days felt more intense positive emotions four weeks later.

**Celebrate good news.** In Chapter 5, I described research on capitalizing or sharing good news with close family and friends. Sharing successes and accomplishments with others has been shown to be associated with elevated pleasant emotions and well-being.[26] So, when you or your spouse or cousin or best friend wins an honor, congratulate him or her (and yourself), and celebrate. Try to enjoy the occasion to the fullest. Passing on and rejoicing in good news lead you to relish and soak up the present moment, as well as to foster connections with others. Researchers advise that you shouldn't shy away from pride: Pat yourself on the back; tell yourself how hard you've worked for this moment; imagine how impressed people might be.[27] Do the same for your spouse or cousin or best friend.

**Be open to beauty and excellence.** This strategy involves allowing yourself to truly admire an object of beauty or a display of talent, genius, or virtue. Strive even to feel reverence and awe. Positive psychologists suggest that people who open themselves to the beauty and excellence around them are more likely to find joy, meaning, and profound connections in their lives.[28] It may appear immensely challenging to experience awe in response to mundane daily life—reading the sports pages, watching a movie, walking through the park—but it's an ability well worth cultivating. Don't go through life wearing blinders to everything that is touching, beautiful, virtuous, and magnificent. Consider the example of the poet Walt Whitman, whose "favorite activity was to stroll outdoors by himself, admiring trees, flowers, the sky, and the shifting light of day, and listening to birds, crickets, and other natural sounds." Here's a description of Whitman by a contemporary:

> It was evident that these things gave him a pleasure far beyond what they give to ordinary people. Until I knew the man, it had not occurred to me that any one could derive so much absolute happiness from these things as he did. . . . Perhaps, indeed, no man who ever lived liked so many things and disliked so few as Walt Whitman. All natural objects seemed to have a charm for him. All sights and sounds seemed to please him. He appeared to like (and I believe he did like) all the men, women, and children he saw.[29]

**Be mindful.** Many philosophical and spiritual traditions stress the cultivation of mindfulness as a critical ingredient of well-being. The practice of Zen Buddhism, for example, emphasizes clearing one's mind and grounding oneself in the present moment. Given the vast anecdotal evidence of the benefits of mindfulness, psychological researchers have begun to study this phenomenon in the laboratory. A series of studies conducted at the University of Rochester focused on people high in mindfulness—that is, those who are prone to be mindfully attentive to the here and now and keenly aware of their surroundings.[30] It turns out that such individuals are models of flourishing and positive mental health. Relative to the average person, they are more likely to be happy, optimistic, self-confident, and satisfied with their lives and less likely to be depressed, angry, anxious, hostile, self-conscious, impulsive, or neurotic. Furthermore, people who are habitually mindful of their current experiences are more likely to experience frequent and intense positive emotions, to feel self-sufficient and competent, and to have positive social relationships, while those who are *not* usually mindful report more illness and physical symptoms.

In the words of William James, "Compared to what we ought to be, we are only half awake."[31] So how does one wake up to the present moment? As it happens, researchers have begun to train people to develop the habit of mindfulness, showing, for example, that a standardized eight-week mindfulness-based intervention can boost well-being and reduce psychological distress, pain, and physical symptoms in ill persons.[32] The intervention teaches specific techniques, like learning relaxation, paying attention to breathing through stretches and postures, and becoming aware of bodily sensations, thoughts, and emotions. Many of these techniques are integrated in the practice of meditation, described in greater detail in Chapter 9.

**Take pleasure in the senses.** Luxuriating, or indulging the senses, is one of the key ways to promote savoring.[33] Pay close attention to and take delight in momentary pleasures, wonders, and magical moments. Focus on the sweetness of a ripe mango, the aroma of a bakery, or the warmth of the sun when you step out from the shade. Take in the cool, fresh air after a storm, the brushstrokes of an impressionist painting, or the crescendo of a symphony. One laboratory experiment revealed that people who focused their attention on the sensory experience of consuming chocolate reported more pleasure than those who were distracted while eating.[34] This means making eating (whether chocolate or steak or a banana) into a ceremonial occasion, with an attractive presentation, a quiet and comfortable setting, and no distractions (no TV, reading material, or intrusive thoughts). To sharpen your perceptions, you may need to focus concentrated attention on certain elements and completely block out others. For example, close your eyes and keep still when listening to music or enjoying a massage, or wear ear plugs to a museum. Stay absorbed in the present—in a state of flow—and try not to think of anything else. Some people call this rolling in the moment, just sensing.

An extraordinary illustration of this strategy comes from a story of prisoners in a concentration camp who met regularly to share a fancy dinner in their minds, imagining all the details of the lighting of the room, the stiffness of their clothes, and the flavors of the food:

> My friend, a French painter and Resistance fighter, was put in a concentration camp by the Nazis. Every evening during his long incarceration,

he and two or three of his fellow prisoners . . . entirely by means of con-versation and gestures . . . dressed for dinner in immaculate white shirts that did not exist, and placed, at times with some difficulty because of the starched material that wasn't there, pearl or ruby studs and cuff links in those shirts. . . . They drank Châteauneuf-du-Pape throughout the meal and Château d'Yquem with the dessert pastry.[35]

Remarkably, these individuals were able to experience "pleasures of the mind" even under conditions of severe deprivation. With practice, we all can learn how to luxuriate and transport ourselves, using our five senses, no matter how ordinary or unstimulating our current setting.

**Create a savoring album.** Whenever I travel for business, even for a day, I carry a little photo album that has pictures of my kids at different ages (the husband is relegated to the back). I look at it a lot—in planes, hotel rooms, and the audience of conference talks—and it never fails to give me a happiness boost. You can create such a savoring/memory album yourself. It can have photos of your favorite people, places, or things—family, friends, pets, famous paintings, etc. (One of my friends has a beautiful panorama of her hometown, Barcelona, Spain.) Or it can have other happy-inducing or meaningful items—your acceptance letter to college, a love note, a favorite recipe, a niece's drawing, or an article about your favorite actor. Look at this album on a regular basis but not too often, so as to stave off adaptation to its pleasure. You don't want the same thing to happen to the items in your savoring album as might happen to a special photo on your nightstand or computer screen; when it's up for a long enough time, you fail to notice it altogether. This savoring album is essentially a strategy to create and savor the memories (the mental photographs) of your positive experiences. It's also valuable to review the album in less happy times, when you're especially needful of a boost.

**Savor with your camera.** An innovative idea is to train yourself to use a camera as a savoring tool.[36] Many people take numerous photos while traveling or on vacation or during significant life celebrations to preserve the experience for the future, but the role of photographer may actually detract from their delight in the present moment. I know a father who devoted himself earnestly to photographing the birth of his first and only child. The photos were beautiful but, he lamented afterward, he felt that he missed out on the most important first moment of his son's life. Looking through the camera lens made him detached from the scene, an observer and not an experiencer. Teach yourself to use your camera in a way that enhances your ongoing experiences, by truly looking at things and noticing what is beautiful and meaningful. Don't just create as many pictures as possible; try to take, print, and frame the best picture you know how. This will make you more mindful and more appreciative and will lead you to enjoy your experiences more.

**Seek bittersweet experiences.** A bittersweet experience is one that involves mixed emotions, usually happiness and sadness mixed together. Such events are usually characterized by the fact that they will soon end— a vacation, a friendship, a phase of life, a sojourn in a particular place or time. When we are fully mindful of the transience of things—an impending return home from an overseas adventure, a graduation, our child boarding the school bus for the first day of kindergarten, a close colleague changing jobs, a move to a new city—we are more likely to appreciate and savor the remaining time that we do have. Although bittersweet experiences also make us sad, it is this sadness that prompts us, instead of taking it for granted, to come to appreciate the positive aspects of our vacation, colleague, or hometown; it's "now or never."

Researchers have attempted to foster savoring in the laboratory by drawing people's attention to the bittersweet or transient nature of some positive life experiences—that is, by pointing out that many such experiences will eventually end. To test this notion, they recruited college seniors nearing the close of their undergraduate careers to participate in an experiment.[37] These seniors were instructed to write about aspects of their college experience (e.g., their friends, the campus, etc.) twice a week over a two-week period. Furthermore, while writing, some of the students were asked to focus on the fact that graduation was imminent (i.e., that they had only "1200 hours left"; this was the bittersweet group), whereas others were asked to focus on the fact that it was still far away (i.e., that they had "1/10 of a year left"; a control group). The researchers expected that pondering the imminence of one's graduation from college would elicit feelings of appreciation for college life and prompt students to savor the present moment (because there was so little time left). By contrast, the "graduation is far away" group would not be compelled to savor the present, inasmuch as they would be made aware that there was plenty of time left to enjoy college. The results confirmed these expectations: Compared with the control group, the bittersweet ("graduation is soon") group was more likely to show increases in happiness and to engage in savoring behaviors (e.g., spending time with friends, taking photos, participating in college clubs, or taking a scenic route to class).

So don't shy away from the bittersweet. In some sense, all our life experiences are bittersweet ones. All good things (and bad things) come to an end, and the acknowledgment of this truth can prompt you to stop and smell the roses.

**Wax nostalgic.** Although many people associate nostalgia with homesickness, it is actually a positive emotion, albeit a poignant one. Being Russian-born, I should know; Slavic peoples are famous for their nostalgia. When you feel nostalgic about a past time in your life, a person you were close to, a seashore you once haunted, you may feel a wistful pleasure, a yearning that is at one and the same time joyful, affectionate, and tinged with sadness, as you are fully aware that it is bygone. From time to time, nurture those nostalgic feelings; they will make you feel warm about your past and bring back cherished memories of beauty, pleasure, goodness, and love. Don't compare these feelings with the present; focus only on the positives and how they have enriched your life. My students and I have found that when recalling their most wonderful moments from the past, the happiest people are apt to put them in their "psychological bank accounts" or experiential treasure chests—that is, to experience them as adding meaning and richness to their lives—rather than focus on how the good old days were so much better than today.[38] "Nostalgia is memory with the pain removed."[39] Studies have shown that nostalgic experiences spawn positive feelings, reinforce our sense of being loved and protected, and even boost our self-esteem.[40]

Nostalgia can be triggered spontaneously—e.g., by a conversation with an old friend, a birthday party, a photograph, an e-mail—or deliberately, through active reflection. It makes us feel good not only because of the positive memories we might recall but because it protects and strengthens our identities (e.g., by putting together pieces of the past into a coherent whole), fosters pride (e.g., through memories of a past triumph), regenerates a sense of meaning (e.g., through an improved understanding of where we fit in our culture and generation), and buttresses social connections (by celebrating past and present relationships).

**A note about writing.** Some psychologists advise savoring through writing, perhaps by keeping a journal in which you describe a memorable past experience or an exciting time in the present. I recommend against this. The reason is that writing, while an invaluable tool to foster gratitude or come to terms with traumas, stresses, or hurt feelings, is counterproductive for savoring or relishing the present. Research from my and other laboratories shows that writing is inherently a structured process that forces a person to organize and integrate his thoughts, to reflect on what causes what, to create a coherent narrative about himself, and to consider systematic, step-by-step solutions. As we saw in Chapter 6, writing is an effective strategy when one needs to cope with negative experiences because it helps a person make sense of them and to get past them, but you don't want to "get past" a positive event! When it comes to the best experiences in life, it's repetitive replaying and savoring of the experiences that maintain the positive emotions surrounding them and enhance your happiness.[41] In contrast, writing about a positive life event may very well prompt you systematically to analyze that event—for example, by breaking it down into its component parts—resulting in your probably reducing the pleasure associated with it and perhaps even evoking negative emotions, such as guilt or worry. So, don't savor through writing, but instead, reflect, relish, and share with others.

---

*Reading Guide*

⌒

If you benefit from this activity, you may also want to try:

1. Increasing flow experiences (Happiness Activity No. 8, p. 181)
2. Committing to your goals (Happiness Activity No. 10, p. 205)

---

# Final Words

It's possible to overdo living in the present. A flourishing life involves contemplating and planning for the future and learning from the errors of the past. One study found that homeless individuals live almost completely in the present,[42] and observations of Alzheimer's patients suggest that they do as well.[43] People whose orientation is overwhelmingly present-focused have been found less capable of delaying gratification and more likely to engage in a host of risky behaviors.[44] As with anything, strive to strike a balance between absorption in the here and now and, as I discuss in the next chapter, the conscious appraisal of the progress you're making toward your goals.[45] As a famous statesman once described how he had changed after a brush with his own mortality, "I try . . . in a funny way, simultaneously to think more about the future in constructive ways but to live more in the moment."[46]

# 8.

# Happiness Activity No. 10: Committing to Your Goals

*An aim in life is the only fortune worth finding.*

—*Robert Louis Stevenson*

In 1932, weighed down by the sorrows and agonies of his self-absorbed and aimless clients, an Australian psychiatrist named W. Béran Wolfe summed up his philosophy like this: "If you observe a really happy man you will find him building a boat, writing a symphony, educating his son, growing double dahlias in his garden, or looking for dinosaur eggs in the Gobi Desert."[1] He was right. People who strive for something personally significant, whether it's learning a new craft, changing careers, or raising moral children, are far happier than those who don't have strong dreams or aspirations.[2] Find a happy person, and you will find a project.

Some devote themselves to lifelong goals vis-à-vis their work, while others commit themselves to making their family, social, or spiritual lives more meaningful. It turns out that the process of working toward a goal, participating in a valued and challenging activity, is as important to well-being as its attainment.[3] Indeed, numerous anecdotes reveal that people often feel enormous letdowns after having attained something that they have been striving toward for years. After spending a decade helping build the architecturally exquisite Walt Disney Concert Hall, the seat of the Los Angeles Philharmonic, music director Esa-Pekka Salonen recounted feeling joy but also a "sadness that he doesn't seem able to shake. Now that the impossible dream has been realized, how to move on to the next thing? And what could possibly top this."[4] Although most of us don't share the problems of famous composers, we are privy to the general phenomenon, that working toward a meaningful life goal is one of the most important strategies for becoming lastingly happier.

Committed goal pursuit is different from the other eleven happiness activities that I describe in this book. The reason is that no matter what our levels of happiness and fulfillment, *all* of us have some kinds of goals. Furthermore, our goals vary from one person to another and across time. So, how do you adapt this happiness strategy to your unique situation? Perhaps you have plenty of goals, but you lack motivation and passion for them. Your priority should be to develop that missing passion and impetus. Perhaps you are following the wrong kinds of goals. The goals that you have set for yourself may be ones sold to you by the larger culture—"Make money! Own your own home! Look great!"—and while there may be nothing inherently wrong with striving for those things, they mask the pursuits more likely to deliver true and lasting happiness. In this case, your priority should be to discern which goals will make you happy in the long term and to follow them.

# Six Benefits of Committed Goal Pursuit

Our first charge is to turn to the question of why the process of pursuing goals in the first place is so critical to our happiness. One way to think about this question is to consider what happens when a person doesn't hold any significant dreams or aims in life. Such a person is lost, with no direction, no incentives to act, no raison d'être. First and foremost, committed goal pursuit provides us a sense of purpose and a feeling of control over our lives.[5] Whether our valued activity is becoming a musician or having a baby, it gives us something to work for and to look forward to. In author G. K. Chesterton's words, "There is one thing which gives radiance to everything. It is the idea of something around the corner."

Second, having meaningful goals bolsters our self-esteem, stimulating us to feel confident and efficacious. Furthermore, the accomplishment of every subgoal (on the way to the big goal) is yet another opportunity for an emotional boost. Such lifts in joy and pride are important not only because they reinforce happiness but because they motivate us to continue striving. Consider the unhappiest people you know. They are likely to be apathetic, bored, unmotivated, and devoid of aspirations, whether it's the idea of changing careers or changing wardrobes. Some of goal striving might require tedium or hard work, but the boosts along the way are worth it.

Third, pursuing goals adds structure and meaning to our daily lives. Notwithstanding the myth of the man in the gray flannel suit, structure and meaning are good! It grants responsibilities, deadlines, timetables, opportunities for mastering new skills (e.g., building a wooden deck) and for social interactions with others (e.g., taking a wood turning class). This is valuable for just about everyone, but it's particularly critical if you are older and retired (and thus may lack the structure and sense of purpose supplied by a profession) or if you have disabilities or health problems that prevent you from doing what you used to do. If you find yourself in one of those situations, you would likely benefit emotionally from pursuing goals with a social, cultural, or political flavor—for example, strengthening friendships and family relationships, participating in cultural events, fund-raising for a political cause, or enrolling in an online class.

A fourth fringe benefit to being committed to our goals is that it helps us learn to master our use of time: to identify higher-order goals (e.g., to visit every continent), to subdivide them into smaller steps or subgoals (e.g., to plan the next trip to South America), and to develop a schedule to accomplish them (with electronic or paper datebook in hand). This is a genuine life-simplifying and life-improving skill. Your life can fall apart pretty quickly if you bungle to-do lists and make a mess of well-laid plans.

Some of us may wonder whether it is feasible or even possible to continue striving toward our goals during times of crisis. Research suggests that not only is it possible, but commitment to goals during such times may help us cope better with problems. So there is the fifth benefit of goal pursuit. Of course, sometimes traumatic or challenging situations may require surrendering no longer tenable goals. A serious injury or grave financial loss will have us rethinking whether we should relinquish our dream of becoming a ski instructor or attending law school. If we can bring ourselves to replace the old goals with new ones, we'll be happier.

Finally, the pursuit of goals often involves engaging with other people—teachers, clients, friends, colleagues, and partners—and such social connections can be happiness-inducing in and of themselves. As I discuss in Chapter 5, human beings have a strong "need to belong" and participating in relationships, social groups, and networks not only makes us happy but contributes to our continued thriving and survival.

# What Kinds of Goals Should You Pursue?

There is persuasive evidence that following your dreams is a critical ingredient of happiness. But does it matter what the dream is and how you follow it? Indeed, it does. It turns out that the type of goal or valued life task (in psychological jargon terms) that you pursue determines whether the pursuit will make you happy. Consider whether your life goals and dreams have the properties depicted in this section.

## INTRINSIC GOALS

As self-evident as it may sound, working toward goals that are personally involving and rewarding to you is more likely to bring you happiness than working toward goals that are not freely chosen. Numerous psychological studies have shown that across a variety of cultures, people whose primary life goals are intrinsically rewarding obtain more satisfaction and pleasure from their pursuits.[6] Intrinsic goals are those that you pursue because they are inherently satisfying and meaningful to you, which allow you to grow as a person, to develop emotional maturity, and to contribute to your community. For example, one of the most intrinsic activities has to be the pursuit of goals while on vacation. People are more and more choosing to engage in worthwhile and effortful tasks while away from work—for example, traveling to Rome for an architecture class, helping build a house for Habitat for Humanity, training for a triathlon, or doing an internship to learn how to run a winery. After all, no one besides yourself is rewarding you or pressuring you into such efforts. You do it because it's diverting, it's pleasurable, and it's meaningful.

By contrast, extrinsic goals reflect more what other people approve or desire for you—for example, pursuing goals for such superficial reasons as making money, boosting your ego, seeking power or fame, and bowing to manipulation or peer pressure. People usually aim for extrinsic goals as a means to an end—for example, working hard to obtain a reward (e.g., wealth or social approval) or to avoid a punishment (e.g., shame or loss of income).

Knocking the pursuit of money, beauty, and fame may smack of a value judgment, but my argument is based squarely in research. The truth is that following intrinsic goals makes us happier, in part because they are relatively more inspiring and enjoyable; hence we are more likely to invest in them, persevere at them, and succeed at them. Another reason is that personal goals that we intrinsically value directly satisfy our most basic psychological needs in life. I'm not talking about food and sex here but, rather, about our need for autonomy (i.e., feeling in control of our behavior), for a sense of competence (i.e., feeling efficacious in dealing with the world around us), and for relatedness (i.e., feeling satisfied with our interpersonal relationships). Researchers have shown that the pursuit of intrinsic goals is more likely to fulfill *all* these needs.[7] Let's say that your intrinsic goal is to become more fit and qualify for the Boston Marathon. Training for the marathon is hard and even painful at times, but you persist and relish the runner's high (which we learn in the next chapter is probably a myth, but you enjoy the feeling anyway). Running brings a sense of independence and mastery, you connect with others training for the same event, and your high spirits spill over to your marriage. You are killing not just two birds with one stone but three or four. The benefits of intrinsic goal pursuit are indeed great.

Does this mean that extrinsic goals are always bad? Not necessarily. Sometimes we pursue extrinsic goals (like material wealth) in order to obtain the resources and opportunities that will allow us to pursue our cherished dreams or intrinsic goals. For example, I'm friendly with a guy, an entrepreneur, who works very hard to earn a high salary and bonus, because, he says, it will permit him to take time off from his work (which is not very satisfying) to write short stories (his true love), to garden (a second passion), and to spend more time with his fast-growing tweens (whom he adores). At other times, we need extrinsic motivation in the form of awards, money, or social recognition to persist at an important but difficult goal (e.g., survive the grinding work required to attain the job we really want) or simply to pay the rent.

## AUTHENTIC GOALS

Do you value and truly "own" your goals, or are they really the goals favored by your parents, spouse, or neighbors? I knew a lot of people in college in the latter category, who were premed because their parents really, really wanted them to be doctors. For the better part of a decade, Ken Sheldon and Andrew Elliot have been studying what they call self-determined, or authentic, goals—that is, goals that are rooted in a person's lifelong deeply held interests and core values. Not surprisingly, they find that people are happier, healthier, and more hardworking when they are following goals that *they* own and that these people show bigger increases in happiness after attaining their authentic goals.[8] Presumably realizing authentic goals satisfies our true values and innate needs, thus delivering powerful emotional benefits. If you have ever met a happy premed, she probably genuinely and authentically desires to minister to the sick. She owns that goal.

One way that you can own your goals is to choose ones that fit you well. We are happier and more likely to persist at a goal when our striving toward it consistently makes us feel good. The more a goal fits your personality, the more likely that its pursuit will be rewarding and pleasureful and increase your happiness. For example, if you are an extravert, you may do well pursuing goals that involve interactions with other people. If you have a dominant personality, you might wish to take on a leadership activity. If you are on the nurturing side, choose a goal that allows you to take care of others. If you are competitive and achievement-oriented, strive for something that satisfies that spirited drive in you, like winning an athletic tournament or being the most productive worker in your division. Knowing which goal will fit you best takes a bit of self-awareness and emotional intelligence. If you understand your guiding values and have a clear sense of your preferences and desires, you will likely instantly recognize when there's a match between you and a particular activity or life task. If you don't, then contemplate whether you feel "authentic" when pursuing a particular goal. When you're doing your thing—writing a song, playing with children, telling a joke, learning about global warming—do you feel as if you're more the person that you want to be . . . or less?

## APPROACH GOALS

Consider as an exercise the most important and meaningful goal that you are currently pursuing, whether big or small. Does this goal involve *approaching* a desirable outcome (e.g., seeking novel and thrilling experiences, redecorating your bedroom, or making three new friends) as opposed to *avoiding* an undesirable outcome (e.g., trying not to feel guilty, preventing an argument with your girlfriend, or making sure your house doesn't fall apart). Interestingly, the same goal can be conceptualized as an approach goal (e.g., to be a fit and healthful eater) and an avoidance goal (e.g., not to be fat). A growing number of studies have shown that people who chiefly pursue avoidant goals (or construe their goals in avoidance terms) are less happy, and more anxious, distressed, and unhealthy, than people who generally pursue approach goals.[9] Not surprisingly, people with many avoidance goals perform relatively more poorly on whatever it is that they're pursuing.[10] One of the reasons may be that it's relatively easy to identify a single path for an approach goal (e.g., to eat three healthy meals per day); an avoidance goal, by contrast, usually requires many paths (e.g., to avoid all obstacles to snacking). Focusing on avoidance goals may also lead you to view things with a negatively biased perspective (e.g., "I'm prone to feeling guilty") and to be ultrasensitive to threats or failures,[11] which could become self-fulfilling. All that thinking about how you don't want to feel guilty may backfire on you, and soon you'll *really* start feeling guilty.[12]

## HARMONIOUS GOALS

It is fairly self-evident that your goals should complement one another. Simultaneously striving for conflicting goals (like "build my business" and "spend more time outdoors") will make you so annoyed and discouraged that you'll relinquish both goals and end up feeling stressed out and unhappy.[13] Unless your business is construction or kayaking, the adaptive solution is to change one or both of the goals to make them more harmonious with each other (e.g., resolving to work on your paperwork in the sun or partitioning your day into work and leisure). That's easier said than done. If it's not possible, you may very well have to give up on one of those goals, but that's preferable to sacrificing both.

## FLEXIBLE AND APPROPRIATE GOALS

As we get older, our opportunities for pursuing goals are bound to change, sometimes opening up and other times diminishing. An empty nest suddenly affords time for travel or new hobbies or changing careers. A chronic illness prompts us to rearrange our entire perspective and face new roles and challenges. Furthermore, our culture (our native country, ethnicity, or religion) "expects" certain life tasks to be accomplished during certain stages of life—for example, establishing our identities and sense of self, finishing school, getting married, buying a home, attaining career success, having children, retiring, and so on. It's no surprise that we obtain maximum happiness when we take on flexible and appropriate goals—that is, the "right tasks at the right time."[14] Of course, if we don't fulfill the cultural prescriptives, we are not necessarily doomed to failure or misery, but we must adapt our goals to the opportunities that we do have.

As we get older, what is important to us also changes. The goals that we set for ourselves in our twenties are different from those we set for ourselves in our forties and our sixties. Studies have shown, for instance, that young people are more likely to have goals that involve seeking new information, acquiring knowledge, and experiencing novelty.[15] When faced with a choice between having dinner with their favorite author and their favorite aunt, they choose the former. Older people, by contrast, make the opposite choice.[16] They are more concerned with emotionally meaningful goals—maximizing positive emotions and avoiding unpleasant ones—than with expanding their informational horizons. In sum, the priorities that we place on our goals change with time, but no matter what the substance of the goals, one certainty remains across every age: Pursuing goals brings greater happiness than abandoning them.

## ACTIVITY GOALS

Which goal is more happiness-inducing: seeking to better your circumstances or taking up a new activity? Research suggests, and we already know, that when people strive to change their circumstances (e.g., buy high-definition televisions, move to Florida, acquire tidier roommates) by defining and then achieving their goals, they certainly feel happier, but they risk experiencing hedonic adaptation. In other words, you are likely to adapt quickly to your new situation and begin to desire ever-higher levels of pleasure (e.g., an ever-bigger HDTV, a home in Florida with a view, a tidy roommate who doesn't play loud music, etc.) simply in order to recapture your previous level of happiness. However, the process of pursuing "activity" goals (e.g., joining a wilderness club, volunteering at a blood drive, learning about art) allows a person continually to experience new challenges, take on new opportunities, and meet a variety of experiences. So, to answer my previous question, sustained pursuit of activities that you value is more happiness-inducing, with its ability to deliver a stream of positive events and regular boosts in happy mood.

Ken Sheldon and I demonstrated this phenomenon empirically in a field study.[17] Participants were instructed to describe two goals that they had recently pursued and realized, one goal that involved a positive change in their circumstances (e.g., moved to a nicer apartment or received some unexpected income) and one goal that involved taking on a new activity (e.g., started studying to gain admission to graduate school or made God a bigger part of life). The participants actually told us that they had "gotten used to" their positive circumstantial changes much *more* than to their positive activity changes. Accordingly, the results showed that both activity changes and circumstantial changes made our participants happier six weeks later, but that only activity changes continued to make them happier twelve weeks later. The reason, I'm convinced, is that despite the fact that circumstantial changes are often more momentous than activity changes, the participants adapted to their positive circumstantial changes (such that they no longer boosted their happiness) but not to their activity changes (i.e., to following activity goals). Pursuing new activities can indeed produce a steady inflow of positive feelings and experiences.

# Recommendations for Committed Goal Pursuit

At the heart of this chapter is a happiness-boosting strategy that involves picking one or more significant goals that are meaningful to you and dedicating time, effort, and passion to pursuing them. Obviously, there are as many ways to accomplish this as there are different goals. However, research suggests that the most successful "strivers" share several characteristics. I've designed a set of suggestions, see pp. 215–16, to help you begin and maintain a program of committed goal pursuit.

## CHOOSE WISELY

To revisit the previous section: The pursuit of goals that are intrinsic, authentic, approach-oriented, harmonious, activity-based, and flexible will deliver more happiness than the pursuit of goals that are extrinsic, inauthentic, avoidance-oriented, conflicting, circumstance-based, or rigid. This mouthful of words is based on decades of research. As a first step, then, consider your significant goals and strivings.[18]

---

## MY MOST IMPORTANT GOALS

INSTRUCTIONS: Please think about the goals that are currently important to you or have been important in your life recently. "Goals" include intentions, wishes, desires, and motives. List at least one (1) and up to eight (8) of your most significant and meaningful goals below.

Date: _____

---

Now, for *each* of the goals that you wrote down, check off which attributes listed in the left-hand column characterize it and which attributes on the right.

| Choose These Types of Goals: | . . . Not These: |
|---|---|
| ____ intrinsic | ____ extrinsic |
| ____ authentic | ____ inauthentic |
| ____ approach-oriented | ____ avoidance-oriented |
| ____ harmonious | ____ conflicting |
| ____ activity-based | ____ circumstance-based |
| ____ flexible/appropriate | ____ rigid/inappropriate |

If any of the descriptors on the right apply to your goals, you may need to reconsider them: modify them, perhaps, or grant them lower priority. For example, if you discover that your goals at work are generally extrinsically motivated and inauthentic, contemplate how you might change your perspective. Keep a diary of the ways that your work has made the world a better place today. Perhaps you've comforted a troubled coworker or client, made a room, garden, or street more beautiful, clarified something that was inscrutable, increased neighborhood safety, helped someone solve a problem, improved the environment, and so on. A study of 1,018 working women found that they spent almost exactly 50 percent of their waking hours working.[19] You may do well either to change your perspective about your work or to change the nature of your work. You'll know if you're successful if hearing that statistic fills you with joy (or at least reassurance) rather than regret.

In general, you are more likely to persevere and succeed at goals that have a larger purpose or long-term importance. Make sure that your goals are meaningful to you. Is your only motivation to become an artist the fact that you consider painting fun, or do you additionally find a sense of purpose while engaging in it? Pleasure is not enough to sustain most people's interest and commitment for extended periods of time.[20] Value and meaning are vital.

## CHOOSE WISELY: REPRISE

What if you read the preceding section and realized, with dismay, that you don't have a list of goals to consider, let alone to reconsider? What if you are unsure about what you want to dedicate yourself to, what worthy purpose to pursue? Don't despair; there are a number of exercises that can help you discover the goals that are most meaningful for you.[21] The first is to contemplate and describe in writing the personal legacy that you would like to leave after you die. For example, you might imagine how you would want to be remembered  by your grandchildren or great-grandchildren. Write a summary of your life, your values, and your accomplishments as you would like them known to your descendants in the format of a first-person letter or even an obituary. "A man should choose with careful eye the things to be remembered by."[22]

Another approach is to write down what kinds of lives you would want your children (or future children) to lead as adults: what kinds of people you wish them to become, which values to hold, which goals to attain. Keep working on your summary, adding and subtracting, until you are satisfied with it. This process will prompt you to reexamine your life and priorities and help you gain clarity on what you consider most important. In this way, your goals will naturally be revealed to you. Reread the summary on a regular basis, and remind yourself what really matters.

## OWN YOUR GOALS

How do you come to have authentic goals—namely, to own them? Ken Sheldon once attempted to enhance the authenticity of people's personal goals (such as achieving academic success, improving a romantic relationship, or mastering a sport).[23] If you had been a participant in his study, you would have been asked to attend two sessions during which you would have been encouraged to think of ways to make your goals more interesting and challenging and to try to value them more, identify with them more, and find them more meaningful. You would have been advised to reevaluate goals that you were forcing yourself to pursue—that is, goals you held only because either somebody else was pressuring or coercing you or because you would feel guilty or anxious if you abandoned them. Trying to "own the goal" and "make it rewarding" would have been suggested to you as being especially important during those inevitable periods when pursuing the goal was frustrating or burdensome and you were tempted to give up. For example, if you are having great difficulty maintaining commitment to preparing an office presentation, you could try reflecting on the deeper value that the goal expresses (e.g., developing your potential in your career, lifelong learning, etc.). You might also try strategies that make the labor more rewarding, such as practicing the presentation with a friend, learning an inventive new software program to create your slides, or finding a particular setting or time of day when the work is more enjoyable.

The results of Ken's study showed that those who were able to transform their goals into authentic ones not only were more likely to attain their goals but felt themselves happier and more authentic with time. It appears that people who have goals they truly own are continually growing and developing and are particularly prepared to take advantage of new opportunities to grow even more. Those who do not own their goals, by contrast, appear "stalled" and stagnant in their growth.

## COMMIT, WITH PASSION

The pursuit of goals, even intrinsically motivated ones, isn't always a cakewalk. To fulfill your dream of becoming a mathematician or a costume designer or a parent, you must endure a great deal of drudgery and hard work, obstacles and stress, and, at times, personal sacrifice and failure. Indeed, developing skills in almost any activity requires a great deal of practice, patience, and labor. Sometimes you must take risks. Thus it may be obvious why it's important to commit to your goals, better yet, to commit to them with passion, ardor, and zeal. If you don't commit or if you do but lack enthusiasm, then you may quit on a whim or give up when you're feeling particularly tired, bored, or fearful of continuing.

Passionate commitment in and of itself carries many benefits. It fulfills people's needs to belong and to connect with others, as it often involves social duties and obligations (helping a neighbor's teenager with his college essay, listening to a despondent friend, nursing a sick child, etc.). Committing to important goals also reinforces our sense of autonomy, because while it may appear at first sight as a constraint to our freedom, the choice to commit is, and should be, made freely. Following through on our decision to strive toward something also helps shield us from social pressures (e.g., "Don't be such a workhorse; come party with us!") as well as from our own self-doubts (e.g., "This is so hard; maybe I should just give up"). When we avidly dedicate ourselves to the pursuit of a dream, we are taking charge of our destinies and gaining insight into ourselves.

Not surprisingly, commitment is especially potent when made in front of other people. Teens who tell their friends that they will abstain from sex are more likely to keep their pledge,[24] and citizens who tell a survey researcher that they intend to vote are more likely to actually do so.[25] A University of Scranton study found that people who made public New Year's resolutions were a remarkable ten times more likely to succeed at their goal (e.g., quitting smoking, improving their relationships, becoming a vegetarian, etc.) than those who had not.[26] Making public our commitment to a particular goal raises the likelihood that we will carry through that goal, in part because we want to appear consistent to ourselves and others (e.g., "I claimed I'd apply for the managerial position, and so I did") and avoid embarrassment or awkwardness.

## CREATE SELF-FULFILLING PROPHECIES

If my grandmother, Baba Valya, had lived long enough, she would have undoubtedly admonished me with something like (roughly translated): "The one who makes no mistake is the one who does nothing." The converse being, if you don't try, if you don't make an effort, you'll achieve zilch. So, in the words of Nike, "just do it." If you believe in yourself and are optimistic—"I can become a successful doctor," "I'll be a good parent, despite my traumatic childhood," "I know I can ask her out"—you will increase the chances that you will persevere and that whatever you're aiming for will ultimately come to pass. For example, a study of people who resolved to carry through an important new goal for their New Year's resolution found that those who were confident that they could change were significantly more likely to maintain their resolutions over time.[27] This is called a self-fulfilling prophecy, a belief that confirms itself, leading to its own fulfillment.

Social psychologists have amassed piles of evidence that simply doing something can change how we feel about it.[28] For example, helping someone can lead us to feel that the helping was worthwhile, and raising money for a political cause can lead us to believe more firmly in that cause. So, take action toward your goals, even when you have lingering doubts. The actions in and of themselves are likely to diminish those doubts or dispel them altogether.

Furthermore, once you begin to succeed at a goal—for example, making one new friend (if the goal is improving your social life) or having a rudimentary conversation in Italian (if the goal is to learn Italian)—you will feel jubilant and satisfied with your progress, thus bringing about more and more success.[29] The result is an upward spiral, something to aim for. Consciously rewarding yourself for achieving milestones can also increase your chances of future success and happiness.[30]

## BE FLEXIBLE

The ability to be flexible with regard to your activities and your goals is a valuable skill. After all, if an obstacle or constraint or opportunity suddenly arises, you may need to change or adapt your aspirations.[31] Say that one of the chief goals that you've been working on for the past several years is to spend more time with your daughter's family. However, you learn that she will be moving soon with her children to another city two hours away.

Psychology researchers describe two kinds of control that people can exert over a situation, primary control and secondary control.[32] Primary control, which is often unfeasible, refers to trying to change the situation (e.g., convincing your daughter to stay or moving yourself), whereas secondary control refers to changing how you *view* the situation (e.g., shifting your goals). Studies show that if you are able to adapt your goals to the new challenge, you will be happier. For example, although your overall higher-level goal (to spend more time with the grandchildren) might remain the same, your subgoals might be different—for example, to purchase and learn to use a webcam to stay in touch, to learn to ride the train to their new city, etc. In another example, a person who has suffered an injury may be unable to continue his regular exercise routine, but he may substitute other goals. The jogger could take up yoga or the stationary bike. This way the higher-order goal (exercise) is maintained, but the lower-order subgoals are adjusted.

The same logic applies when new opportunities develop. Being flexible involves keeping your eyes and ears open to new prospects and possibilities. If you do so, you'll be more likely to take advantage of such opportunities and to derive greater happiness from them. So, if you learn about a new program that allows you to earn a valued degree on the weekends, consider acting on it. Effective secondary control also entails viewing constraints or threats as challenges or opportunities. Your daughter's moving farther away might inspire you to learn to drive so that you could visit her more often. One door may close, but another may open.

## Don't Undermine Intrinsic Motivation

When you do find a pursuit that is both enjoyable and meaningful, be careful not to do anything to undermine your intrinsic motivation. The reason is that we can lose interest and enthusiasm even for the most valued and gratifying activities *if* we feel pushed or coerced to engage in them. Social psychologists have persuasively shown that rewarding people for what they already enjoy may undermine their enjoyment—that is, it can turn play into work. A woman I know loved reading great works of literature and decided to earn a Ph.D. in English. A couple of years later she was accepted to a graduate program with a good reputation and began taking the sequence of required literature courses. Suddenly she found herself being rewarded for doing something that she already enjoyed (and punished for slacking off). The rewards—A grades, impressing the professors—essentially gave her a second (and extrinsic) reason for working on her Ph.D. "I'm finding myself reading novels so that I could get a good grade and not because I love it," she told me the last time I saw her. "I don't look forward to reading anymore." This is how extrinsic rewards can undermine intrinsic motivation.

A classic and elegant study demonstrated this phenomenon with kids.[33] Nursery school children (all of whom liked drawing) were divided into two groups. Children in the first group were told that if they played with Magic Markers, they would receive an attractive "Good Player Award." The other group was just given the opportunity to play with markers (with no promise of reward). A couple of weeks later the researchers returned to the nursery school and observed what the children were doing during their classroom "free play." Interestingly, the kids who'd previously anticipated the reward now played less with the Magic Markers than those who had not been offered an award. For the "Good Player Award" group, what was once play had been transformed into a duty, something they did to receive a reward and not because they sincerely enjoyed and valued it.

## "Baby Steps": Break Down Your Goals

To make progress toward your higher-level goals, you must break them down into lower-level, concrete subgoals. Before you can master French cooking, you must learn how to braise Belgian endives. This means creating plans to take specific steps regarding where, when, and how to pursue a goal. People who have such implementation intentions are more likely to realize their bigger, more abstract goals.[34] But always keep the more abstract goals in the back of your mind.

Researchers in Montreal wanted to help young community-living retirees identify, plan, and pursue personal goals.[35] So they did an intervention. Over the course of about three months the participants met in small groups with a group leader for two-hour weekly "workshops" to "learn how to manage their life goals." The intervention was extremely successful; relative to a control group, the retirees who participated in the workshops became significantly happier after the intervention and maintained that improvement for a remarkable six months after. Given how well the intervention worked to teach people to follow and realize their goals, let's consider what it encompassed. Bear in mind the steps taken by the individuals enrolled in this study; you might want to draw on them yourself.

During the first few sessions participants generated a list of their personal aspirations, intentions, and projects (e.g., to socialize more, to become more spiritual, to raise a pet, etc.), and brought up any irrational beliefs about these goals (e.g., "My friends don't like me around anymore" or "I could never afford a pet").

Second, they identified their highest-priority goals and contemplated them at some length. Suppose that your highest-priority goal is to move to the city. How much effort will this require? What kinds of resources do you need? How much would you enjoy the move? And so on.

Third, they selected a single goal (e.g., learning Spanish), described it in concrete terms (e.g., gaining fluency in speaking and some facility in writing and reading), and personally committed themselves to it. You could consider writing your goal down in a journal, posting it in a visible place, or announcing it to your family or circle of friends.

The fourth step involved developing implementation intentions— where, when, and how actions would be taken (e.g., complete a Spanish language workbook, take a Berlitz language course downtown on Monday nights, etc.). A critical element here was to anticipate obstacles (e.g., boredom, lack of time, frustration, family disapproval) and to think of strategies to manage them (i.e., switch gears, prepare your family, set aside time to study when energy levels are high, etc.). For example, you might try to watch out for thoughts of quitting or feelings of low motivation and make a conscious effort to return your attention to the task at hand.

Fifth, participants carried out their plans, persisting through challenges and difficulties, with the group's emotional support. Indeed, at times it's necessary to revise or change your chosen goal and even to question its priority ("Is moving really the right thing for me right now?").

For example, one of the participants, a Mrs. M, began the intervention with a lot of challenges (her husband had passed away five months earlier, leaving her feeling helpless and astray, and she had recently retired) but, according to the researchers, ended up successfully involving herself in goal pursuit and becoming considerably happier as a result.[36] Her original inventory of priorities comprised four different goals—"Put my talent to good use," "Recover my self-confidence and autonomy," "Reestablish myself either through work or a charitable cause," and "Join a new circle of friends"—and she selected the last one to focus on. During the planning phase Mrs. M broke up her goal into concrete terms—specifically, "to attend breakfasts for retirees, to find new activities to participate in . . . with others," and "to take the initiative to call people instead of waiting for them to call."

The obstacles that Mrs. M faced included moments of feeling like giving up and persistent grief over the two major losses in her life, her husband and her work. In the process, she was encouraged by hopeful thinking, supported tangibly and emotionally by the workshop group, and additionally decided to undertake psychotherapy to work out her grief.

The leaders of the workshops noted that Mrs. M demonstrated "exemplary courage" in pursuing her goal of making new friends (as well as her broader goal of rediscovering the high-energy, decisive woman that she once was). By the end of the intervention she reported having achieved 75 percent of her objective. She also felt strongly that she was progressing toward "finding the woman from before" and became happier in the process.

So you see that committed, passionate goal pursuit consists of many elements. Although the process may be difficult, it's not really very complicated. All the required steps are logical: You begin with a dream or vision of what you want to do, you break it up into smaller, concrete subgoals, you identify in advance (and prepare for) the doubts or challenges that might compel you to quit, and you go do it. Whether your goal is to get married, to read every great work of literature, to be an expert skateboarder or scrapbook maker, or simply to become a happier person, it's within your power to make it happen. Just remember that happiness will come from pursuing goals, and not necessarily from achieving them.

## MR. SCHWENGEL

Before I end this chapter, I want to tell you a story about a guy I interviewed who happens to be a teacher. His name is Kurt Schwengel, and he is well known as one of the most innovative and talented teachers in his school district. I had heard from a variety of sources that he is a fantastic kindergarten teacher, winner of a Crystal Apple ("Best Educator") Award, who has developed his own curriculum, which he constantly updates and reworks on his Web site. "Mr. Schwengel doesn't follow the rules," a little girl from his school had warned me, so I should have guessed that he'd be a genuinely happy person. And he is. He is pure energy, enthusiasm, ingenuity, hard work. "I love my job. I'd do it for free," he told me, and it shows. His job is a calling.

The happiness-enhancing strategy of committing to goals may sound boring, but it is anything but. To say that Mr. Schwengel has committed to goals is an understatement. He is fairly bursting with goals. He makes digital movies of his pupils and creates new games that make them "explode with happiness." Every three weeks he changes the curriculum to a new theme, with accompanying costumes, music, thematic schoolwork, and field trips ("Star Wars" is the kids' favorite, but so are "baseball," "Japan," and "The mystery of the missing swordfish.") He takes the kindergartners to college basketball games, the beach, and the dinosaur museum and introduces them to bowling and sushi. Every morning, when the classroom door is opened promptly at eight-thirty the kids rush in as if he were a rock star. He plans and designs and writes and imagines and talks all day long. He is a phenomenal disciplinarian. ("You never, *ever* hear a kid say, 'So-and-so was mean to me today,' in his class," a former

Schwengel mom informed me.) He's teaching five-year-olds how to read, how to use scissors, how to play Uno, and how to putt. And when he's not working hard, he's playing hard.

Let me make something clear. Mr. Schwengel is not manic or off his rocker. He doesn't even necessarily *look* happier than you or I. He is just engaged, in flow, in constant interaction with children and adults, making his work and life as enjoyable and meaningful as anyone could imagine. I'm sure excellent public school kindergarten teachers are underpaid. Also, I'm sure that some of them, unlike Mr. Schwengel, bemoan the drudgery, the bratty kids, and the anxious, pushy parents. Elsewhere in this book I've raised the notion that there are multiple perspectives of the world, of yourself, your family, your job, your living situation. Deciding to become happier entails making a choice about which perspective you take and acknowledging that the choice is *in your hands*. Mr. Schwengel has made the choice to commit to being the best teacher he can be. You make your own choice.

---

## *Reading Guide*

If you benefit from this activity, you may also want to try:

1. Savoring life's joys (Happiness Activity No. 9, p. 190)
2. Developing strategies for coping (Happiness Activity No. 6, p. 151)

# 9.

# Taking Care of Your Body
# and Your Soul

This last chapter on happiness-increasing activities covers a set of strategies that appear, at first glance, qualitatively different from the rest. After all, most people don't commit to a religious faith, join a gym, or smile at strangers *in order* to become happier. Happiness, however, happens to be a significant by-product of all these behaviors, true regardless of how fortunate (or unfortunate) you have been with regard to your "happiness genes" or your position in life. This very fact makes the strategies described in this chapter a vital part of a program to maximize the amount of happiness in our day-to-day lives. If any of them happen to fit your traits and lifestyles, choose one today, and begin implementing it without delay.

# Happiness Activity No. 11: Practicing Religion and Spirituality

Psychological researchers have often been hesitant to study spirituality and religion. On the face of it, science and religion cannot mix. God cannot be investigated in the laboratory, and the sacred cannot be quantified. Just because religious beliefs can't be empirically tested or falsified, however, doesn't mean that the *consequences* of having religious beliefs, participating in religious life, or searching for the sacred cannot be studied. Indeed, a growing body of psychological science is suggesting that religious people are happier, healthier, and recover better after traumas than nonreligious people.[1] In one study, parents who had lost a baby to sudden infant death syndrome were interviewed three weeks after their loss and then again after eighteen months.[2] Those who attended religious services frequently and who reported religion as being important to them were better able to cope eighteen months after the loss, showing relatively less depression at this time and greater well-being than nonreligious parents. Two reasons were found to underlie the benefit of religion on adjustment: Those active in their churches reported greater social support (perhaps through the church itself) and were able to find some meaning, however elusive, in their children's deaths.

## RELIGION'S RETURNS FOR HEALTH AND WELL-BEING

Other studies have shown that relative to nonreligious folks, those active in their religions live longer with a variety of diseases and are healthier in general.[3] For example, if you are having serious cardiac surgery and receive strength and comfort from your religious faith, you'll be almost three times more likely to be alive six months later.[4] The trouble is that we don't really know why. One seemingly obvious reason could be that religious people are more likely to practice healthy behaviors. Indeed, many religions prohibit such unhealthy practices as excessive drinking, drug use, promiscuous sex, and smoking. Religious people smoke and drink less than their less religious peers.[5] Certain religious groups (like Mormons and Seventh-Day Adventists), which encourage healthy diets and prohibit premarital sex, alcohol, tobacco, and drug use, are healthier than other groups.[6] Religious groups also encourage positive, low-stress lifestyles— for example, by advocating moderation (versus extreme, illegal, or risk-taking behavior) and by fostering a harmonious family life. Indeed, some studies show that religious involvement is related to reduced risk of crime, delinquency, and marital conflict.

This potentially explains the finding that religious people are physically healthier, but what about the fact that they're happier, more satisfied with their lives, and cope better with crises? For instance, 47 percent of people who report attending religious services several times a week describe themselves as "very happy," versus 28 percent of those who attend less than once a month.[7] The social support and sense of identity provided by belonging to a close-knit religious organization (church, temple, or mosque) could be the operative mechanisms. After all, religion is usually not practiced in isolation but within a "fellowship of kindred spirits," who share one another's burdens, reach out to those in need, and offer friendship and companionship. To be sure, people who attend religious services on a regular basis have larger social networks—that is, more friends and acquaintances on whom they can rely—and actually do receive tangible help from members of their religious group.[8] This isn't surprising; religious services and the many activities associated with them (such as charities, volunteer programs, and outreach initiatives) bring together people who have a lot in common. Members share not only the basic assumptions and beliefs inherent in their religion but important political and social values. This fact enables one-to-one social, emotional, and material support, and creates a sense of community among the members of the church, synagogue, or mosque, leading people to feel appreciated, respected, and provided for. This sense reinforces your identity and affirms your lifestyle. After all, it feels good when people whom you respect and admire share similar roles and values and your approach to daily life.

So it's possible that the fact that religious people are happier than the nonreligious has nothing to do with the substance of their religious and spiritual beliefs—with God, with living life in accordance to their holy texts, with the sanctity of life, or with the sense of meaning that religious faith gives their lives—and everything to do with the simple fact that their religions bring them into contact with other similarly minded and caring people. It could be true, but I don't believe it.

First, we shouldn't ignore the one "ultimate" supportive relationship for many religious individuals, one that doesn't require any formal participation in religious services or programs, and that is their relationship with God. This relationship is not only a source of comfort in troubled times but a source of self-esteem, feeling unconditionally valued, loved, and cared for. Those of you who feel this way have a sense of security that others only wish for. Your belief that God will intervene when needed gives you a sense of peace and calm. Your identification with God or particular biblical figures can help you interpret and guide your own life (e.g., "What would the divine other do in this situation?") and even fuel a sense of vicarious control (i.e., "With an omniscient and omnipotent deity, all things are possible").[9]

Second, your sense that God has a purpose in everything helps you find meaning in ordinary life events as well as in traumatic ones. This is critical. Regardless of whether you are involved with a formal religious organization, your health and happiness may benefit simply (or perhaps not so simply) from your having religious faith. This becomes particularly important during challenging times. A health crisis or a death in the family, especially one that is unexpected or premature, may lack a clear secular explanation and can severely challenge your basic assumptions about the fairness and justice of the world. "Religious coping," which includes praying, reexamining one's sense of meaning, and collaborating with a divine other, can help you understand that the event is part of a broader divine plan or that it offers an opportunity for spiritual growth or that you have the ability to handle things. The sense of meaning that you derive from your religion can provide hope (e.g., "God will ensure that things will get better"), a satisfying explanation via a broader, benign purpose (e.g., "God brings hardship to make you strong" or "The will of a loving

God cannot be fully understood"), and solace (e.g., "We are more than just a momentary blip in the universe"). Indeed, such religious coping is so powerful that during hard times it is the single most frequently used form of coping by older people.[10]

A mother who lost her firstborn son and later gave birth to a healthy second child was able to find meaning in the death in the following way: "They say there's a reason for God to do everything, you know. I think that's very true because I think I love [my second child] a lot more than I would [have] had our first son been here."[11] Similarly, studies show that "God had a reason" is one of the most common responses by victims of a range of traumas, such as paralysis, to the question, Why me? Furthermore, those of us who are able to apply benevolent religious frameworks generally adjust better to our ordeals. For example, in a study of patients undergoing chemotherapy, those who believed that God had a measurable control over their cancers had higher self-esteem and were rated as better adjusted by their nurses (e.g., more happy, serene, and active, and relating better to others).[12] Interestingly, the belief in God as a controlling force helped these cancer patients cope better than did belief in their own personal control. But the control they were talking about wasn't a passive submission to an external force; rather, the patients spoke of using prayer and faith, as well as their own efforts at managing the disease, as a means of obtaining control from God. It was an active and interactive give-and-take process between the individual and a higher power.

Even beyond negative or traumatic life events—when our days are merely ordinary—religion and spirituality undoubtedly help us find meaning in life. Why do we need a sense of meaning? Because we need to feel that we matter, that our suffering and our hard work aren't futile, and that our life has a purpose. Because we need to feel a sense of control over our fates. Because we need to be able to justify our actions: why we should forgive, what we have to be grateful for, why we should turn the other cheek, and so on. Because we need a reason to focus beyond just ourselves. Finally, because a sense of meaning fuels our sense of self-worth. It makes us feel good about our belief systems, our identities, and the communities of like-minded individuals to which we belong.[13]

It's also worth noting that religious faith gives rise to a number of positive emotions and experiences that are associated with happiness, and this in itself can partly explain why religious and pious people are happier than nonreligious ones. One such attribute is the disposition to forgive. A slew of studies has shown that highly religious and spiritual individuals see themselves as more forgiving and value forgiveness more than do their peers.[14] Finally, the practice of religion—private prayer, spiritual pursuit, and collective worship—can engender hope, gratitude, love, awe, compassion, joy, and even ecstasy, all being happiness-increasing feelings.[15]

## BENEFITS OF SPIRITUALITY

So far I have been muddling a bit the words *spiritual* and *religious*. What's the difference? There is certainly a lot of overlap, but the overlap isn't complete.[16] *Spirituality* is defined as a "search for the sacred"[17]—that is, a search for meaning in life through something that is larger than the individual self ("self-transcendence" is a good label). Spiritual individuals refer to God or to related concepts like divine power or ultimate truth. Religion also involves a spiritual search, but this search usually takes place in a formal, institutional context. However, because the majority of spiritual people define themselves as also religious, the benefits of spirituality are essentially identical to the benefits of religion. Spiritual people are relatively happier than nonspiritual people, have superior mental health, cope better with stressors, have more satisfying marriages, use drugs and alcohol less often, are physically healthier, and live longer lives.[18] People who perceive the divine being as loving and responsive are happier than those who don't.[19]

However, those of you who do not believe in God may still be able to sanctify ordinary things on earth. If you think of your work as a calling (divine or not), if you perceive your children as blessings, if you understand love as eternal, or if you believe that the body is holy, you are imbuing aspects of life with sacred or divine qualities. Sanctification, it turns out, can provide motivation, meaning, and satisfaction. Couples who sanctify their marriage are more satisfied and invested, parents who sanctify parenting are more effective disciplinarians, and college students who pursue goals concerned with transcending the self and committing to a higher power (e.g., "Be aware of the spiritual meaningfulness of my life" or "Learn to tune into higher power throughout the day") are relatively happier.[20]

So spirituality offers something for those of us who are not, or do not want to be, affiliated with any formal religious institution. Instead of attending church or temple, we can work at searching for the sacred in many different ways—through meditation, prayer, or by instilling a spiritual dimension into our daily lives.

First, as I describe in the next section, meditation is a powerful technique that can boost both physical and psychological well-being, and many people who practice it do so by using a spiritual mantra. The ability to transcend your ordinary life through meditation appears to be one of the reasons for its many benefits.

Although undoubtedly there are different ways to pray, the type of prayer most closely linked with spiritual practice, and the most beneficial, is meditative prayer. This is a type of prayer through which you try to maintain a divine relationship. For example, you might spend time just being "in the presence" of God. People who practice meditative prayer are happier overall and feel closer to God than those who practice other kinds of prayer, such as petitioning for relief or beseeching for forgiveness.[21]

Finally, people for whom spirituality is important try to experience a sense of the divine in their day-to-day existence—for example, by cultivating feelings of awe, inspiration, and wholeness, by fostering a sense of the vastness of God's love, by nurturing belief in a power greater than oneself, and by developing a connection with the transcendent. This sense of spirituality may come more easily with practice and during extraordinary circumstances, such as childbirth.

## FOR WHOM ARE RELIGION AND SPIRITUALITY MOST BENEFICIAL?

The first answer to this question is consistent with a key theme of this book, which is that particular happiness-enhancing activities will be most effective for people who are open to them and are motivated to practice them with effort and commitment. In other words, if it feels natural to you to practice religion and spirituality, then by all means do it.

In addition, researchers have made several interesting discoveries, including the fact that religiosity is more strongly tied to happiness among women (relative to men), among African-Americans (relative to whites), among older people (relative to younger ones), and among North Americans (relative to Europeans), possibly because their religious faith is relatively stronger. Furthermore, people who actively and publicly participate in religious activities (e.g., attending church or praying) are happier than those who simply espouse religious beliefs. (This finding underscores the key role that a support community may play in the happiness-boosting effects of religion.) Finally, and not surprisingly, those who pursue religion for intrinsic reasons (i.e., as a way of life) are happier than those who pursue it as a means to an end (i.e., for instrumental, extrinsic reasons, such as career or status).[22]

## ARE THERE DOWNSIDES TO RELIGION?

Freud argued that religion can create an "obsessional neurosis," whose symptoms include suppressed emotions, repressed sexuality, and guilt.[23] The popular media sometimes suggest that religious people are more prejudiced and closed-minded than their less religious peers, or are rather passive about their lives and health (relinquishing all control to God), or are incapable of rational scientific thought, or have maladaptive beliefs in divine vengeance, "righteous anger," and original sin. Furthermore, just like intimate relationships, which can deliver a person's highest highs and lowest lows, religious congregations can similarly be a source of stress and conflict. They may demand a great deal of time, energy, money, sacrifice, and conformity to strict expectations for moral conduct and family life.

Do these represent genuine drawbacks and harms of a religion, or are they myths perpetuated by a secular public? Yes and no. Studies support some, but not all, of these observations. For example, people who strongly believe that prayer can cure their ills are less likely to exercise and are less involved in their own health care, and those who passively defer their problems to God show lower levels of mental health.[24] People who perceive God as distant and punitive are more likely to be distressed and ill, and individuals angry at God backslide in their health. Guilt, shame, and fear may be experienced when people believe that negative events represent God's punishment for their sins (or, worse, the work of demonic forces), and such beliefs are associated with greater depression and worse health and quality of life.[25] Finally, beliefs in original sin are associated with low self-esteem, perhaps because it's hard to feel good about yourself if you feel incompetent and shameful out of the conviction that you are inherently a wicked person.

Regarding the question of whether religious beliefs can foster prejudice, this has been found in some studies of religious fundamentalists, who sometimes agree with statements like "The reason the Jews have so much trouble is because [*sic*] God is punishing them for rejecting Jesus"[26] and "The AIDS disease currently killing homosexuals is just what they deserve."[27] However, these findings are fairly weak and the results not very generalizable to today's diversity of views, indicating that the vast majority of religious and spiritual individuals are more likely to be inclusive, compassionate, and open-minded than the reverse.

Finally, the search for the sacred can be unsuccessful, triggering anxiety and distress, or, in rare cases, can lead to absolute submission to a cult or hostility toward nonbelievers. To be sure, these are extreme examples. If you choose religion and spirituality as one of the activities to increase and sustain your happiness, you're unlikely to confront such problems. As with all the happiness-boosting strategies I have discussed, moderation and common sense are wisest.

## PRACTICING RELIGION AND SPIRITUALITY

I had considered leaving this section blank, as most people who are religious or spiritual have a pretty good idea of how to observe their faith. But perhaps a few suggestions can galvanize someone who is uncertain, at a loss, or feeling despondent and inert. I'll start with a brief list and expand on a couple of strategies in detail. For now, for today, you need choose only *one* activity to try. Join (or recommit to) a temple, church, or mosque, a spiritual program, or a Bible study group. Set as your goal attending a religious service once a week or even daily. Spend fifteen minutes every day reading a spiritually themed or religious book, flipping through a volume of affirmations, listening to a spiritual radio program, or watching a religious show. Volunteer for a faith-based charity. Finally, learn about other religions by doing research at the library or on the Web or by talking to friends and acquaintances about their faiths. Not only will you be enlightened and perhaps stirred to try something new, but you may end up building or strengthening friendships.

**Seek meaning and purpose.** Researchers believe that a genuine sense of meaning in life must be rooted in a person's own thoughts, feelings, and experiences. Blindly embracing someone else's sense of meaning won't bring about happiness and growth. Creating meaning is one of the most difficult things that you can do, and the meaning that you do create is likely to change over the course of your life. Here are six suggestions from researchers on how to strive to find it.[28]

First, life is more meaningful when you are pursuing goals that are harmonious and within reach—for example, when you have the time, the ability, and the energy to devote to your most important goals, whether those goals involve rearing children or developing as a writer. If you're not sure what your goals are or how to follow them, read Chapter 8.

Second, greater meaning comes from having a coherent "life scheme." Sit back and write down, or share with someone, your own life story. Who are you now, and who were you before? What future do you imagine for yourself? What are the obstacles in your path? What assumptions do you hold about the world and why things are the way they are?

Third, creativity—in the arts, humanities, *and* sciences and even in self-discovery—can impart a sense of meaning to many people's lives. Here again, self-transcendence may be critical. What you create may be not only a joyful process for you personally, which lends your life significance, but something, if you're lucky, you may pass on to others—for today and for future generations.

Fourth, for many, there is sometimes powerful meaning in anguish and trauma (see Chapter 6). Suffering may bring about posttraumatic growth, including spiritual growth, a timeless perspective on possible life paths, and a sense that life has renewed meaning.

Fifth, at the heart of religion and spirituality are strong emotional experiences, like the comfort you feel at a religious service or the awe and wonder you feel when in the presence of the mystery and majesty of the divine or when confronted with the intensity of love, the immensity of the universe, or scenes of exquisite natural beauty. Such religious experiences, including conversion and near-death experiences, which may contain profound feelings of spiritual awakening, ecstasy, or being "bathed in light," all serve to deepen your faith and endow your life with greater meaning.

Finally, an essential path to finding meaning in your life is, almost by definition, to work on developing your faith. In a sense, faith provides the answer to the "big" questions: Who am I? What is my life for? Where do I fit in? Who is the creator? How do I live a virtuous life and improve the world around me?

**Pray.** A universal way to practice religion and spirituality is through prayer. Indeed, almost seven out of ten Americans report praying every single day, and only 6 percent report never praying.[29] Every religion has its own form and tradition of prayer, its own ways of communicating with God or the divine. The following ideas are for how to make prayer a bigger part of life.

- Dedicate a period of time each day—from five minutes to an hour—to prayer. You may use the time to petition God for something for yourself or others or simply to be "in his presence," or to read a prayer book.
- Alternatively, you may choose to pray spontaneously throughout the day and in specific situations—for example, when you feel depressed or tense or judgmental, or when you witness a beautiful object or a kind act, or when something particularly good (or bad) has happened.

- Say a prayer upon waking or before bedtime or prior to each meal. A prayer of gratitude, if you are so inclined, may be particularly comforting and happiness-inducing (see Chapter 4).

Rosa, a young woman I met at my university, decided to change her life by actively practicing prayer. Although she was raised to believe in God and to attend church on Sundays, she told me that she did it only because she was dragged there. When she became an adult, she had stopped doing something that she used to do a lot, and that was praying. This is how Rosa describes her experience of trying to accomplish her new goal and the multiple benefits she incurs:

The past week I have been praying when I go to bed and when I wake up. I pray for my day, and I give thanks for everything that has happened. I tell God of all the things that have bothered me during the day, finding myself wiser and happier when I finish praying, as if I had just told a friend everything that has bothered me for a while. Before I started praying, I felt awkward, as I had to do it in front of my roommate and I did not know how she would take it, yet when I engaged in praying to God and closed my eyes, I stopped being aware of my surroundings. I completely let myself free of all opinions and biases and thanked him for my day, thanked him for all he had done for me, and prayed for strength to continue in his path in the following days. As I finished praying, I felt relieved, as if a huge weight had left me, and I felt satisfied.

The activity itself was not hard per se, but doing something I have not done in many years was hard to pick up, especially since I started doing it every morning and every night. However, I enjoyed doing it. . . . I did not feel alone anymore. . . . I have and will make a habit of repeating my prayers every day, as I know that every time I do, I engage in better conversations with people, act more thankful, forgive easier, and make the ones around me feel like they are in good company. I believe that God is capable of many great things and he will watch over me wherever I am. He is my father, my friend, and my brother, and the feeling that I receive from talking to him is joyous as I get to share with him all my secrets, and he rids me of all my doubts and anxieties. I am definitely going to continue doing this every day as it gives me strength when I wake up and I rest easier as I go to sleep.

**Find the sacred in ordinary life.** Develop an ability to see holiness in everyday things, both beautiful and plain. A meal can be holy, and so can a child's laugh or a new snowfall. The big sky above Montana looks to many people as if it has God's fingerprints on it, but so can ordinary scenes and situations. Sanctifying day-to-day objects, experiences, and struggles takes a great deal of practice, but it's at the heart of spirituality and its rewards.

## Closing

Scientists can no longer ignore the powerful influences of spirituality and religion on health and well-being. If nothing else, the statistics should compel them. In the United States alone the vast majority of individuals, about 95 percent, believe in God.[30] If you so choose, and in your own way, you can harness the benefits of faith to improve your happiness and your life.

## Reading Guide

If you benefit from this activity, you may also want to try:

1. Taking care of your body (Happiness Activity No. 12, p. 240, 244, 250)
2. Developing strategies for coping (Happiness Activity No. 6, p. 151)

# Happiness Activity No. 12: Taking Care of Your Body (Meditation)

*Half an hour's meditation each day is essential, except when you are busy. Then a full hour is needed.*

—*St. Francis de Sales*

One of the limitations of the existing research on religion is that almost all of it has focused on Judeo-Christian faiths. Eastern religions—Hinduism, Buddhism, Taoism—offer a distinct perspective. At the core of these religions is an explicit contemplative spirituality. In Buddhism, this discipline is achieved through meditation, which helps a person accept life's "irrefutable truths"—that our lives are constantly changing and that our grasping to control our lives is futile. The regular practice of meditation is said to produce true happiness by realizing a state of awareness and detachment.

Meditation actually comprises a family of techniques that go by different names (Zen meditation, Transcendental Meditation, Vipassana meditation) and different categories (concentrative, mindfulness, contemplative, loving-kindness). The core ingredient that underlies them all is the cultivation of attention.[31] Of course you can focus attention in many different ways—for example, nonanalytically and nonemotionally on a single object (on a flame, your breath, a sound, or a single word, such as is done in concentrative meditation), or nonjudgmentally on all thoughts, sights, and sounds without ruminating on them (such as is done in mindfulness meditation), or more broadly by opening yourself up to God to contemplate the big questions of life (such as is done in contemplative meditation). Meditation is a very personal experience and may be performed in many different ways, but experts have put together several crucial elements to aim for during its practice:[32]

- Be nonjudgmental: Observe the present moment impartially, with detachment, without evaluation.

*240*

- Be nonstriving: Although, at first glance, this instruction may appear inconsistent with what I advise in the chapter on committed goal pursuit, it's not because it encourages you not to be too focused on achieving (as opposed to *progressing* toward) your goals.

- Be patient: Don't rush or force things, but allow them to unfold in their own good time.

- Be trusting: Trust yourself, and trust that things will work out in life.

- Be open: Pay attention to every little thing, as though you were seeing it for the very first time.

- Let go: Set yourself free of ruminations. This is what's called nonattachment.


## WHY MEDITATE?

I honestly was surprised to learn how many controlled laboratory and field investigations have been conducted to explore the consequences of the practice of meditation.[33] An avalanche of studies has shown that meditation has multiple positive effects on a person's happiness and positive emotions, on physiology, stress, cognitive abilities, and physical health, as well as on other harder-to-assess attributes, like "self-actualization" and moral maturity.

Researchers who study the bodies of people during the practice of meditation have confirmed that meditators are able to attain both a profound state of physiological rest (indicated by a reduced respiration rate, for instance) and a heightened state of awareness and alertness (indicated by such things as increased blood flow and other relevant markers in the brain). In my favorite meditation study, healthy workers underwent an eight-week training program in mindfulness meditation.[34] At the end of the eight weeks, those who had practiced meditation (compared with a control group) showed increases in activity in their left prefrontal cortex, relative to the right. If you recall from Chapter 2, this particular pattern of greater brain activation in the left versus right part of the brain is observed in happy and approach-oriented individuals; thus this finding nicely corroborates other research revealing that a series of regular meditation sessions produces greater happiness and less anxiety and depression.[35] Furthermore, in the same meditation study, meditators showed a stronger immune response to the influenza vaccine (with which they had been injected), and the greater the increases in their left-right brain asymmetry, the stronger the immune response. Amazingly, even a short-term practice of meditation can affect your brain activity and your immune system.[36]

Not surprisingly, such physiological effects may translate into and influence a person's health. Meditation interventions have been shown to be effective in patients with heart disease, chronic pain, skin disorders, and a variety of such mental health conditions as depression, anxiety, panic, and substance abuse. Besides its direct physiological effects, meditating can help people who are ill (and everyone else, for that matter) because it reduces their reactivity to stress and boosts positive mood, self-esteem, and feelings of control. For instance, one study showed that a six-week meditation workshop made working adults happier by augmenting their daily positive emotions, producing, in turn, such benefits as more savoring of the present moment, enhanced quality of their relationships, more social support, and a reduction in their illness symptoms.[37]

A number of intriguing studies have even revealed benefits of meditation for such seemingly intractable characteristics as intelligence, creativity, and cognitive flexibility in the elderly. In two different studies, college students who undertook a program to learn about and practice meditation showed bigger improvements on an intelligence test as well as in their course test grades, relative to control groups. Another study, with premedical and medical students, found that those who were instructed to practice mindfulness meditation reported greater spiritual experiences and empathy for others—and lower anxiety and depression, even during the stressful exam period—than those in a control group placed on a wait list.

These studies make meditation look like a panacea. If the evidence were only anecdotal, I'd be skeptical, but it's based on years of empirical work. The data are persuasive that there's something powerful about this technique—*if* you learn to apply it with sedulous effort and commitment. Successful practicers of meditation cultivate it like physical exercise: as a daily way of being. A woman friend who swears by meditation as the secret to her happiness described it to me this way: "I meditate every morning for twenty minutes. It is a sacred time that I protect from all intrusions or commitments, and for the rest of the day I am more centered and open-minded, not as sensitive or irritable or tense. I feel a sense of well-being that lasts all day. A day that I miss doing it is not the same, somehow wrecked."

People meditate for a variety of reasons: to gain inner peace, to explore a higher reality, to heal themselves of disease, to release their creativity or intuition, or to attain insight. And to achieve happiness.

## How to Meditate in Fewer Than Three Hundred Words

Teachers of meditation advise that meditating involves sitting alone in a comfortable place, back straight. Close your eyes, and focus on breathing in and out. As you breathe out, silently repeat a short word (like *one, aum,* or *be*). Or if you prefer, focus on a specific object, sound, or task, like a candle, a tone, or your breath. If your mind wanders (e.g., "I have to start dinner in twenty minutes," "Jack looked so handsome yesterday," "I feel a sore throat coming on"), let your thoughts pass, and then restart by bringing your attention back to your breath. The key is to notice your mind wandering and then to turn inward and "detach" from your thoughts. Don't let your ruminations and fantasies and plans and memories control you; take charge of them. This will take practice and repetition; beginners usually can only "quiet" or "still" the mind for no more than a few seconds at a time. A common experience is that the moment you think you've emptied your mind, it starts to fill up again.

Build the length of time you are able to meditate from five to twenty minutes, and try to do it every day. Ideally, arrange for a meditation space. It can be modest or large, decorated—with photos, artworks, or inspirational quotes—or completely spare. It should be comfortable and, if possible, free of distractions.

Meditation has many rewards, but it doesn't come effortlessly for everyone. Pascal wouldn't have contended, "All of humanity's problems stem from man's inability to sit quietly in a room alone," if sitting quietly alone were easy. For a boost or encouragement, consider taking a class on meditation, visiting a meditation Web site, or buying a how-to CD or book.

# Happiness Activity No. 12: Taking Care of Your Body (Physical Activity)

An impressive study of physical activity was published in the *Archives of Internal Medicine* in 1999.[38] The researchers recruited men and women fifty years old and over, all of them suffering from clinical depression, and divided them randomly into three groups. The first group was assigned to four months of aerobic exercise, the second group to four months of anti-depressant medication (Zoloft), and the third group to both. The assigned exercise involved three supervised forty-five-minute sessions per week of cycling or walking/jogging at moderate to high intensity. Remarkably, by the end of the four-month intervention period, all three groups had experienced their depressions lift and reported fewer dysfunctional attitudes and increased happiness and self-esteem. Aerobic exercise was just as effective at treating depression as was Zoloft, or as a combination of exercise *and* Zoloft. Yet exercise is a lot less expensive, usually with no side effects apart from soreness. Perhaps even more remarkably, six months later, participants who had "remitted" (recovered) from their depressions were less likely to relapse if they had been in the exercise group (six months ago!) than if they had been in the medication group.[39] The researchers named the study the Standard Medical Intervention and Long-term Exercise study. SMILE.

The proverbial feel-good factor in exercise is well known. But the fact that the psychological benefits of physical activity trumped those of anti-depressant drugs surprised even me. Could the exercise program in this study have boosted participants' self-esteem and sense of mastery over their training? Could the antidepressant medication, by contrast, have given participants a less self-affirming explanation for their personal improvement (i.e., "The drugs lifted my depression" versus "It was my own effort and commitment to the exercise program that helped me beat this thing")? In any case, the SMILE study epitomizes a flood of research corroborating the multiple benefits of physical activity for health and well-being. Physical activity reduces anxiety and stress; protects us from dying in general (and from dying of heart disease or cancer, in particular); reduces the risk of numerous diseases (diabetes, colon cancer, hyperten-sion); builds bones, muscles, and joints; increases quality of life; improves sleep; protects against cognitive impairments as we age; and helps control weight.[40] In sedentary older adults, a very low-intensity exercise pro-gram (walking or resistance/flexibility training) reduces depression and increases confidence and maintains the improvement for an astonishing five years.[41] Finally, surveys show, and large-scale randomized interven-tions confirm, that exercise may very well be the most effective instant happiness booster of all activities.[42] Is that enough?

## WHY DOES PHYSICAL ACTIVITY MAKE PEOPLE HAPPIER?

Psychologists believe that several explanations underlie the well-being rewards of exercise. First is the self-esteem/mastery explanation I just mentioned. Taking up a sport or fitness regimen makes you feel in control of your body and your health. Seeing yourself get better at something—faster, farther, stronger—provides a terrific sense of agency and self-worth. Second is the possibility that physical activity offers potential for flow as well as a positive distraction that turns away worries and rumina-tion. It essentially serves as a time-out from your stressful day, with positive spillover effects for hours afterward. Interestingly, this view of exercise makes it sound a lot like meditation, and indeed, the few studies that have directly compared meditation with exercise show that the two activities often show identical effects, including reduced anxiety and increased mood-lifting hormones.[43] Of course the *experience* of exercise and meditation is very different, most notably, one generally producing so-called high-arousal emotions (energy, enthusiasm, and vigor), the other producing low-arousal emotions (serenity, peace, and calm). But they all are positive emotions that not only make you feel good but distract you from hassles and anxieties.

Third, physical activity, when performed along with others, can provide opportunities for social contact, thus potentially bolstering social support and reinforcing friendships. It can even lift the burden of loneliness or isolation. A former avid footballer (soccer player) in Birmingham, England, described how taking up the sport allowed him to take on a new social identity separate from his current one—namely, a person with a mental illness:

> When you have had a bad day . . . then you can go out for football for an
> hour and a half with complete strangers and they don't know what I do,
> they just know me to play football with and that's how I like it. I've got
> friends who know about my illness but these people don't know nothing
> about me, they just respect that I am a good footballer and they like me
> because of that. It's kind of a therapy for myself because I don't have to
> justify who I am and what I have done in the past in terms of illness and
> they just respect me for being a damn fine soccer player because I am the
> captain of the team.[44]

The feel-good consequences of exercise could be physiological in origin. When you exercise, not only do you feel good that you're accomplishing something, but you also experience the fringe benefits of improved physical fitness, including greater cardiovascular endurance, flexibility, and strength. You may be able to lift heavier objects, walk farther, and avoid health problems into old age. This in itself can bring about greater happiness. Indeed, exercise has been shown to elevate serotonin levels, similar to the effects of Prozac.[45]

But what about the endorphin hypothesis? Doesn't vigorous physical activity elevate endorphins, the brain's natural pain-killing and euphoria-inducing opioids, leading to the familiar runner's high? Unfortunately, there is not a great deal of support for this theory, although central opioids *have* been found to suppress the unpleasant symptoms of physical exertion, thus presumably reducing discomfort (though likely not producing an actual high).[46]

Finally, I should mention that physical activity really has two kinds of benefits. The first is the "acute" immediate boost you gain from a single bout of exercise, and the second involves the "chronic" improvements from an ongoing exercise program. These benefits are not one and the same. For example, you may feel wretched *during* exercise but experience feelings of motivation, exhilaration, lifting of anxiety, or general well-being immediately afterward. Alternatively, you may not encounter any enduring effects (such as the sense of mastery from sustaining your training or bolstered body image from dropping a pant size) until much later. The first time I resolved to become fit, back in school, I read in a running manual that it takes eleven weeks for a running program to "stick" and to obtain benefit. Eleven weeks are a long time to wait and endure, and unfortunately, many people give up before they reach that mark. But when you reach it, physical activity becomes a natural extension of your life, a habitual act that requires no decision making to initiate. When the alarm goes off, you don't contemplate whether you should drift back to sleep or get up and start moving; you just do it. It sure is worth it.

## What if Exercise Makes You Feel Bad?

Rigorous physical activity, no matter what it is, may cause you to feel terrible. Does this make you a bad person? No, but it probably means that you should change your exercise routine. First, consider finding an exercise that—magic word—fits your lifestyle, resources, and personality. Don't jog if you live in a rainy climate and hate being wet. Don't join a gym if it strains your budget. Don't participate on a team if you're allergic to competition. Don't do aerobic exercise (e.g., elliptical machine) if you prefer anaerobic (e.g., stretching and toning). Do something that affirms some part of you. If you're a social person, acquire a running buddy or join a golf club. If you need more time with your children, buy a jogging stroller or join a baby yoga class. If you like nature, take up hiking or skiing. If you love the water, do a water-based sport. If you have only slices of time during the day, exercise in ten-minute chunks, or take the stairs everywhere you go, or do calisthenics in your office.

Second—and this is a crucial one—if exercise makes you feel bad, you are very likely overdoing it. Learn to measure your maximum heart rate (see below), and when you set out for your first session, do *not* exceed 60 percent of that limit. For some people, this may be walking briskly (running will come later) or simply walking. Too many start out an exercise routine working out too hard, leaving them feeling discouraged, frustrated and generally unwell, and so they quit.

In one study, participants were asked to cycle at 60 percent of their maximum heart rate. Over the course of thirty minutes, half the participants reported feeling progressively better, and half claimed to feel progressively worse. Researchers, who tend to study the average person, don't yet know why some people experience pleasure while exercising, and others displeasure, but you can take steps to figure out why you in particular feel good or bad.

## How to Do It

*Physical activity* is defined as "energy expenditure above that of resting level,"[47] so the field is really wide open, the options limitless. Researchers chide people who use the terms *physical activity* and *exercise* interchangeably (the latter is only a subset of the former, exercise being a specific kind of planned and structured physical activity, usually with the goal of improving physical fitness or health), but I choose to confound them anyway. If you resolve to undertake a program of physical activity after reading this chapter, you'll essentially be *moving* more. It's that simple. The moving can be done as part of a formal, organized, and refereed sport or at home alone on a yoga mat.

Exercise professionals traditionally advise that you calculate your maximum heart rate (most simply defined as 220 minus your age) and strive to work out at a level between 65 and 80 percent of that figure. So, if you are thirty-two years old, your maximum heart rate is 188, and the range to aim for is between 122 and 150.[48] Don't be a slave to this range, however; it's approximate because the formula is designed for an average person of your precise age,[49] and at least those of us who've grown up in a Western culture know that we are definitely not average.

Few of us don't already have a pretty good idea how to start and implement a physical activity routine. But it doesn't hurt to add these several recommendations:

- Start slow—in the 60 to 65 percent range of your maximum heart rate.
- Decide ahead of time on specific dates, starting times, and durations of your exercise, and pencil or stylus them in, treating them like fixed appointments. Would you ever miss a meeting with your boss or to pick up your kid from school? Yes, but rarely and only in exceptional situations.
- If possible, choose a time to exercise during a time of day when you feel most energetic.
- Current guidelines recommend thirty minutes of moderate physical activity on most days of the week. But better to exercise for ten minutes than not at all. The most important thing is to stick with your plan.
- If you already engage in regular physical activity, up the ante. Run faster and longer; lift heavier weights; join a more advanced swim or dance class.
- An exercise routine is like a diet. It's okay to break it, but don't let guilt and shame so overwhelm you that you give up the whole thing. Get back on the horse (literally or figuratively) the following day.

## ACTIVITY AND REST

I don't know if it was ironic, coincidental, or completely predictable if you knew me, but I found myself reading scientific papers on the benefits of physical activity while exercising on a stationary bike. Admittedly, I'm a bit addicted to exercise, and my commitment (if not always my performance) is very high. But one thing that I *don't* get enough of is sleep. "The world belongs to the energetic," according to Ralph Waldo Emerson, but the energetic also need to reserve time for rest. No matter how active and vigorous and successful we are during wakeful hours, if we don't obtain an adequate amount of sleep, we'll suffer in terms of our moods, energy, alertness, longevity, and health. One prominent sleep researcher argues that if people got just one more hour of sleep each night, our Western "sleep-sick" society would be much happier and healthier.[50] It's like those ads professing that you can "Lose weight while you sleep!" You can say you've read it here that you can become happier while you sleep.

## LAST WORD

No one in our society needs to be told that exercise is good for us. Whether you are overweight or have a chronic illness or are a slim couch potato, you've probably heard or read this dictum countless times throughout your life. But has anyone told you—indeed, *guaranteed* you—that regular physical activity will make you happier? I swear by it.

# Happiness Activity No. 12: Taking Care of Your Body (Acting Like a Happy Person)

It is somehow fitting to complete our discussion of specific strategies for how to become happier with the prescription simply to *act* like a happy person. Remarkably, pretending that you're happy—smiling, engaged, mimicking energy and enthusiasm—not only can earn you some of the benefits of happiness (returned smiles, strengthened friendships, successes at work and school)[51] but can actually *make* you happier. In poet Marge Piercy's words, "Live as if you liked yourself, and it may happen."

## FACIAL FEEDBACK

This wisdom has been supported by decades of research and by the facial feedback hypothesis in particular, an idea foreshadowed by Darwin's view that "the free expression by outward signs of an emotion intensifies it."[52] In other words, show the physical manifestations of happiness (or fear or disgust), and you will come to feel it—at least in mild form. Smooth (or furrow) your brow, fashion smile (or frown) lines, open your hands (or clench them), and you might just experience more joy or more irritation. According to this notion, your face, (and body and voice), send signals (feedback) to your brain, informing it that you are experiencing a particular emotion and leading you—surprise!—to feel it. If you ever took a course in introductory psychology, you probably learned about a study in which participants were asked to hold felt-tip markers in their mouths, either gripped directly between their teeth (simulating a smile) or between their puckered lips (simulating a frown).[53] (For those concerned about the hygienic aspects of this procedure, the pen was first disinfected with an alcohol-dipped swab.) The participants were not aware that the marker holding would have any particular impact on them, nor were they truthfully told why exactly they had to do this. Instead, they were instructed to examine a set of *Far Side* cartoons and to judge how funny they found them. Those whose facial muscles were (unknowingly to them) manipulated to resemble a smile found the cartoons more humorous than those whose facial expressions mimicked a frown.

This study, and many others like it, suggest that simply taking on the facial expressions and postures of happiness can go a long way to make you experience joy. Admittedly, the effects are modest. When trained actors were obliged to manipulate their facial muscles (most of us average folk aren't able to do this) into the configuration required for a genuine smile—to be exact, this involves the contraction of the orbicularis oculi, the muscle that encircles the eye, and contraction of the zygomaticus major muscles, pulling the corners of the lips upward—the actors reported feeling positive and happy, though their feelings were closer to *"as if* I were happy" than to the real thing.[54] In spite of this, some people swear by a strategy of regular smiling. Recently a reader named Marsh wrote to me that he makes use of a special wristwatch designed to vibrate several times a day to prompt people to take their medication. He has it set to 10:00 A.M., 12:00 P.M., 2:00 P.M., 4:00 P.M., and 6:00 P.M. to remind himself to smile. "Am I happier?" he wrote. "I think so."

## PERMANENT SMILES OR FROWNS

Another intriguing sort of evidence for facial feedback comes from research seeking to understand the effects of permanent facial expressions on emotion. Mobius syndrome is a birth defect that causes those afflicted with it to lack the ability to move their facial muscles; in a real sense, they have frozen neutral expressions on their faces. Such patients claim that they cannot *experience* emotions, only think them. "I . . . think happy or I think sad, not . . . actually feeling happy or feeling sad," reported one man with the condition.[55] So the inability physically to express emotions powerfully influences the ability to feel them.

Have you noticed that as people age, they tend to develop facial lines that match their personality? A very old and very happy person appears to have a happy expression fixed on her face, and a person who has been sad (or angry) all his life is trapped with a sad (or angry) look. This is a scientifically supported fact. For example, repeated contractions of the orbicularis oculi muscle, which constricts both sides of the eyes, raising the cheeks and gathering the skin in toward the bridge of the nose, causes eye wrinkles, the familiar crinkly eye lines that characterize a smile. So, what if you took away the "sad" or "angry" wrinkles, would you actually become happier? If the facial feedback hypothesis is right, the answer is yes. A study to test this directly was done not long ago.[56] The participants were ten clinically depressed patients whose depressions had not responded to treatment by either drugs or psychotherapy. In other words, nothing had worked. They all were women, thirty-six to sixty-three years of age, and they had been depressed for periods ranging from two to seventeen years. All the patients were administered muscle-paralyzing botulinum toxin A—aka Botox—to their frown lines (on the bridge of the nose, between the eyebrows, and slightly above them). Two months later, nine out of the ten participants were no longer depressed, and the tenth had much improved. Although it comes from an admittedly preliminary study, this is a stunning finding. Undoubtedly, removal of the frown lines makes other people perceive you as happier (and more attractive), and as this investigation shows, people actually do *feel* happier.

## SOCIAL INTERACTIONS AND COPING

Of course, in the real world, outside the laboratory, if you smile, the world smiles with you. People respond to you more positively; they may initiate a conversation, engage with you, help you out or comfort you, become your new best friend or the future parent of your child. The smiles of infants have been shown to procure love and attachment, ensuring that the caregiver will continue to care for the child and secure his well-being. Mothers who express positive emotions have infants who begin to express positive emotions as well, an observation that led Erich Fromm to go so far as to contend that "A mother must not only be a 'good mother,' but also a happy person."[57]

Even—or perhaps especially—in the face of stressful events, smiling and laughter can help "undo" negative emotions, distract, and bring about feelings of peace, amusement, or even joy. In one study, people who had lost their spouses six months earlier were interviewed and asked to reminisce about their marriages.[58] Those who laughed spontaneously during the interviews reported coping much better with their bereavement and experiencing more enjoyment in their lives, less anger, and more positive relationships with others. It was as though the laughter helped them "dissociate" from their distress. Other work has shown that laughter can lower stress hormones, and even the *expectation* of laughter can elevate beneficial hormones. Men who anticipated watching one of their favorite humorous videos had 27 percent more beta-endorphins in their blood and 87 percent more human growth hormone than a control group.[59] And these physiological changes happened before the videos even rolled.

In sum, smiling and laughter—even the insincere "I don't want to pose for this photo" smile or "This joke's not that funny" chuckle—gives rise to a mild feeling of positive well-being. Even more, that little boost jump-starts a powerful upward spiral of consequences for coping and social relationships, thereby reducing anxiety and distress and bringing you ever-greater happiness and joy.

So go for it. Smile, laugh, stand tall, act lively, and give hugs. Act as if you were confident, optimistic, and outgoing. You'll manage adversity, rise to the occasion, create instant connections, make friends and influence people, and become a happier person.

## Reading Guide

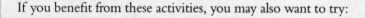

If you benefit from these activities, you may also want to try:

1. Committing to your goals (Happiness Activity No. 10, p. 205)
2. Savoring life's joys (Happiness Activity No. 9, p. 190)

*Part Three*

Secrets to

Abiding Happiness

# 10.

# The Five Hows Behind
# Sustainable Happiness

I t's relatively easy to become happier for the short duration, just as it's a
piece of cake to quit smoking for a day or to temporarily keep a tidy
desk. The challenge lies in *sustaining* the new level of happiness. You
know this intimately if you've tried to turn your life around before (perhaps numerous times) but have found that "nothing works." I would
wager that your previous attempts *have* worked, just not for long. Why
not? This chapter explains that long-term increases in your level of happiness can be attained, but only if you abide by the five hows (or keys)
behind sustainable well-being. The six chapters of Part II described in
detail a set of twelve activities from which you can adopt one, or two or
four, to launch the process of making yourself a happier person. On the
other hand, some of you may choose to read about all twelve activities
and benefit from each and every one.

With the intentional activities, you have the power to harness the
promise of the 40 percent of our feelings of well-being that are within
our control, to improve that large part of your happiness that *can* be
improved. You may have begun carrying out these happiness activities

already or you may have not. In either case, you may be wondering about the essential secrets of their success. If you understood better *how* and *why* the happiness strategies worked, would you be more effective in practicing them? Would you be more likely to persist in engaging in them? Absolutely. In this chapter, I describe the critical mechanisms of action (or reasons) for the success of the book's core program. The five hows, grounded in the scientific literature, are assembled and interpreted together here for the first time.

# The First How: Positive Emotion

Happiness consists more in small conveniences or pleasures that occur every day, than in great pieces of good fortune that happen but seldom.

—*Benjamin Franklin*

Say that you are reasonably comfortable materially. You may not have everything you desire, but you have a roof over your head, plenty of food to eat, clothes that fit and keep you warm, and some security in your income. What if seventy-five thousand dollars suddenly fell out of the sky and onto your fortunate head. How should you spend the money to maximize the happiness that you will obtain from it?

This is by no means a frivolous question; the answer gets to the heart of one of the primary ways that particular happiness activities, or behaviors, make people happier, and that is by creating many happy moments. Indeed, frequent positive emotions—feelings of joy, delight, contentment, serenity, curiosity, interest, vitality, enthusiasm, vigor, thrill, and pride—are the very hallmark of happiness.[1] Although all human beings endure negative emotions, happy people experience positive states more frequently than do their less happy peers. It can even be said that positive emotions make happy people who they are.

Fortunately, each of the twelve intentional happiness activities described in Chapters 4 through 9 has the ability to generate a cascade of positive experiences. To be sure, one of the desirable features of such activities is that they can be frequently initiated, reinitiated, and adjusted to yield a continual flow of positive experiences and positive feelings. For example, a person who has resolved to undertake the twin strategies of committing to goals and increasing flow may decide to return to school in middle age. Accordingly, he may vary his reading choices and course selections in order to develop expertise in multiple areas. In the process he will feel strong intrinsic motivation and flow and experience the joy of discovering fascinating new areas of knowledge, the pride of mastering new skills, and the enjoyment of meeting new people. These ongoing positive experiences, brought about by conscious effort on his part, may help him remain particularly happy over a long period of time.

Consider another individual who embarks on practicing the three strategies of gratitude, kindness, and religion. If she places sincere effort into these activities, she will feel the gratification and peace that come from appreciating life's blessings, the satisfaction that comes from helping others and from forging new relationships, and the serenity and awe that come from being in the presence of God. Notably, however, these surges of positive feeling won't be singular but recurrent. No happiness–enhancing strategy would be capable of successfully sustaining happiness if it made a person feel happy only once and only briefly.

If you contemplate each of the twelve happiness-boosting activities, you will observe that every one of them has the potential to produce a stream of positive experiences, to increase the number of transient bursts of happiness in your life. Because positive emotions are typically short-lived, many people believe they are trivial. This is a mistake. As Barbara Fredrickson has eloquently argued, moments of pleasure don't just make you *feel* good. They broaden your horizons and build your social, physical, and intellectual skills.[2] In this way, positive emotions beget upward spirals. For example, you feel invigorated after aerobic exercise, which boosts your creativity, which gives you a new idea about how to enchant your partner, which strengthens your marriage, which shores up your satisfaction and commitment, which leads you to be more grateful and forgiving, which fuels optimism, which creates a self-fulfilling prophecy, which buffers the sting of a setback at work, and so on. Some of the changes produced by small boosts of positive emotion are small, and some are big, but they add up. Positive emotions truly *make* you into a happier person. "We live in an ascending scale when we live happily," said the author of *Treasure Island*, Robert Louis Stevenson, "one thing leading to another in an endless series."

So, if you suddenly experienced a financial windfall, you would ultimately be much happier if you spent the money on numerous pleasant, mood-boosting things occurring on a day-to-day or weekly basis—a daily lunch of expensive sushi, a weekly massage, a regular delivery of fresh flowers, or Sunday-morning calls to your best friend in Europe—rather than spend it all on a single big-ticket item that you believe you would really love, like a new top-of-the-line Jaguar or the remodeling of a bathroom with hand-painted tile. By now you should appreciate the fact, as Ben Franklin did, that you would swiftly adapt to the new automobile or bathtub but not to the bursts of intermittent happiness.

But why do we continue to *believe* so strongly that it's the large and dramatic events of our lives—the earthquake, the overseas adventure, the wedding, and the divorce—that are the ones that matter? Because those are the events we anticipate, remember, chew over, and discuss with others. We tend to notice and recall only special and important episodes from our lives, the one day that something went very wrong (or extremely right) instead of the remaining 364 ordinary days. However, don't underestimate the positive emotions experienced during those ordinary days, because properly understood, they can change your entire perspective and open your mind to new possibilities that you hadn't known were there just moments before. Consider the famous madeleine cookie consumption experience of French novelist Marcel Proust:

> I raised to my lips a spoonful of the tea in which I had soaked a morsel of the cake. No sooner had the warm liquid mixed with the crumbs touched my palate than a shudder ran through me and I stopped, intent upon the extraordinary thing that was happening to me. An exquisite pleasure had invaded my senses, something isolated, detached, with no suggestion of its origin. And at once the vicissitudes of life had become indifferent to me, its disasters innocuous, its brevity illusory—this new sensation having had

on me the effect which love has of filling me with a precious essence; or rather this essence was not in me, it was me. I had ceased now to feel mediocre, contingent, mortal.[3]

Yes, Proust definitely feels a positive emotion upon eating the madeleine, perhaps more intense and transcendent than that experienced by most of us ordinary folk, but we all have had our share of positive emotions. The fact that the experience feels *good,* however, doesn't end there. It changes him, providing new insight and new understanding. It prompts him to look at the world in an entirely different way. This is an elegant analogy for what happens when you resolve to craft daily kindnesses or smile more or consider the brightest possible future for yourself. By enacting these strategies, you will create happy moments in your life that will not only make you feel happier but alter your whole way of thinking and being. They will create a sense of possibility and promise, and who knows where that will take you?

## POSITIVE EMOTIONS AND DEPRESSION

If you've ever had long-lasting or intense periods of feeling down or blue, you may be surprised at the role that positive emotions can play in depression. To be sure, depression has been described as a syndrome distinguished by a *deficit* of positive emotions: a lack of joy, curiosity, contentment, enthusiasm—that is, an empty cup.[4] Indeed, inability to take pleasure in joyful events is a hallmark of depression. This positivity deficit is also evident in how depressed people think about the future and the past. Their problem, it turns out, is not so much that they anticipate bad things will come to pass as that they cannot believe that good things will.[5] They also have great difficulty recalling anything pleasant that has ever happened to them.[6] The experience of positive events is also important; surprisingly, recovery from depression appears to be jump-started by positive events even more than it's thwarted by negative events. For example, researchers in the UK carefully analyzed forty-nine instances when women improved or recovered from depressive episodes.[7] These changes of fortune were found to be galvanized by a positive experience, especially something that gave these women the feeling of a "fresh start."

All these observations and findings point to multiple ways that happiness-enhancing activities can alleviate the symptoms of depression. The activities that will be most effective in lifting depressive symptoms should be those that increase positive emotions (e.g., joy and relief at overcoming an obstacle), their surrounding positive thoughts (e.g., "I'm tougher than I thought"), and positive experiences or events (making an important deadline at work). It's worth noting that in our day-to-day lives, emotions, thoughts, and experiences are connected and typically occur together. Researchers, however, usually disaggregate them, so that they can show the value of each separately. In any case, it's no coincidence that the twelve happiness strategies described in Part II of the book—activities like practicing daily gratitude, focusing on the best person you can possibly be, being generous, and spending quality time with loved ones—all are designed to accomplish exactly what is needed to ward off depression: Increase positive emotions, foster positive thoughts, and fuel positive experiences.

First, we have already seen that happiness activities boost positive emotions, but researchers have also shown that positive feelings can foil the effects of negative feelings.[8] In one study, participants were given only one minute to prepare a speech on the topic "Why you are a good friend." (Unbeknownst to them, the speech never actually took place.) Immediately, these participants reported being extremely anxious, felt their hearts racing and their blood pressures rise. Then they were divided into four groups, and each group was simply shown a movie that made them feel joyful, content, neutral, or sad. After the films, all the groups eventually returned to their original emotional and physiological states (i.e., no anxiety, normal heart rate, etc.), but the two groups that had experienced positive emotions—namely, joy and contentment—showed the fastest recovery in their cardiovascular symptoms.[9] Recent data from my lab extended this finding to depression.[10] People who were instructed to practice various happiness activities reported experiencing more frequent positive emotions, such as contentment and pleasure, for as long as three months after our study had ended. Critically, our analyses revealed that those very positive emotions, in turn, led the same individuals to show reduced depressive symptoms as long as six months after the study.

Researchers argue that positive emotions possess the ability to undo the lingering cardiovascular effects of negative emotions. Indeed, feelings of joy, satisfaction, or pride can help people see the "big picture" of their lives and provide a sort of "psychological time-out" in the midst of stress or trauma, thus lessening the sting of any particular unpleasant event. In these ways, positive feelings marshaled in the face of adversity can build resilience, by helping people bounce back from stressful experiences.[11]

A second benefit of happiness activities is that they boost positive thinking. As I discuss in the "Postscript," the most widely held theories of depression posit that negative, dysfunctional thoughts are at the root of this disorder.[12] This is because pessimistic, downbeat attitudes and memories fuel negative emotions—sadness, anger, jealousy, fear—which spawn more negative thoughts, and so on, in a vicious downward spiral. In contrast, happiness activities can counteract the negative bias by helping us unlearn our patterns of negative thinking. For example, hopeful predictions that result from the optimism strategy replace thoughts of hopelessness and powerlessness. Joyful memories brought to mind by the savoring strategy replace bitter and angry recollections about old hurts. Pleasant, distracting thoughts prompted by the avoiding overthinking strategy replace fretful ruminations about current troubles. Indeed, a study from my laboratory confirmed this reasoning. People who actively and regularly practiced either gratitude or optimism over an eight-week period came to regard their routine experiences in more positive ways and to find everyday events (meeting a friend, commuting to work, cooking dinner) more satisfying.[13] These more positive thoughts and interpretations, in turn, triggered improvements in well-being.

Third, happiness activities encourage positive experiences. Practicing the nurturing relationships activity yields periods of relaxation and contentment in the company of family and friends. Practicing acts of kindness produces moments in which we suddenly feel efficacious and appreciated. Having more flow at home, school, and work can lead us to be more successful and productive, producing greater engagement and enjoyment of our daily life.

The majority of conventional depression therapies aim for "remission"—or the virtual absence of depressive symptoms—as their end point.[14] Most people recognize, however, that relief of symptoms is not the depressed person's ultimate objective. If you are depressed, your goal is not just *not* to be depressed; your goal is to be happy. However, even after therapy has successfully assuaged sadness, guilt, fatigue, and apathy, you still may not be happy, and you almost certainly wouldn't be flourishing or thriving. The latest estimate is that 11 percent of us are "languishing"—that is, not clinically depressed yet living stagnant, empty lives or, to quote Thoreau, leading "lives of quiet desperation."[15] Thus recovery from depression will likely return you to a hedonic "neutral" point, to "languishing" at best. The goal of practicing happiness activities is to bolster positive emotions, thoughts, and experiences, such that they eventually lift you and sustain you above that neutral point.

If you are currently receiving treatment for depression, the combination of the treatment and the use of happiness-increasing strategies will, I hope, have the double whammy effect of relieving depressed mood and elevating happiness. The reasons should be plain by now. The happiness strategies are expected to trigger pleasant emotions and uplifting thoughts, which serve as an antidote to depressive symptoms. They are also expected to bring about a stream of positive experiences, which are inconsistent with depression.

## POSITIVE EMOTIONS VERSUS LIFE MEANING

Are transient positive emotions really as important to strive for as honor, integrity, or meaning in life? The answer is that the very question is misleading. It sets up a false dichotomy between so-called hedonistic pleasures and the well-deserved gratifications of the mind, heart, and soul. In truth, positive emotion is positive emotion, joy is joy, contentment is contentment. Who is to compare the thrill of a helicopter ride with the ecstasy of spiritual awakening, the joy of a lemonade in the high desert to the delight of hearing your baby's first laugh? Experiences that forge a sense of life meaning, whether they involve helping a friend in need, worshiping a higher power, or developing a superior expertise, are *happy* moments, even if the positive emotions surrounding them may not always be evident immediately or if they differ (as they undoubtedly do) from the positive emotions induced by a sugar high.

So don't pooh-pooh pleasure. You can find pleasure in a silly TV show or in being wholly absorbed in a lecture on astrophysics. Both types of pleasure contribute to a happy life, and both types of pleasure can give rise to the multiple benefits of positive emotions, like feeling more sociable, more energetic, and more resourceful. An avalanche of studies has shown that happy moods, no matter the source, lead people to be more productive, more likable, more active, more healthy, more friendly, more helpful, more resilient, and more creative.[16] This means that positive emotions actually help us achieve our goals (reinforcing the feeling that we are working toward something important) as well as help us strive for meaning and purpose in life. Indeed, a series of intriguing studies at the University of Missouri found that happy moods lead people to perceive their lives as more meaningful; for example, the more positive emotion people experience during a particular day, the more meaningful they judge that day.[17] That seriousness and greatness must be accompanied by grumpiness is a myth.

## WHENCE THE SOURCE

I confess now that I did gloss over something. The *source* of the happy moments does in fact matter, for it influences the ability of the experience to be self-sustaining. Although the bliss of a sinful pleasure can trigger the same kinds of intellectual, social, and physical benefits as the bliss of hard-earned effort, the sinful pleasure is over quickly and, what's more, can leave guilt or other negative feelings in its wake. But the pleasure borne of any of the dozen happiness-inducing strategies described here, whether they involve practicing optimism, nurturing relationships, developing coping strategies, or living in the present, is lasting, recurring, or self-reinforcing. One of the chief reasons for the durability of happiness activities is that unlike the guilty pleasures, they are hard won. You have devoted time and effort to meditating or avoiding overthinking or committing acts of kindness. You have made these practices happen, and you have the ability to make them happen again. This sense of capability and responsibility is a powerful boost in and of itself. When the source of positive emotion is yourself (as opposed to a televised World Cup game or chocolate or a glass of wine), it can continue to yield pleasure and make you happy. When the source of positive emotion is yourself, it is *renewable*.

# The Second How: Optimal Timing and Variety

To be interested in the changing seasons is a happier state
of mind than to be hopelessly in love with spring.

—*George Santayana*

Discovering which exact strategies you can undertake to become happier won't necessarily blow your mind. Many people intuitively grasp that being grateful for what they have, savoring the moment, strengthening relationships, and coping well with hardship all are activities that ultimately bolster happiness. Knowing what to do is an important step, but you also need to know precisely *how* to do it. Fortunately, research has something to say about specifically how a happiness-increasing program must be carried out to achieve maximum success. In this section, I describe two elements that are critical, timing and variety.

## TIMING IS IMPORTANT

Love is brief, but frequently recurring.

—*François de La Rochefoucauld*

The pie chart theory of happiness predicts that no attempt at making yourself happier can work if you eventually adapt to the happiness-boosting effects of your effort. This is why, as we see in Chapter 2, the strategy of changing one's circumstances—earning more money or switching jobs—is ultimately fruitless. But can't you also adapt to the *activities* you do in order to be happy—for example, to counting blessings, to dispensing kindnesses, or to pursuing life goals? Yes, you can, unless you respect the second how of sustainable well-being. As the French author La Rochefoucauld intuited, activities, by definition, are episodic; they happen at irregular intervals. Intentionally cultivating optimism, for instance, might be something that you do on mornings that you wake up gloomy, or on your way to social get-togethers, or each time you receive an e-mail from your boss. Alternatively, you might choose to practice optimism every Sunday night by writing in a journal about your best possible future self. The bottom line is that for happiness activities, as for humor, timing is important. Accordingly, it's essential to consider your strategies' frequency and duration and to strive to time them in ways that deliver you greatest satisfaction, serenity, or joy— in other words, to time them in ways that thwart adaptation. For example, you might choose to count your blessings only after braving a difficult period, or only when you're especially needful of a boost, or only at week's end. A friend of mine actually keeps a handwritten list of the strategies that work especially well for her during particular times (e.g., meditate and practice gratitude before in-laws visit, focus on goal pursuit and avoid over- thinking when dealing with supervisor, etc.) and consults that list during those times. This way you strive to discover the optimal timing for each activity—that is, a frequency of engagement that allows each activity to remain fresh, meaningful, and positive.

How do you accomplish this? Through self-experimentation. Earlier I described a couple of experiments from my laboratory in which we induced people to practice different happiness-boosting strategies.[18] These experiments offer some ideas for how one might achieve optimal timing. One study showed that people were more successful at increasing their happiness when they counted their blessings every Sunday night than when they did it three times a week. A second study showed that people were more successful at increasing their happiness when they com- mitted five acts of kindness on a Monday than when they spread them throughout the week. Both these observations may be true for you as well. However, these findings represent averages—that is, *on average,* people who count their blessings only on Sundays and those who do five acts of kindness in one single day are happiest—and they may not apply to every reader of this book. Furthermore, these general rules may not apply to *other* ways of expressing gratitude or kindness (such as writing gratitude letters or volunteering weekly for a charitable organization) or to other happiness activities (such as learning coping strategies or practicing optimism, forgiveness, or flow). You need to try different ways of timing your happiness activity, manipulating when and how often you perform it, until something clicks and it begins to work for you.

Interestingly, religious practices and prohibitions make clever use of optimal timing. Orthodox Jewish married couples, for example, are forbidden to touch each other—let alone be intimate—during the seven days surrounding the woman's menstrual period. To ensure that inadvertent physical contact doesn't occur, even such mundane acts as passing the salt must be conducted with forethought and care; the wife must place the salt shaker on the table in front of her husband, leaving just enough time to pull back her hand before his comes close to hers. This might seem absurd to some of us, but the unintended (or perchance intended?) fringe benefit is the maintenance of the flames of love and passion. How wonderful it must be to be able to resume physical contact after the period of prohibition each month! Notwithstanding the origins for such practices, we can borrow their spirit, if not their substance, to enhance the love and happiness in our own lives.

## VARIETY, THE SPICE OF LIFE

Activities, by definition, are also dynamic—that is, they don't tend to stay the same.[19] Being generous and charitable to others on a regular basis requires a multitude of diverse behaviors every week: One day you might leave an extra-large tip for a weary waiter; another day you might visit a grieving friend; the following week you might do the dishes even when it's not your turn. The same applies to expressing gratitude or striving for goals or any other strategy you might undertake. This is why we don't adapt very quickly or easily to an activity (and its shifting nature), and this is why another important way that you can bolster the effectiveness of a happiness activity is to vary it. By varying it, we ensure that we don't adapt to it. For example, by alternating attention among several projects at work, by changing the route, time of day, and speed of your running regimen, or by exploring a variety of software programs and Web sites, your activities could remain intrinsically enjoyable and conducive to many rewarding flow experiences. Or if in expressing gratitude, you choose to vary the domains of life in which you count your blessings (i.e., in relationships, in your profession, in your health, or in whatever area of life you've recently been fortunate), then the strategy may remain fresh and meaningful and work indefinitely. Conversely, if you count the very same blessings every day, in a nonvarying routine, you may become bored with the routine and cease to extract any meaning from it. Supporting this notion, psychological research suggests that people tend to seek variety in their behavior, perhaps because change, in both thoughts and actions, is innately pleasurable and stimulating.[20] No doubt aware of this, the German philosopher Immanuel Kant was said to shift his routine on his daily walks, in order to forestall boredom.

The importance of variety is demonstrated by both empirical and anecdotal evidence. In a kindness intervention from my laboratory, participants given the opportunity to vary their acts of kindness over a ten-week period (do an extra household chore, help a stranger change a tire, help a niece with homework, etc.) became happier and stayed happier. For the participants who performed similar acts each week, however, the kindness strategy completely backfired.[21] An analogous observation was made by "obesity czar" Robert Jeffery.[22] Having developed an obesity intervention that is incredibly effective, he soon learned that it works great for about six months, at which point his clients get burned out or bored with the regimen and can't stick to it. Consequently, he has begun to retool the intervention every six months or so in order to give a booster shot for its effectiveness, encouraging his clients to try new and different weight loss routines.

These observations underscore the notion that a crucial method of maximizing the impact of an activity is to attend to its variety. So sprinkle a little of this and a little of that, revivify your happiness strategies on a regular basis, surprise yourself sometimes. Regard finding happiness as an adventure, full of enterprise, developments, and detours. Work on several happiness activities at once, so if one is not going so well, you can relish another.

I was reading a novel not long ago and came upon the assertion that "to be happy you have to find variety in repetition."[23] It may seem like puzzling phrasing, even an oxymoron, but it actually comes close to what I mean here by the suggestion to vary the way you implement your happiness activities. On the one hand, there's routine and habit—the habit of initiating the behavior in the first place—and on the other hand, there's *how* you do it, which cannot always be the same or you'll adapt to it and end up feeling the same as when you started.

My friend Stephanie told me of a guy in her acting class who had "tried everything" in his attempts to become a happier person. Every day he listened to motivational tapes, he prayed, he wrote in a journal, and he went on a bike ride to the beach. He was incredibly assiduous about this routine and never wavered from it. But it wasn't working. He was sinking lower and lower, and my friend was just bewildered. Then a lightbulb went off. The guy had created such a rigid routine that he was going through the motions in exactly the same way every day. He listened to the same tapes every morning, and using identical words, he prayed for the same individuals. His route to the beach never strayed. When you take up a happiness activity, be sure to jazz up your routes to the beach, both literally and figuratively. Effort matters, without question, but so does *how* you put it into practice.

# The Third How: Social Support

Most of us are involved in a wide web of relationships and social connections. We are dependent on other people, and we could not accomplish many of our goals if we didn't receive help and cooperation from others. It's not surprising, perhaps, that the third critical factor underlying the success of a happiness activity is social support. This jargon is used by psychologists to represent all kinds of help and comfort provided by others, especially those with whom we have strong, meaningful relationships. Say you are embarking on a happiness-enhancing program, which involves the three strategies of regularly expressing gratitude, avoiding overthinking, and engaging in regular aerobic exercise. Having a buddy with whom to carry out the program, or simply the validation of people close to you, is an enormous benefit. Social support partners can offer informational support (e.g., suggesting a new way to show gratitude or cautioning that your current approach might lead you to get stuck), tangible support (e.g., giving you rides to the gym), and emotional support (e.g., providing reassurance, solace, and inspiration).

We learned in Chapter 6 that social support is invaluable in helping people cope with life's challenges and misfortunes. Women who have at least one friend are better able to cope with problems than those without friends.[24] Whether you're suffering a breakup, a chronic illness, or the threat of layoffs, talking to a caring friend or family member can significantly ease the pain and provide a push to address problems. Confiding your worries and troubles to others can reduce stress if you learn that they have endured similar experiences and have survived or thrived. It can reduce anxiety when other people comfort and reassure.

Emotional or tangible support, whether this involves a sole confidant, a circle of friends, your family, or a psychotherapeutic group, may also be crucial in helping people persist at and realize their goals in general.[25] Social support helps motivate and guide you along your path, thus ultimately promoting the realization of a wide variety of goals, including those concerning work, relationships, and personal growth. Indeed, many organizations, such as Alcoholics Anonymous (AA) and some large religious congregations, emphasize the importance of having "teammates" or "small-group members" who work together toward goals, be they abstaining from alcohol or worshiping. Whether they are teammates, buddies, mentors, or big sibs, supportive and validating others can make the difference between short-term success and long-term success in your goal of becoming happier. Indeed, group support, such as the kind found in AA, can be extraordinarily powerful in galvanizing conviction, commitment, and perseverance: "An alcoholic could lose his job and his family, he could be hospitalized, he could be warned by half a dozen doctors—and go on drinking. But put him in a room of his peers once a week—make him share the burdens of others and have his burdens shared by others—and he could do something that once seemed impossible."[26]

What does this have to do with trying to become happier? Any change in behavior that requires effort and dedication will be made easier if your spouse, children, friends, parents, siblings, and coworkers are supportive. They can motivate you and remind you to continue to practice your happiness activities, an indispensable boost when you start to lose momentum or simply forget. They can offer positive feedback, encouragement, and warmth: "Hey, you seem so much happier lately," "You look great," or "I know what it's like to feel like quitting." Sometimes it's necessary to establish ties with a new group of people—perhaps from happiness-relevant chat groups or Web sites—who might share similar goals and concerns as you. Or you might want to seek out new friends in your own work, school, and neighborhood communities, as a way to find partners who support each other's efforts. Remember, you don't need a posse; often just one caring friend will do.

## The Research Evidence

The importance of social support is demonstrated in copious empirical investigations. In the domain of health, for example, sick patients who have strong social support are relatively more likely to cooperate with their medical treatment.[27] Studies have found that patients with hypertension (who must take medication every day and eat low-salt diets) are much more likely to adhere to their strict regimens if they have family support, especially from spouses.[28] Those with social support are more motivated to cooperate with their doctors' orders, more knowledgeable about their treatments, and more likely to maintain their blood pressures.

In the self-help domain, people who make New Year's resolutions are much more likely to persevere for two years, and even for six years, if they have social support.[29] One of my favorite studies investigated the extent to which social support can help people with the goal of losing weight.[30] Participants undertook a four-month-long weight loss program (involving diet, exercise, and behavioral changes) either alone or with three acquaintances, friends, or family members. Of those who embarked on the program alone, 76 percent completed it, and 24 percent maintained their weight losses in full for an entire six months. In contrast, of those who engaged in the weight loss program with social support, 95 percent completed it, and 66 percent maintained their weight losses in full. Furthermore, those with social support lost more weight and kept more of it off. These numbers are compelling, to say the least.

Like these participants, I expect that those of us who attempt happiness-enhancing programs without much social support are unlikely to commit for very long, to carry it through. Think of social support as essentially a force that works with the behavioral change. Your spouse, friend, life coach, or other buddy can encourage you to work hard toward your goals and serve as a sounding board when you lose motivation or get stuck in a rut.

# The Fourth How: Motivation, Effort, and Commitment

> You have to participate relentlessly in the manifestations of your own blessings. And once you have achieved a state of happiness, you must never become lax about maintaining it, you must make a mighty effort to keep swimming upward into that happiness forever, to stay afloat on top of it.
>
> —*Elizabeth Gilbert*

Another vital key to a successful happiness-increasing program, as you already well know, is committed and dedicated effort. When it comes to achieving greater happiness, the steps you need to take are not altogether different from those required for learning French or changing careers or any other goal you might pursue.

1. You must *resolve* to undertake a program to become happier.
2. You must *learn* what you need to do.
3. You must put weekly or even daily *effort* into it.
4. You must *commit* to the goal for a long period of time, possibly for the rest of your life.

The first and second steps you have already initiated by picking up this book or others like it. They are critical steps because the sense of mastery and possibility that accompanies the launch of a new chapter for yourself is immensely powerful and transporting. Just think of it, you are on the threshold of altering your life! "Every time you make a choice," wrote C. S. Lewis, "you are turning the central part of you, the part of you that chooses, into something a little different from what it was before."

The third and fourth essential steps in this process—concerted effort and commitment—may be the hardest. Without them, your journey will be altogether brief. You may become happier for a day, a week, perhaps a month, but it won't last. Most people have had such experiences with New Year's resolutions; come January 1, they know exactly what they need to do, they're determined and motivated to do it, they try for a time, and then they give it up. Following through on new intentions isn't easy, but neither is the work required for all the best and most meaningful things in life.

## THE WONDERS OF MOTIVATED
## AND COMMITTED EFFORT

Motivation, or the drive and inspiration to accomplish something, plays an indispensable role in all four steps of resolving, learning, effort making, and committing. You know that you have high motivation for a new endeavor when you find yourself brimming with enthusiasm and ideas about it. You know that you have high motivation when you do something because you truly believe that the experience (or its consequences) will ultimately be interesting and challenging and enjoyable. The desire comes from deep within you. My collaborators and I have tested directly the question of whether the more motivated a person is to become happier, the more successful he or she will be. For example, in one study we directly recruited participants who wanted to improve their happiness levels (e.g., "Do you want to be happy? This is the study for you!") and compared them with participants who signed up for a generic psychology experiment.[31] The effects were striking. Regardless of whether they were asked to write gratitude letters on a regular basis or to keep a journal about their best possible futures, the motivated participants became a great deal happier, whereas the nonmotivated participants improved only slightly or stayed the same. Another happiness intervention that we did, in which we also induced people to practice either gratitude or optimism, corroborated this result.[32] Those participants who found the happiness-enhancing activity most motivating and rewarding were those most likely to practice it and therefore the ones most likely to benefit from it.

There you have it, the secret ingredient of motivation: The more motivated you are to do something, the more likely you'll invest effort in it! And it doesn't take a rocket scientist (or a social psychologist) to persuade you that without effort, there is no result. Plenty of studies confirm this intuitively obvious observation. Even, after the experimenter has hung up her coat and packed up the lab, those participants who continue to perform the happiness-enhancing activity and integrate it into their lives are more likely to show long-term benefits than those who quit.[33] Without effort, without trying, without striving, without tenacity, without constancy of purpose, there is only failure, hesitation, "a faint heart and a lame endeavor."[34]

When my students and I first started conducting happiness interventions, it didn't take long for us to notice that the benefits lasted only as long as the participants practiced their assigned strategies. We initially received tough criticism for this: "Gee, your interventions must not be very strong." But my colleague down the hall (and the acclaimed methodologist) Robert Rosenthal came to our rescue. He pointed out that the pattern of our results characterizes every single kind of pharmaceutical, including lifesaving meds and therapeutic drugs taken by millions. The drug may be lifesaving while you take it, but interestingly, the moment you stop, it "fails" to work. Yet I've never heard someone argue that insulin, aspirin, Lipitor, Claritin, Vicodin, and Viagra must be weak because they don't have long-term benefits. Again, the lesson here is the importance of practicing the life-changing program you have undertaken, whether that program involves your becoming a happier person, quitting smoking, or treating an illness. Effort and commitment are king.

## WHAT IF YOU'RE TOO BUSY?

"I'm too stressed out to think about anything else but how to get through the day," a not-so-happy acquaintance told me when I suggested that she try some happiness activities. She was indeed busy, with two teenagers in the house, volunteer work, and a real estate practice taking off. I empathized. But when it comes to the important things in life, are we ever really too busy? When you decided to have a baby, did you reserve just one hour a month to contemplate it? When you fell in love, did you set your relationship aside to make more time for your job? When you obtained an incredible career opportunity, did you say no because it would spoil your schedule? I hope not. Besides, many of the happiness activities do not actually require you to make time. They are simply ways of living your life: observing your job, partner, and children with a new, more charitable and optimistic perspective, saying a kind word to your spouse, distracting yourself when you find yourself dwelling on something, uttering a short prayer before a meal, smiling at strangers during your commute, empathizing with someone who has hurt you, and so on. Most of these strategies aren't a time drain but, by deliberate choice and with some effort, can be woven seamlessly right into your day.

## WHAT IF YOU BACKSLIDE?

There surely will be times when your commitment wavers, when you forget, and when you fail to practice the happiness-enhancing strategy you have determined to undertake. This is normal and inevitable and human; none of us is perfect. Furthermore, know that circumstances will arise when being ungrateful, unforgiving, self-focused, pessimistic, traumatized, lethargic, or indecisive is completely understandable and acceptable. A continual and perfect state of bliss is not only impossible to achieve but also maladaptive.[35] Plenty of situations (deaths, failures, abuses of power) call for negative emotions, which have the valuable function of promptly triggering action and reaction, whether it's grieving, persistence, or work toward reform.[36] In any case, the point for you to remember is that when you lose motivation to continue engaging in your happiness activity, and when you stop engaging in it, you need not feel that all is lost and that your individual situation must be hopeless. There is no crisis here. Your complicated life likely interfered, or maybe the strategy you were using lacked variety, or maybe you needed more encouragement from friends. Simply renew your motivation—reconsider the reasons that you want to become happier—and get back on track. Sometimes at this point substituting a new happiness-enhancing strategy might be of value, and sometimes it's altering how you practice the strategy you originally chose. Research suggests that the right combination of optimal timing and optimal variety, strong social support, and determined effort can be effective for the vast majority of people.

## Recommit Today . . . and Tomorrow

I'm not usually in the habit of quoting Oprah Winfrey, but here I go. When she was reportedly once asked how she is able to run five miles per day, even when traveling, she replied that she has to recommit to the goal every day of her life. The same applies to strategies to make yourself a happier person. Renew your commitment every day. Not only the strategy but the very act of recommitment will become easier and more automatic with time.

# The Fifth How: Habit

I hope you are now convinced that it takes a great deal of effort and determination to become happier. This may be disappointing news for some, especially if lately you've been feeling disheartened, insecure, or overwrought and simply aren't sure if you have the energy that this effort calls for. Here I get to deliver the good news, which is that the effort is greatest at the beginning, but it diminishes with time, as your new behaviors and practices become habitual through repetition.

## How Do Habits Form?

We all have habits—some good, some bad. Most people associate the word *habit* with annoying behaviors like chewing fingernails, sucking thumbs, twisting hair, or interrupting conversations. Smoking is a familiar habit, and so is changing lanes without using blinkers or buying a latte every morning on the way to work. Healthy or "good" habits are behaviors like always cutting the fat off a piece of chicken, flossing after every meal, carrying a water bottle wherever you go, or recycling.

What do these behaviors have in common? They are labeled "habitual" because you don't have to make the decision to do them. They are not intentional acts. When I wake up in the morning, I immediately get out of bed and put my running clothes on. I don't usually—well, not often—ever think, "Should I get up and go running, or should I stay here under the bed sheets?" There's really no decision to make. Similarly, if you have the habit of singing show tunes in the car or getting takeout every Friday night, you don't debate the act—"Should I sing this time or not?"—you just do it.

Habits form with repetition and practice. Researchers theorize that every time you repeat a behavior (such as going jogging in the morning), associations develop in your memory between the behavior and the context in which it occurs.[37] For my morning jogging, that context would be the alarm clock going off, my bedroom, my running gear by the door, etc. With repetition, the contextual cues (the alarm clock ringing) automatically trigger the habitual behavior (donning running shoes), such that the behavior eventually switches from the direction of controlled processing to automatic processing.[38] To apply this to happiness strategies, the more often you initiate a positive activity—for example, savoring meals with family or appreciating your life during bad moments—the stronger the connection becomes between that activity (savoring or appreciating) and the cues around you (family dinner or daily hassles). So the next time (or more likely the tenth time) you get together with your family, you might be prompted into savoring simply by the situation of being around your loved ones, and the next time you get stuck in traffic, you might be prompted into an appreciative mode by the surrounding cues. Of course, such connections take time and a great deal of practice to build. As you might expect, habits take time to form and endure.

## But Aren't Habits Hard to Establish?

When it comes to losing weight or quitting smoking, media reports and research articles are full of failure stories. Indeed, well-controlled treatment studies show incredibly high recidivism rates for people who try to change their behavior. We're told that 86 percent of those who try to quit smoking eventually take it up again, and 80 to 98 percent of those who try to lose weight gain it back (and often gain more than they lost).[39] However, don't we all know people who've successfully turned their lives around, people who have successfully lost weight, quit drinking, given up drugs, renounced lives of crime, gone back to school, or become less grouchy? How can we reconcile these two facts, the high recidivism rates from studies of weight control and smoking cessation programs and the relatively high success rates among our acquaintances and friends?

In a classic study, social psychologist Stanley Schachter tried to resolve this paradox.[40] Talking to staff at his Columbia University office and to acquaintances and strangers on the beach at Amagansett, where he spent his summers, he observed that a large percentage used to be overweight or smokers. So the anecdotal evidence—the "real-world" evidence—suggests that lots of people successfully kick bad habits and form new ones. Indeed, this is what Schachter found in his wide-ranging beach and office interviews—namely, a 63 percent success rate for self-cure of smoking and obesity. He concluded that the published recidivism data are biased by the fact that they represent the outcomes of the "hard-core cases"—that is, people who come in for treatment. The rest, who are able to cure themselves, don't seek treatment. In addition—and this is a seemingly obvious but very important observation—in trying to accomplish something (like quitting smoking), people may try (and fail) many times before they ultimately succeed. The 63 percent of success stories that Schachter found had tried several times before finally accomplishing their goal.

Schachter's informal investigation was replicated in a more recent, much larger, and more representative study of 784 people with extensive histories of being overweight.[41] These individuals were able to keep off a minimum of thirty pounds for at least five years. Most tried many weight loss methods and yo-yoed in their weights until they were finally successful. It took most of them until their forties to lose the weight and to maintain it; however, once they found what worked for them, the task became much easier. Indeed, the researchers were surprised to learn that 42 percent of the sample reported that maintaining the weight was much easier than losing it. By the time they reached their weight goal, their weight loss strategies likely had already turned into true habits.

## Two Kinds of Habit

Clearly, everyone's goal should be to turn positive thinking and behavior strategies into habits. But be wary of the wrong kind of habit! Your aim should be to create the habit of *instigating* a happiness activity: Go ahead and forgive, savor, thrive, look on the bright side, and count your blessings. Aim to do it unconsciously and automatically. This kind of habit helps you get over the hump of implementing a happiness activity on a regular basis. Conversely, the other kind of habit—doing the activity the same way each time (contemplating forgiveness for the same person in the same way at the same time each day)—eventually becomes monotonous, prone to adaptation, and deficient in any happiness-boosting potential.

# Conclusion

This book's message can be understood as the exhortation to establish new, healthy habits. Because such activities as looking on the bright side, savoring the moment, practicing forgiveness, and striving for important life goals make a difference in your happiness, it is certainly a good idea to make a habit of doing them. It may be exasperating to know that naturally very happy people, those fortunate to have high set points, seem to have inherited such habits. They don't need to *try* to be optimistic or grateful or forgiving; it's second nature to them. However, if your set point for happiness is not as high as theirs and you were blessed with fewer of those good habits, know that with some time and determination, you can develop the same exact habits for yourself.

In the past you may have felt trapped in the tunnel of your unhappy inheritance, your pessimistic thoughts, or your maladaptive habits. I hope the journey that this book has introduced you to will liberate you from the heavy weight of those negative perceptions. You'll find that there's a tremendous freedom in understanding the unifying theory of happiness put forth here, not only in knowing what are the most powerful determinants of happiness but in recognizing how to access that portion of happiness that's in your power to achieve a real and lasting change.

# The Promise of Abiding Happiness:
# An Afterword

It is never too late to be what you might have been.

—*George Eliot*

Writing this book knocked me for a loop. I'd been investigating happiness for eighteen years. I'd been engrossed in the broader subject of psychology for longer. Much of the research I describe in these pages I know like the back of my hand, and I am fairly well familiar with the rest. Yet immersing myself in the data about the various activities that people can use to become happier had an unexpected impact on me, an impact that quickly became almost laughingly predictable. When I was working on the gratitude section, I wound up penning a gratitude letter to a colleague (not something that comes naturally to me), and when I was working on the kindness section, I was unusually considerate of and thoughtful toward my acquaintances and friends. My husband was pleasantly surprised when he found me practicing on him the techniques I wrote about in the section on nurturing relationships, and during the writing of the spirituality section, I (the least spiritual person I know) started thinking about the larger questions on meaning and purpose and reading messages into some of the major events of my life. These experiences genuinely surprised me not only because of my intimate familiarity with all these recommendations to boost happiness, such that they were really nothing new, but because I honestly had never been the best subject for receiving these recommendations. I am not the type of person to pick up a self-help book or to try to count her blessings. Yet this is precisely what working on this book made me want to do. If I, the ultimate reluctant subject, can be transformed in her recognition of the power and efficacy of this book's suggestions, then some of you reluctant readers can be transformed too.

In hindsight, I now understand why certain chapters affected me more than others. Writing about the strategies that I was already good at—optimism, goal pursuit, coping, physical activity, and flow—didn't influence me as much as those for which I needed improvement. For example, the section on living in the present was especially compelling and valuable in teaching me to focus on what really matters in the moment as opposed to fretting about daily irritations. But why would it have such an impact, given that I am *already* well aware (as you might also be) of the copious anecdotal evidence that living in the present makes people happy, not to mention the empirical work supporting it? In some seemingly magic way, seeing all the evidence converge together in one chapter, in one place, magnified its impact. Today a frustrating, disappointing, or painful moment does not go by when I don't ask myself: Will this matter in a year? And it passes.

I hope that you will have a similar experience. You may already be vaguely aware (or even certain) that such activities as meditating, expressing gratitude, pursuing significant life goals, and doing random acts of kindness would make you a happier person. But how can you be sure that these strategies would work for you, and how precisely should you carry them out? Furthermore, why haven't you committed to practicing such activities, or practicing them effectively, up until now? Perhaps *The How of Happiness* will be the catalyst that you've been waiting for to remake your life. The foundation of science should bolster your confidence that you can be happier, *if* you practice happiness activities in an optimal way and with dedicated effort. You may not have known how to do that before, and I hope you have a better idea now. You may not have been as fulfilled and happy as you wanted to be for your entire life and now are assured, from the potential of the 40 percent of happiness that can be controlled, that changing your happiness level is entirely in your hands, that your "unhappy genes" do not doom you to unhappiness or, worse, to depression.

The recommendations in this book for how to become a happier person turned out to possess a surprising power, even for a seasoned happiness researcher like me. Without a doubt, writing the book has changed my life in some anticipated and many unanticipated ways. I hope that reading it will change yours and help you get the life you want.

# Postscript

## *If You Are Depressed*

I f you scored in the "depressed range"—that is, 16 or above on the depression scale (the CES-D) printed in Chapter 2—you may be wondering what you need to know immediately and what special steps you can take in addition to those described here. I should stress, however, that although a program to become happier can positively be attempted by those who are depressed, relief from depression is not what this book promises. We'll now take a closer look at depression, what causes it, and what can be done about it.

## What Is Depression?

Depression is an illness, not a failing. It's what psychologists call a syndrome—that is, a group of signs and symptoms that form a pattern. Many of you are undoubtedly already familiar with these symptoms. Some of you may only have a few of them, while others may have many. There are nine classic symptoms, with the first two being most diagnostic of depression:[1]

1. Sad mood for most of the day: feeling down, anxious, or "empty," though some of you may feel tense or irritable instead
2. Being less interested and finding less pleasure in almost all hobbies or activities that you used to enjoy (including sex)
3. Feeling excessively guilty, worthless, or helpless
4. Having little energy and feeling fatigued much of the time
5. Having a hard time concentrating, remembering, or making decisions
6. Having trouble sleeping: experiencing insomnia, early-morning awakening, or oversleeping
7. Having trouble eating: overeating and gaining weight *or* losing your appetite and losing weight
8. Feeling either agitated or slowed down
9. Having thoughts of death or suicide, making suicide attempts

It's important to distinguish clinical, diagnosable depression from a passing sad mood. Full-fledged depression involves your whole body and person—your feelings (e.g., "I feel wretched"), your thoughts (e.g., "I'm ugly"), and your physical state (e.g., "I can't sleep"). To make things more complicated, there are also different types of depression. The most common are the following:

• Major depression, which involves one or more episodes (or periods of time) during which the depression is intense and you suffer a large number of symptoms. These symptoms interfere with your work and your relationships, in addition to disturbing your sleeping, eating, and enjoyment of once pleasurable activities.
• Dysthymia, a less severe but more chronic (longer-lasting) type of depression. Your symptoms aren't as numerous or as disabling as in

major depression, but they keep you from feeling good or functioning very well. If you're particularly unlucky, you may have both major depression and dysthymia, a condition researchers call double depression.

- Subsyndromal depression, in which you have some symptoms of depression, but they are not so intense or so long-lasting to earn you a formal diagnosis of either major depression or dysthymia. However, this type of depression deserves attention too, inasmuch as you may still feel miserable and impaired in your daily life.

Even within these classes of diagnoses, you may suffer from particular types of symptoms. For example, when women are depressed, they are more likely than men to experience weight gain, a boost in appetite, and increased need for sleep, called reverse vegetative symptoms. Men are more likely to experience the opposite and to feel angry and discouraged instead of hopeless and helpless. Furthermore, approximately one in ten adults (men and women) has depressed moods that cycle with the seasons, inflaming during the winter months. About one in twenty women has depressive symptoms that tend to appear during the week before her menstrual periods. Depression in women is also common after giving birth. Depression in older people is often triggered by a taxing illness or the loss of a loved one.

But no matter what kind of depression or what unique constellation of symptoms you have in particular, you must know that you *can* get better. Amazingly, the typical depressed person doesn't seek treatment for an average of *nine years* after experiencing her first symptoms.[2] So, even if you're pretty sure you are depressed or if you have been in the past, you may have never received help from a mental health professional. I urge you to do so without delay, for several reasons.

First is a problem called comorbidity. This means that if you are depressed, you are very likely to be experiencing one or two or even more *other* physical or emotional problems. Do you have persistent worries and tension or irrational fears that you just can't shake? Have you ever had a panic attack, when you've felt that you might die? Do you have frightening nightmares or memories of a terrifying event? Do you have an eating disorder or a problem with smoking, drinking, or drugs? These are just some of the conditions that tend to accompany depression and must be managed and treated as soon as possible. Fortunately, several kinds of anti-depressant medications have proved helpful not only in effectively relieving depressive symptoms but also in treating some of these accompanying conditions.[3]

The second reason to seek help for your depression is that it can wreak lasting damage on your life. Research shows that the toll depression takes is as great as that of a chronic physical disorder like diabetes, arthritis, or high blood pressure.[4] Because the average age at which people develop depression is in their mid-twenties, the illness can have a profound effect on important life transitions, like finishing school, starting out in a career, becoming a parent, and getting and staying married. Furthermore, in the United States alone, the loss of productivity engendered by depression costs thirty-three billion dollars per year in salary.[5]

Some people argue that depression is "normal," that feeling sad or inadequate or hopeless about everything is not a sign of irrationality or illness. Some even argue that good things can come out of it. There is a kernel of truth in this. Some of the low moods we feel may be what Freud termed ordinary human unhappiness, and sometimes pessimism has value. That is, people with negative outlooks may be more vigilant about threats and dangers and thus heed warnings that optimists will not. But if you are depressed, you know all too well that what you are experiencing is not just a pessimistic view of yourself and the world. What you are experiencing is utter suffering and pain. Much of this suffering is unrelenting and awful and undeserved, and this is the biggest reason that depression needs to be resolved and relieved.

# The Causes of Depression

## SUSCEPTIBILITY AND STRESS (OR NATURE AND ENVIRONMENT)

Many physical diseases develop when two things are present at the same time: First, we have an inborn susceptibility or predisposition toward the disease, and second, we experience some kind of event or stress in our lives that triggers it.[6] Likewise, depression appears to be a result of both "nature" and "environment." Like heart disease or diabetes or arthritis, it is rooted in our biology. This is the nature part, involving our genes and brain function. The heritability of depression—that is, the extent to which it is genetically determined—ranges from 20 to 45 percent[7] for milder forms and is likely much higher for severe forms. Indeed, a parent, child, or sibling of someone with depression has a two to four times higher probability of becoming depressed than the average person.[8] It's clear that some of us are born with a susceptibility to depression. This susceptibility, which could be inherited or simply ill fated, is likely expressed in what happens in our brains. Many studies have found that people suffering from depression show unique symptoms in their bodies.[9] These symptoms include too low amounts of various brain chemicals (norepinephrine, serotonin, and dopamine), a too high amount of a stress hormone (cortisol), and disturbance of deep dream-related (REM) sleep. Furthermore, new technologies allowing researchers to image the brain have revealed that severely depressed patients have abnormalities in the prefrontal cortex (the region of the brain responsible for thinking and managing emotions) as well as in the limbic regions (i.e., areas involved in sleep, eating, sex, motivation, memory, and responses to stress), including the mysterious-sounding Area 25.[10] In sum, there is now a great deal of evidence that depression is partly rooted in those parts of our physical bodies over which we have minimal control.

However, a genetic or biological predisposition is generally not enough to precipitate depression. It's not the whole story. A stress or some kind of trigger is necessary as well. If your predisposition is very strong, then a relatively minor stress could lead you to fall into a full-fledged depression. If your predisposition is small, then only a major stress or trauma will bring about depression.

What do I mean by *stress*? The trigger that makes you depressed could be stress in your life, although it's likely to be severe stress—for example, the stress of poverty or a traumatic life event (like experiencing violence, a natural disaster, or the loss of one's home), separation or divorce, serious or chronic illness, caring for a sick child or aging parent, and many others.[11] Alternatively, some researchers focus on bad experiences in childhood as the stressors that trigger depression in adulthood. Indeed, many different kinds of poor parenting, including whether your mother was depressed or anxious while pregnant, as well as whether your parents were neglectful, intrusive, harsh, inconsistent, or abusive, have been blamed for later depression. Unfortunately, researchers don't know whether it's the inadequate parenting that leads to later depression in their kids or something else entirely, like depression-prone genes shared by the whole family.

## PSYCHOLOGICAL VULNERABILITY

What else can cause or activate a depression? Many tomes have been written on this subject, and I shall only mention the two theories backed, in my judgment, by the most scientific evidence. The first is Aaron Beck's cognitive theory of depression, which forms the basis for the most commonly used psychotherapy for this illness, cognitive-behavioral therapy. Beck is a psychiatrist who argues that some people have dysfunctional attitudes that make them vulnerable to becoming depressed in the face of a negative event. These maladaptive attitudes often involve the notion that our happiness and self-worth depend on our being perfect or hinge on other people's approval. For example, we might think, "My teacher's critical comment means that I'm a total failure" or "If my girlfriend doesn't love me, then I am nothing." If we share these beliefs, then when something truly bad happens, we tend to have automatic negative thoughts about (1) ourselves (e.g., "I'm not lovable"), (2) our present experiences (e.g., "My boss always prefers my coworkers"), and (3) our futures (e.g., "I'll never outgrow my shyness"). Beck calls these types of thought a nega-tive cognitive triad.

A related explanation for depression, called hopelessness theory, came out of the work of Martin Seligman and his students. According to this theory, having expectations that bad things will happen to us and that really good things will *not* happen, and that we cannot do anything to improve the situation, can cause depression. Thus hopelessness is thought to lie at the root of a depression. How does a person become hopeless? When confronted with stressful or otherwise negative experiences, some people draw harmful inferences or conclusions. For example, when a man fails to get an expected promotion, he may conclude that being passed over (1) "means I don't have talent," (2) "will prevent me from ever advancing in my career," and (3) "proves that I'm unworthy." These are symptoms of hopelessness, and they are likely to trigger depression in such a person. In contrast, another person in the exact same situation may be protected from hopelessness, and thereby from depression, if she alter-natively concludes that (1) "I haven't been putting much effort into my job lately," (2) "I should work harder, so I could get the promotion next year," and (3) "this has no bearing on my self-worth."

Both hopelessness theory and Beck's cognitive theory assume that people who become depressed have a cognitive vulnerability—that is, a dysfunctional way of thinking about negative life events that makes it more likely that they'll become depressed. Simply put, how we interpret our life experiences (e.g., current problems in a relationship) influences our feelings about those experiences (e.g., feeling hopeless and inadequate versus confident and optimistic), which ultimately lead to distress and even full-fledged depression.

An exciting recent project, the Cognitive Vulnerability to Depression Project, has followed participants over time, measuring both their mal-adaptive thoughts and their life stresses. It has found that indeed, those participants with hopeless and dysfunctional attitudes at one time are more likely to suffer a major depressive episode at a subsequent time.[12]

Fortunately, cognitive therapy, as you will shortly learn, has been very effective at attenuating these maladaptive attitudes.

## RISK FACTORS FOR DEPRESSION

A risk factor is something that makes depression more likely, without necessarily causing it. There is now a great deal of scientific support for three risk factors for depression:

1. Poor social skills
2. Shyness or withdrawal
3. Excessive dependency on others

If you recognize any of these qualities in yourself (and it's possible to possess more than one), obtaining professional help may be extremely valuable. First, if your social skills need improvement, you can learn how to express yourself and communicate better, to control your emotions and be sensitive to others' feelings, and to initiate and hold your own during conversations. Researchers have also found that people who have poor social skills have a tendency to seek criticism from friends and family; indeed, they gravitate toward people who reject them. This is also something that a psychotherapist can help you resolve.

Second, if you are the type of person who avoids social situations or is excessively shy, you may be predisposed to experience depression. This is probably because in the face of stress or negative events, shy or inhibited people avoid the very things that can protect them from falling into a negative spiral—namely, companionship and social support.

Finally, if you constantly seek reassurance from other people about your worth and lovability or if you are extremely needy of others' acceptance and support, then you may be characterized by so-called excessive interpersonal dependency. As with the other risk factors, having this characteristic makes you vulnerable to becoming depressed. Again, excessive dependency should be worked out in a therapeutic context.

# The Most Effective Treatments for Depression

This section could take up the space of an entire book—or a shelf-ful—because there are many, many treatments for depression. Hence I shall only discuss the small handful of treatments that, in my opinion, have the strongest empirical support—namely, the four most effective therapies. One is pharmacological therapy, otherwise known as antidepressants or meds. The other three are types of psychotherapy (or talk therapy): cognitive-behavioral therapy, interpersonal therapy, and marriage and family therapy. The current wisdom is that people with mild depression do very well with psychotherapy, but those with moderate or severe depression may significantly benefit from antidepressants.[13] Most, however, do best with a combination of medication and psychotherapy, the medication to provide swift relief from symptoms and the psychotherapy to teach skills so that the depressed person can independently solve her problems and manage her depressed feelings and thoughts. We'll begin with the best psychotherapies.

## COGNITIVE-BEHAVIORAL THERAPY

As mentioned earlier, Beck's cognitive theory of depression gave rise to this, the most widely used depression therapy. The focus here is on your thoughts. Cognitive-behavioral therapists assume that those who are prone to depression are overly negative in their perceptions of themselves, their worlds, and their futures (that negative cognitive triad again) and that such people show distorted thinking. For example, a depressed person might come to the therapist's office and declare that she's a failure because it rained at her son's swim party the day before. The job of the therapist is to teach the depressed patient to recognize and dispute her negative beliefs and to replace them with more adaptive thoughts. The therapist might engage in a dialogue with the patient about the circumstances of the child's party until the patient realizes that her thinking has been irrational and unduly pessimistic. "Homework" may be assigned between sessions to reinforce the therapist's instruction and guidance.

So that's the cognitive part. The behavioral part consists of teaching depressed patients skills that they might lack, such as problem solving (i.e., teaching you how to define life problems and helping you generate possible solutions to those problems and choose among them), self-control (i.e., teaching you to set weekly goals and then to monitor your behavior and reward yourself for meeting those goals), and so-called behavioral activation (i.e., encouraging you to take action rather than avoid difficult situations). The main goal of behavioral therapy, however, is to engage depressed individuals in activities that they enjoy and that afford them a sense of mastery. Not only will this strategy increase positive emotions, but it will also distract the depressed person from overthinking—or ruminating—about her feelings and problems, making the depression even worse.[14]

Cognitive-behavioral therapy is relatively short term, usually lasting from four to fourteen sessions. However, treatment is likely to be longer for those with extensive histories of rigid dysfunctional thinking. Patients with long-standing and entrenched maladaptive beliefs are taught to recognize that much of their distress stems from these beliefs, and not just from the negative life events that they've experienced. In other words, it may not be the breakup six months ago that's making you depressed but your continued maladaptive ruminations about it.

Is cognitive-behavioral therapy effective? The short answer is yes. This type of therapy has been one of the most extensively tested of all depression treatments and has been shown to be equally or more effective than other psychotherapies and roughly comparable to medication.[15] Furthermore, those treated with cognitive-behavioral therapy until their depressions have lifted (i.e., until "remission") are less likely to relapse or to suffer from a future depressive episode.

## INTERPERSONAL THERAPY

If you're depressed, you are likely to have at least one interpersonal problem—for example, you may be grieving the loss of someone close to you, dealing with a failing marriage or a stressful life transition, or suffering from a lack of assertiveness. Although it's loosely based on Freudian psychoanalysis, interpersonal therapy uses an eclectic approach, borrowing the best techniques from a handful of other therapies. For example, when the assumptions of medical doctors are applied, the depressed person is defined in this therapy as having a medical illness, which is treatable and not the result of a personal defect or weakness. Furthermore, like marital therapists, interpersonal therapists help you work on and solve your relationship problems, instilling optimism in you that doing so will both improve your personal situation and relieve your depressive symptoms. Finally, like cognitive therapy, interpersonal therapy is focused on the here and now, not on excavating the unconscious basis of depression in childhood.

This therapy takes three to four months. The focus during the sessions is on addressing your recent and ongoing interpersonal events—whether they involve marital strife, a child's disability, or the loss of friendship—and the therapist's strategy depends somewhat on the type of event that's problematic. For example, if your greatest concern is conflict with your mother-in-law, the interpersonal therapist will talk with you about the disturbed relationship, the exact nature of the conflict, and what you want to do about it. He will help you re-create your situation so that he can fully understand it. The therapist will then go over with you all the options that you have at your disposal to resolve the problem, options that the depression may have kept you from seeing or exploring fully. Together you may engage in role playing at this point to rehearse possible strategies, such as what you would say when confronting your mother-in-law about a grievance.

Studies have shown that interpersonal therapy is very effective at alleviating depression. Its efficacy is close or equal to that of antidepressant medication and even superior to medication at improving social functioning.[16] If you think this type of psychotherapy is a good fit for you, then it could be a vital treatment.

## MARRIAGE AND FAMILY THERAPY

Like interpersonal therapists, marital and family therapists recognize that depressed individuals often have problems with family relationships. Indeed, if you are married *and* depressed, you are very likely to be experiencing distress in your marriage.[17] If you are depressed and have children at home, you are probably experiencing difficulty in the area of parenting.[18] Serious depression can cause pain and suffering not only in the ill person but in his or her family. But is it the family problems that cause depression or vice versa? According to stress-generation theory,[19] whose logic guides most marital and family therapists, the causal arrow runs both ways. There are many ways that depressed individuals can create stress in their interpersonal relationships, and this interpersonal stress can make them even more depressed. For example, depressed women are more negative and pessimistic toward their partners, are more lax and inconsistent mothers, have more strained relationships with their teenage children, and are more likely to withdraw during conflicts. All these factors make it likely that the depression exacerbates these women's family troubles. On the other hand, marital problems (an infidelity or the threat of divorce) and parenting problems (constant strife with kids) increase the risk of depression or aggravate the depression that's already present.[20] This vicious cycle, in which depression leads to problems, which lead to more depression and more problems, is where the marital and family therapist can intercede.

The two most common and successful interventions for the kinds of family troubles commonly experienced by depressed individuals are behavioral marital therapy for marital discord[21] and parent training for child management problems.[22]

Behavioral marital therapy is a relatively brief treatment in which the therapist meets regularly with the depressed person and his or her partner. In the first phase of treatment, the therapist tackles the biggest strains on the relationship and helps the couple have more positive interactions. The couple may be given a homework assignment to figure out what activity they have enjoyed doing together in the past and then going ahead and doing it. When this phase is successful, the depressed person is already feeling brighter and both partners are expressing positive feelings toward each other. This boost serves as the foundation for the second phase, whose aim it is to restructure the relationship—for example, to improve the way that the couple communicates, handles problems, and interacts on a daily basis. Sometimes this is done by having the couple write a behavioral "contract," agreeing to change aspects of their behavior. When successful, this phase will leave the couple feeling more supportive and sensitive to each other's needs, more intimate, and better able to cope with future difficulties. Finally, in the third phase, the therapist helps the two partners prepare for stressful situations that might come to pass and encourages them to attribute their improvement in therapy to their love and caring for each other. Interestingly, behavioral marital therapy has been found to be at least as effective as individual therapy at lifting depression. However, it has the additional benefit of bolstering marital satisfaction. Indeed, a number of studies have shown that the boost in marital happiness (or favorable changes in the marriage related to that boost) is in fact the *reason* that the marital therapy works.[23]

Unfortunately, marital therapy suffers from a considerable obstacle: Its success hinges on the depressed person's partner's not undermining the whole process or refusing to participate altogether. This does happen occasionally (though less often than it did twenty-five years ago), because some people consider such therapy a stigma. An alternative is to consider parent training as a first step because depressed individuals are likely to have difficulties in both the arenas of parenting and marriage. Relative to marital therapy, parent training is much more widely accepted, is considered less embarrassing, and doesn't require the participation of both parents. Different types of parent management training exist, but most teach parenting skills (e.g., the use of reinforcement and time-out with children), provide insight into how parents may be inadvertently reinforcing their children's problem behavior (e.g., by giving attention to negative behavior), model warmth and effective communication, and instill confidence in new and not-so-new parents alike. This type of intervention has been shown to alleviate child management problems *and* relieve depressive symptoms.[24]

## ANTIDEPRESSANT MEDICATION

It would be difficult to find a person who's never heard of antidepressant medications. These drugs have been available to depressed individuals for almost fifty years. Prozac is undoubtedly the best known, but there are many others, and they can be divided into several categories. The first includes the most commonly used antidepressants, called SSRIs. These are the "superstars" you've heard of, like Prozac, Zoloft, and Paxil. The second category are newer drugs that include Wellbutrin and Effexor. The third and fourth categories are older antidepressants, which are still considered effective but have more side effects. These comprise the tricyclics (like Anafranil and Tofranil) and the MAO inhibitors (like Nardil and Parnate).

Our society has witnessed a massive growth in antidepressant prescriptions. In 2005, antidepressants were the third most commonly prescribed medications of any kind.[25] Needless to say, their widespread use has provoked many strong and polarized opinions. Some argue that everyone, even relatively happy people, should be taking Prozac, while others prophesy that its widespread use will deliver terrible ills. As always, however, there is a middle ground. The fact is that 60 to 70 percent of depressed patients improve after using a single antidepressant,[26] although it usually takes three to six weeks for a full response.[27] If one drug doesn't appear to work, many depressed individuals ultimately find another one that does. On the other hand, a sizable percentage of patients do not respond well to such medications or can't tolerate the side effects. You must be careful to choose the treatment that's right for you. Someday, with the help of a new field called psychopharmacogenetics, we may be able to do this by matching the best-fitting drug to our unique genetic makeups.[28]

The choices of antidepressants are indeed overwhelming, but a psychiatrist can help navigate the boundless information and select the type and dosage of drug that are appropriate for each case.[29] Indeed, each class of antidepressants is unique; particular drugs attack different brain chemicals (serotonin or norepinephrine or both), differ in their side effects, show different interactions with other medications that the patient might be taking, and require different doses and schedules.[30] For example, Prozac is taken once daily, and the dosage needs to be adjusted only slightly during the course of treatment. This green pill is believed to work by increasing the amount of serotonin in the patient's brain. Its side effects are minor but include nausea, insomnia, and nervousness at the beginning of treatment; sexual side effects may be problematic throughout treatment. Another downside is that Prozac can block the effectiveness or reduce the safety of other medications (e.g., drugs taken for heart disease, migraine, or epilepsy) more so than other antidepressants in its class (such as Zoloft).

By contrast, the antidepressant Wellbutrin affects the depressed patient's levels of norepinephrine and dopamine (but *not* serotonin), so it's likely to be effective for a different sort of patient from those taking Prozac. Wellbutrin's most common side effects—insomnia, anxiety, tremor, and headache—are also different from those of Prozac, and on the positive side, it has few sexual side effects. However, its drawbacks are that it needs to be taken up to three times daily, and it has a higher chance than other antidepressants of causing seizures. Fortunately, a newer cousin of Wellbutrin, called Zyban, has addressed some of these potential problems; Zyban doesn't carry an elevated risk for seizures and needs to be taken only twice a day.

Effexor XR is yet another antidepressant, which works biologically in a different way from all the other drugs in its class. Interestingly, it raises the patient's levels of serotonin when taken in low to moderate doses and elevates norepinephrine at higher doses. Some studies show that when it comes to more severely depressed patients, Effexor XR is more effective than any other drug of its kind.

Because of their higher rates of side effects and other complications, the older classes of antidepressants are usually not used as first-line agents. However, they may be tremendously valuable for certain types of depressed persons, especially when other drugs don't initially succeed at lifting their depressions. In sum, there are many choices for pharmacological treatment of depression, and the selection process is complex, especially for the roughly one-third of depressed people for whom the first drug tried (the first-line agent) is unsuccessful. The fact that many options exist, however, is good news, as psychiatrists can try various approaches. The most obvious one is to switch to another antidepressant, but other options include increasing the dosage or the length of treatment, adding a second nonantidepressant drug, and giving two antidepressants simultaneously.[31]

Patients are often curious about how long they need to stay on medication and whether the depression will return once they stop. The usual recommendation is that antidepressants be taken from four to nine months (fortunately, they are not habit-forming), at which point the medication will be tapered off over one to two months. If one's depression is severe and recurrent, runs in the family, and started before age twenty, many doctors recommend maintenance treatment—that is, to continue taking the medication even after the depression has fully lifted in order to prevent recurrence. Research confirms that this is indeed good advice. In two studies the vast majority of patients who continued taking the tricyclic Tofranil for five years after experiencing depression did not have a recurrence.[32] Even better news comes from studies showing that antidepressants lower the risk of future depressions even *after* they're discontinued.[33]

Despite the fact that antidepressants now help millions of people, misconceptions about them are still widespread. Some claim, for example, that these drugs provide only "artificial" relief. This is the notion that depressed people need to work out their problems and deal with their depressions by themselves, without help from synthetic agents. A related assumption is that antidepressants prevent people from facing the true sources of their suffering and troubles. In response, I'd like to underscore that depression is an illness that needs treatment. Without treatment, the symptoms of depression can last for weeks, months, or even years. People with depression cannot just "snap out of it" or "pull themselves together." Hardly anyone would ever argue that people shouldn't take "artificial drugs" for cardiovascular disease or cancer or rheumatoid arthritis. It's true that depression is different—it seems to be a disorder of emotion rather than an organ of the body, like the heart or kidney—but in truth, depression is a disorder of the brain. When a drug begins to relieve the suffering of the depressed individual, only then can she begin to confront her pain.

## WHICH TREATMENTS ARE DEBATABLE?

I want to mention two well-known treatments for depression that have been found to be much less effective than the ones I've already described. One is herbal therapy, the most common of which involves taking St. John's wort, a fragrant plant draped in yellow flowers in summer. In Germany this plant is used more for depression than are conventional antidepressants, and most of the research testing its effectiveness has been done there. This work shows that it can be effective, especially for short-term periods for mild depression.[34] However, flaws in the studies that have been done so far prompted the U.S. National Institutes of Health to conduct a much larger and well-controlled three-year study, which found that St. John's wort was no more effective than a placebo at alleviating depression or at boosting overall functioning.[35] Because this herbal medicine can have dangerous interactions with other medications, and because its potency and preparation are not tightly regulated in the United States, depressed people should be vigilant when using it as a treatment.

The other treatment that has had mixed results for depression is psychodynamic therapy, which includes traditional Freudian psychoanalysis. Psychodynamic therapists believe that a depressed person's current problems can be resolved successfully only with an intense self-exploration, the goal of which is to give the person a complete understanding of her conflicted feelings and the unconscious basis of her problems in early family relationships. This type of therapy is very intensive (involving fifty-minute sessions several times a week), lengthy (usually lasting several years), and expensive. Furthermore, it has been found to be useful only for people with mild depressive symptoms or who have already improved with other treatments.[36]

## WHAT TO DO IF YOU ARE DEPRESSED

Amazingly, despite the existence of several highly effective treatments for depression, very few depressed people actually partake of them. For example, of those meeting criteria for major depression—that is, those with the most severe symptoms and disability—only 22 percent of whites and 11 percent of Mexican-Americans receive treatment.[37] The percentages are undoubtedly even lower for people whose symptoms are less severe. If you suffer from depression, I strongly encourage you to try one of the immensely effective treatments that exist. The first step toward getting treatment is to make an appointment with your primary care physician. A full physical examination is necessary because many medications and illnesses (such as infections) can have symptoms that are very similar to depression, and these need to be ruled out. If they *are* ruled out, then the physician (or a psychiatrist or psychologist) will complete a psychological evaluation, asking you questions about the history of your symptoms, your family history, and possible substance use problems and suicidal thinking. Your speech, reasoning, and memory are likely to be tested as well; sometimes these types of abilities are affected by depressive illness. If a diagnosis of depression is made, then you and your doctor will decide on the first-line treatment.

## The Cure for Unhappiness Is Happiness

The cure for unhappiness is happiness, I don't care what anyone says.

—*Elizabeth McCracken*

If you are deeply depressed, you may wonder and perhaps question how a book about how to become happier can help you. On one hand, you are right to be skeptical. Most people need to get a reprieve from the most troubling symptoms of their depression before they are able to muster the energy and motivation to embark on a happiness-increasing program. On the other hand, as Seligman has demonstrated, even the most severely depressed individuals can improve by doing a simple daily happiness-increasing exercise. (His study essentially involved an optimism strategy: taking time to recall three things that went well each day.) Indeed, other studies from Seligman's laboratory are demonstrating parallel results.[38] In one of them, researchers conducted a six-week course of so-called group positive psychotherapy, meeting for two hours per week with eight to eleven depressed individuals at a time. Each week the participants were prompted to do a different positive exercise, such as expressing gratitude, savoring, or using their signature strengths. Compared with participants who hadn't received any treatment, the positive psychotherapy groups showed significant relief from their depressive symptoms over the course of the six-week therapy. Amazingly, their levels of happiness not only increased reliably throughout treatment but continued rising long after the intervention was over, reaching an all-time high after one year. In a subsequent study, patients diagnosed with major depression participated in a ten- to twelve-week *individual* positive psychotherapy. Patients encouraged to focus on their strengths rather than on their pathologies experienced significantly greater relief from depression compared with those receiving "treatment as usual" and even compared with those taking antidepressant medication.

The positive psychotherapy recently developed and applied by Seligman and his collaborators uses some happiness-enhancing strategies that are similar to those described in this book. In this way, their research bolsters our confidence in the value of doing happiness activities that bolster positive emotions, positive thoughts, and positive experiences in order to begin to relieve mild, moderate, and even severe depression. Although the activities illustrated in Part II are not designed to "cure" depression, if you are depressed, trying one or more of these activities affords a strong chance of lightening the burden and darkness of depression *and* producing positive feelings.

Furthermore, you might consider trying one of several existing psychotherapies for depression that aim to increase well-being rather than only to relieve symptoms. These psychotherapies are relatively widely tested and established. For example, the goal of one such treatment, the short-term well-being therapy, is to improve patients' positive functioning—their sense of life purpose, positive relationships, self-acceptance, etc.—and to increase their experiences of mastery and pleasure. This therapy has been shown to be highly effective at reducing so-called residual symptoms of people who've recovered from depression.[39] Other promising positive-focused therapies for depressive and other psychological disorders include Quality of Life Therapy,[40] hope therapy,[41] positive psychotherapy, and personal growth therapy.[42]

# Surmounting Setbacks

A final point needs to be made. Most people experience at least one tragedy or major setback in their lives. Researchers have shown that people are remarkably resilient and, after an initial bout of misery, eventually return to their previous level of well-being.[43] However, while in the throes of their misfortune, some become depressed, insecure, and unable to perceive a brighter future. This type of unhappiness is temporary or reactive, and the happiness exercises described in this book may be particularly helpful at alleviating it. Committed engagement to happiness activities can lift a person out of the rut, first to a neutral point and then onto higher ground.

During the 2004 U.S. presidential campaign, vice-presidential candidate John Edwards revealed having endured the tragedy of losing his sixteen-year-old son, with whom he had been extremely close. After a period of depression and grief, he appeared to have come out of the experience a different person, with new priorities and goals. "I have learned two great lessons," Edwards wrote in his memoir, "that there will always be heartache and struggle, and that people of strong will can make a difference. One is a sad lesson; the other is inspiring. I choose to be inspired."[44] Out of depression, if we beat it, we can emerge stronger, happier, more engaged in life.

# Appendix

## *Additional Happiness Activities That May Fit*

The grid below summarizes which happiness-increasing strategies go together. Ideally, first try your four best-fitting happiness activities established for you by the Person-Activity Fit Diagnostic (see Chapter 3). After exhausting this list of four, use the grid below to help you find additional helpful happiness activities.

| IF YOU BENEFIT FROM THIS ACTIVITY | YOU MAY WANT TO TRY THIS ONE | OR THIS ONE |
| --- | --- | --- |
| Expressing gratitude (Happiness Activity No. 1) | Practicing acts of kindness (Happiness Activity No. 4) | Learning to forgive (Happiness Activity No. 7) |

| IF YOU BENEFIT FROM THIS ACTIVITY | YOU MAY WANT TO TRY THIS ONE | OR THIS ONE |
|---|---|---|
| Cultivating optimism (Happiness Activity No. 2) | Savoring life's joys (Happiness Activity No. 9) | Learning to forgive (Happiness Activity No. 7) |
| Avoiding overthinking and social comparison (Happiness Activity No. 3) | Developing strategies for coping (Happiness Activity No. 6) | Committing to your goals (Happiness Activity No. 10) |
| Practicing acts of kindness (Happiness Activity No. 4) | Savoring life's joys (Happiness Activity No. 9) | Increasing flow experiences (Happiness Activity No. 8) |
| Nurturing relationships (Happiness Activity No. 5) | Practicing acts of kindness (Happiness Activity No. 4) | Taking care of your body (Happiness Activity No. 12) |
| Developing strategies for coping (Happiness Activity No. 6) | Committing to your goals (Happiness Activity No. 10) | Learning to forgive (Happiness Activity No. 7) |
| Learning to forgive (Happiness Activity No. 7) | Developing strategies for coping (Happiness Activity No. 6) | Cultivating optimism (Happiness Activity No. 2) |
| Increasing flow experiences (Happiness Activity No. 8) | Savoring life's joys (Happiness Activity No. 9) | Committing to your goals (Happiness Activity No. 10) |
| Savoring life's joys (Happiness Activity No. 9) | Increasing flow experiences (Happiness Activity No. 8) | Committing to your goals (Happiness Activity No. 10) |

| IF YOU BENEFIT FROM THIS ACTIVITY | YOU MAY WANT TO TRY THIS ONE | OR THIS ONE |
|---|---|---|
| Committing to your goals (Happiness Activity No. 10) | Savoring life's joys (Happiness Activity No. 9) | Developing strategies for coping (Happiness Activity No. 6) |
| Practicing religion and spirituality (Happiness Activity No. 11) | Taking care of your body (Happiness Activity No. 12) | Developing strategies for coping (Happiness Activity No. 6) |
| Taking care of your body (Happiness Activity No. 12) | Committing to your goals (Happiness Activity No. 10) | Savoring life's joys (Happiness Activity No. 9) |

# ACKNOWLEDGMENTS

Somewhere in the foreword I wrote that the star of this book is science. Well, there would be no science without scientists. My deep gratitude goes to my collaborators, my students, and colleagues far and wide who have labored on the research depicted in this book. First and foremost I am infinitely grateful to Ken Sheldon, who is an equal collaborator on the empirical research I describe and who was central to the development of the pie chart model. I thank Ken for our fruitful and rewarding collaboration and hope it will continue for many years to come. David Schkade also deserves major credit for helping develop several ideas at the heart of this book. I am also grateful to Marty Seligman for providing Ken, David, and me with the sublime setting, the funding, and the feedback to germinate and propel our ideas forward and for introducing me to Richard Pine (more on him later).

I am privileged to be mentored and championed by several very special individuals. Lee Ross kindled in me an enduring interest in happiness. I am indebted to his brilliance and warmth, and the many intellectually provoking and thoroughly enjoyable discussions we have had over the years. When it comes to the greater part of my research today, all roads lead back to Lee. My wonderful mentor and friend Susan Nolen-Hoeksema has taught me much about how to do science and has always been an unflagging supporter of me and my work. Barry Schwartz has been a treasured friend, and I am grateful for his encouragement, wisdom, and wit and for giving me much sage advice about how to shepherd this book from the earliest spark of an idea to the end.

I would like to acknowledge my appreciation for my many friends and fellow psychologists for being there intellectually and emotionally: Andrew Ward (first as always), Larry Rosenblum, Shelly Gable, Ed Diener, Becky Collins, Robert Biswas-Diener, Danae Aitchison, Terry Johnson, Carol van Heerden, and many others. Countless thanks are also due to my fabulous students, current and former, without whom none of this research would have been possible (in chronological order): Kari Tucker, Fazilet Kasri, Lorie Sousa, Allison Abbe, Chris Tkach, Rene Dickerhoof, and Julia Boehm. Finally, I am indebted to two friends and department chairs who have supported me unreservedly: David Funder and Glenn Stanley.

Writing this book was a (surprisingly) painless experience and oftentimes even a fun and thrilling one. This was undoubtedly true because of the fantastic direct and indirect help and encouragement I reaped from the terrific team at Penguin Press—the most talented, expert, professional, and supportive group of individuals. The only place to start is by acknowledging my immense gratitude to my editor at Penguin Press, the unparalleled Ann Godoff, who is brilliant, irreverent, and wise. I also had the great fortune to work with two senior editors: Emily Loose, who was the first to recognize the promise of my ideas and to help launch them, and especially Vanessa Mobley, who has been indefatigable in her efforts toward improving the book and unstinting with her assistance, advice, and bounty of thoughtful and penetrating feedback. Late in the publishing process but certainly not least, Tracy Locke has been a superb associate publisher.

Richard Pine deserves his own paragraph. I know lots of people say that theirs is the best agent in the world, but they are wrong. Richard *is* the best agent in the world. Without his manifold virtuosity, this book would have been a figment of my imagination and I would certainly not have stumbled on the fabulous Penguin Press.

A number of individuals read drafts of chapters and made valuable suggestions. My sincere thanks go to Dianne Fewkes and Lisa Terry for giving me honest and discerning feedback from a layperson's perspective; to Jennifer Aaker for her astute suggestions, always made with humility and humor; to Julia Boehm, Irene Chang, and Crystal Schmidt for conducting and writing up interviews; to the students of my fall 2005 Psychology 148 class ("The Psychology of Happiness and Virtue") for sharing their stories and insights; and to a score of incredibly smart, capable, and industrious research assistants, starting with Jessica Geleng and Andrea LaPlante and continuing with Danielle O'Brien, Sapna Mendon, Kimberly Hazelwood, Adrienne Grant, Valerie Laws, Nesha Sharma, Ligia Ceja, Lisa McMoran, and Yazmin Perez.

Although money may not make people as happy as they might think, it positively improves research. I extend my gratitude to the National Institute of Mental Health, the Templeton Positive Psychology Prize, and the University of California for their generous funding for a great portion of my work.

Finally, some extra-special thanks. To my parents and brother for always being there for me, and to my two awesome sisters-in-law. To Peter Del Greco: Although my appreciation, love, and admiration may go without saying (at least publicly), I say them anyway. Peter is many things but, with respect to the writing of this book, he has been my editor, my moral support, and, most of all (as some of my friends have pointed out), the greatest husband ever. Finally, saving the best for last, I thank my two young children who will understand one day that they are not just the hows of my abundant happiness, but the whats, whens, wheres, and whys.

# NOTES

## Foreword

1. Lyubomirsky, S., King, L., and Diener, E. (2005). The benefits of frequent positive affect: Does happiness lead to success? *Psychological Bulletin* 131: 803–55.
2. Seligman, M. E. P., and Csikszentmihalyi, M. (2000). Positive psychology: An introduction. *American Psychologist,* 55: 5–14.
3. Ivins, M. (2000, September 22). The manufactured public schools crisis. *Fort Worth Star-Telegram.*

## Chapter 1: Is It Possible to Become Happier?

1. Diener, E. (2000). Subjective well-being: The science of happiness and a proposal for a national index. *American Psychologist,* 55: 34–43. Diener, E., Suh, E. K., Smith, H., and Shao, L. (1995). National differences in reported well-being: Why do they occur? *Social Indicators Research,* 34: 7–32.
2. Keyes, C. L. M. (2005). Mental illness and/or mental health?: Investigating axioms of the complete state model of health. *Journal of Consulting and Clinical Psychology,* 73: 539–48.

3. This study was conducted by Martin Seligman, professor of psychology at the University of Pennsylvania, and Jeff Levy. Seligman, M. E. P. (2002). *Authentic Happiness.* New York: Free Press.

4. Wilson, T. D., and Gilbert, D. T. (2005). Affective forecasting: Knowing what to want. *Current Directions in Psychological Science,* 14: 131–34. Gilbert, T. D. (2006). *Stumbling on Happiness.* New York: Knopf.

5. This quote is from Harvard University social psychologist Dan Gilbert. Goldberg, C. (2006, February 6). Too much of a good thing. *Boston Globe,* F1.

6. The stories of Neil, in this chapter, and Judith, in Chapter 2 (not their real names), are presented in the television documentary *In Pursuit of Happiness* (www.happycanadians.com), made by Canadian Television, with Sarah Spinks as producer, Jon Dore as host, and me as expert. It first aired on CTV on June 17, 2006.

7. Lyubomirsky, S., Sheldon, K. M., and Schkade, D. (2005). Pursuing happiness: The architecture of sustainable change. *Review of General Psychology,* 9: 111–31.

8. Lykken, D., and Tellegen, A. (1996). Happiness is a stochastic phenomenon. *Psychological Science,* 7: 186–89. Tellegen, A., Lykken, D. T., Bouchard, T. J., Wilcox, K. J., Segal, N. L., and Rich, S. (1988). Personality similarity in twins reared apart and together. *Journal of Personality and Social Psychology,* 54: 1031–39.

9. Stallone, D. D., and Stunkard, A. J. (1991). The regulation of body weight: Evidence and clinical implications. *Annals of Behavioral Medicine,* 13: 220–30.

10. Diener, E., Suh, E. M., Lucas, R. E., and Smith, H. L. (1999). Subjective well-being: Three decades of progress. *Psychological Bulletin,* 125: 276–302.

11. Diener, E., Horwitz, J., and Emmons, R. A. (1985). Happiness of the very wealthy. *Social Indicators Research,* 16: 263–74.

12. Inglehart, R. (1990). *Culture Shift in Advanced Industrial Society.* Princeton, NJ: Princeton University Press. DePaulo, B. M., and Morris, W. L. (2005). Singles in society and in science. *Psychological Inquiry,* 16: 57–83.

13. Three recent studies that examined how people's happiness levels change as they grow older found remarkably similar estimates for this percentage, ranging from 33 to 42 percent: Lucas, R. E., and Donnellan, M. B. (in press). How stable is happiness: Using the STARTS model to estimate the stability of life satisfaction. *Journal of Research in Personality.* Ehrhardt, J. J., Saris, W. E.,

and Veenhoven, R. (2000). Stability of life-satisfaction over time: Analysis of change in ranks in a national population. *Journal of Happiness Studies,* 1: 177–205.

14. Lyubomirsky, S. (2001). Why are some people happier than others?: The role of cognitive and motivational processes in well-being. *American Psychologist,* 56: 239–49. Diener et al. (1999), op. cit. Myers, D. G. (2000). The funds, friends, and faith of happy people. *American Psychologist,* 55: 56–67. (4) Diener, E., and Lucas, R. E. (1999). Personality and subjective well-being. In Kahneman, D., Diener, E., and Schwartz, N. (eds.), *Well-being: The Foundations of Hedonic Psychology* (pp. 213–29). New York: Russell Sage. Argyle, M. (1999). Causes and correlates of happiness. Ibid. (pp. 353–73).

15. Lyubomirsky, Sheldon, et al. (2005), op. cit. Tkach, C. (2005). Unlocking the treasury of human kindness: Enduring improvements in mood, happiness, and self-evaluations. Unpublished doctoral dissertation, Department of Psychology, University of California, Riverside. Lyubomirsky, S., Sousa, L., and Dickerhoof, R. (2006). The costs and benefits of writing, talking, and thinking about life's triumphs and defeats. *Journal of Personality and Social Psychology,* 90: 692–708. Sheldon, K. M., and Lyubomirsky, S. (2006a). How to increase and sustain positive emotion: The effects of expressing gratitude and visualizing best possible selves. *Journal of Positive Psychology,* 1: 73–82. Dickerhoof, R., Lyubomirsky, S., and Sheldon, K. M. (2007). How and why do positive activities work to boost well-being? An experimental longitudinal investigation of regularly practicing optimism and gratitude. Manuscript under review. For interventions from other laboratories, see also Seligman, M. E., Steen, T. A., Park, N., and Peterson, C. (2005). Positive psychology progress: Empirical validation of interventions. *American Psychologist,* 60: 410–21. Fordyce, M. W. (1977). Development of a program to increase happiness. *Journal of Counseling Psychology,* 24: 511–21. Fordyce, M. W. (1983). A program to increase happiness: Further studies. *Journal of Counseling Psychology,* 30: 483–98.

16. Lyubomirsky, King, et al. (2005), op. cit.

17. Diener, E., Nickerson, C., Lucas, R. E., and Sandvik, E. (2002). Dispositional affect and job outcomes. *Social Indicators Research,* 59: 229–59.

18. Harker, L., and Keltner, D. (2001). Expressions of positive emotions in women's college yearbook pictures and their relationship to personality and life outcomes across adulthood. *Journal of Personality and Social Psychology,* 80: 112–24.

## Chapter 2: How Happy Are You and Why?

1. Names, identifying information, and details about interviews have been changed for some of the examples offered in this book.

2. Ed Diener, the most distinguished and most widely published researcher in the field of subjective well-being, told me once that he coined the term *subjective well-being* because he didn't think he would be promoted with tenure if his research were perceived as focusing on something so fuzzy and soft as "happiness." The label caught on.

3. However, it's worth noting that "well-being" is a broader, more holistic construct than "happiness," encompassing people's physical and mental health, in addition to their emotional well-being.

4. Lyubomirsky, S., and Lepper, H. S. (1999). A measure of subjective happiness: Preliminary reliability and construct validation. *Social Indicators Research,* 46: 137–55.

5. Ibid.

6. Radloff, L. (1977). The CES-D Scale: A self-report depression scale for research in the general population. *Applied Psychological Measurement,* 1: 385–401.

7. Nezu, A. M., Nezu, C. M., McClure, K. S., & Zwick, M. L. (2002). Assessment of depression. In Gotlib, I. H., and Hammen, C. L. (eds.). *Handbook of Depression* (pp. 61–85). New York: Guilford.

8. Chwastiak, L., Ehde, D. M., Gibbons, L. E., Sullivan, M., Bowen, J. D., and Kraft, G. H. (2002). Depressive symptoms and severity of illness in multiple sclerosis: Epidemiologic study of a large community sample. *American Journal of Psychiatry,* 159: 1862–68. Unützer, J., Patrick, D. L., Marmon, T., Simon, G. E., and Katon, W. J. (2002). Depressive symptoms and mortality in a prospective study of 2,558 older adults. *American Journal of Geriatric Psychiatry,* 10: 521–30.

9. Burt, V. K., and Stein, K. (2002). Epidemiology of depression: Throughout the female life cycle. *Journal of Clinical Psychiatry,* 63: 9–15.

10. Kessler, R. C., McGonagle, K. A. Zhao, S., Nelson, C. B., Hughes, M., Eshlman, S., Wittchen, H. U., and Kendler, K. S. (1994). Lifetime and 12-month prevalence rates of DSM-III-R psychiatric disorders in the United States: Results from the National Comorbidity Survey. *Archives of General Psychiatry,* 51: 8–19.

11. Klerman, G. L. (1988). The current age of youthful melancholia: Evidence for increase in depression among adolescents and young adults. *British Journal of Psychiatry,* 152: 4–14.

12. Üstün, T. B., Ayuso-Mateos, J. L., Chatterji, S., Mathers, C., and Murray, C. J. L. (2004). Global burden of depressive disorders in the year 2000. *British Journal of Psychiatry,* 184: 386–92. Disease burden is measured by the World Health Organization via the number of disability-adjusted life years. In Africa the share of disease burden for unipolar depressive disorders is 1.2 percent; in the Americas they are the leading cause, representing 8 percent of the total burden. The ranking of depression as a disease burden is thirteenth in Africa, fifth in the eastern Mediterranean region, fourth in Southeast Asia, first in the Americas, third in Europe, and second in the western Pacific.

13. Murray, J. L., and Lopez, A. D. (1996). *The Global Burden of Disease: A Comprehensive Assessment of Mortality and Disability from Diseases, Injuries and Risk Factors in 1990 and Projected to 2020.* Summary. Boston: Harvard School of Public Health: World Health Organization.

14. Schwartz, B. (2000). Pitfalls on the road to a positive psychology of hope. In Schwartz, B., and Gillham, J. (eds.). *The Science of Optimism and Hope: Research Essays in Honor of Martin E. P. Seligman* (pp. 399–412). Philadelphia: Templeton Foundation Press. O'Connor, R. (1999). *Undoing Depression.* New York: Berkley. Machoian, L. (2005). *The Disappearing Girl: Learning the Language of Teenage Depression.* New York: Dutton. Charney, D. S., and Nemeroff, C. B. (2004). *The Peace of Mind Prescription: An Authoritative Guide to Finding the Most Effective Treatment for Anxiety and Depression.* New York: Houghton Mifflin. Seligman, M. E. P. (1990). Why is there so much depression today?: The waxing of the individual and the waning of the commons. In Ingram, R. (ed.), *Contemporary Psychological Approaches to Depression: Theory, Research, and Treatment* (pp. 1–9). New York: Plenum.

15. Klerman, G. L., and Weissman, M. M. (1989). Increasing rates of depression. *Journal of the American Medical Association,* 261: 2229–35. Lavori, P. W., Warshaw, M., Klerman, G. L, Mueller, T. I., Leon, A., Rice, J., and Akiskal, H. (1993). Secular trends in lifetime onset of MDD stratified by selected sociodemographic risk factors. *Journal of Psychiatric Research,* 27: 95–109. Lavori, P. W., Klerman, G. L, Keller, M. B., Reich, T., Rice, J., and Endicott, J. (1987). Age-period-cohort analysis of secular trends in onset of

major depression: Findings in siblings of patients with major affective disorder. *Journal of Psychiatric Research,* 21: 23–35.

16. Weber, R. (1991, June 3). "I can't wait to grow up and be happy." *New Yorker.*
17. Diener et al. (1999), op. cit.
18. In 2005 the national median household income for a family of four was $46,326. DeNavas-Walt, C., Proctor, B. D., and Lee, C. H. (August 2005). U.S. Census Bureau, Current Population Reports, P60-231, *Income, Poverty, and Health Insurance Coverage in the United States: 2005.* Washington, DC: U.S. Government Printing Office.
19. Paul Bellew, executive director for market and industry analysis at General Motors, quoted in Scott, J., and Leonhardt, D. (2005, May 15). Class in America: Shadowy lines that still divide. *New York Times.*
20. Goodwin, D. K. (1994). *No Ordinary Time.* New York: Touchstone, pp. 42–43.
21. Lane, R. E. (2000). *The loss of happiness in market democracies.* New Haven: Yale University Press. See Figure 1.1, p.5.
22. Ibid.
23. It's worth noting that people whose basic needs *aren't* being met—needs for such requisites as safety, food, and shelter—report being very unhappy. For this group, more money (for medical care, nutrition, toys for their children, etc.) does indeed make a substantial difference to their well-being and quality of life. So the small correlation between happiness and wealth holds only for individuals above the "basic needs," or poverty, threshold. For example, see Biswas-Diener, R., and Diener, E. (2001). Making the best of a bad situation: Satisfaction in the slums of Calcutta. *Social Indicators Research,* 55: 329–52.
24. Lopez, S. (2004, May 26). Neighbors' ire equals scale of Ovitz plan. *Los Angeles Times,* B1.
25. *Sun,* August 2002.
26. Nickerson, C., Schwarz, N., Diener, E., and Kahneman, D. (2003). Zeroing on the dark side of the American dream: A closer look at the negative consequences of the goal for financial success. *Psychological Science,* 14: 531–36.
27. Cohen, P., and Cohen, J. (1996). *Life Values and Adolescent Mental Health.* Mahwah, NJ: Erlbaum.
28. Sheldon, K. M., and Kasser, T. (1998). Pursuing personal goals: Skills enable

progress, but not all progress is beneficial. *Personality and Social Psychology Bulletin,* 24: 1319–31.

29. Richins, M. L. (1995). Social comparison, advertising, and consumer discontent. *American Behavioral Scientist,* 38: 593–607.

30. Campbell, A. (1981). *The Sense of Well-being in America.* New York: McGraw-Hill.

31. Pryor, J. H., Hurtado, S., Saenz, V. B., Lindholm, J. A., Korn, W. S., and Mahoney, K. M. (2006). The American Freshman—National Norms for Fall 2005. Working paper, Higher Education Research Institute.

32. Rich think big about living well (1987, September 24). *Chicago Tribune,* 3. Pay nags at workers' job views (1987, October 18). *Chicago Tribune,* 10B.

33. Kristof, K. M. (2005, January 14). Study: Money can't buy happiness, security either. *Los Angeles Times,* C1.

34. Kahneman, D., Krueger, A. B., Schkade, D., Schwarz, N., and Stone, A. A. (2006). Would you be happier if you were richer?: A focusing illusion. *Science,* 312: 1908–10.

35. The quote is attributed to Warren Buffett. O'Brien, T. L. (2006, September 17). Fortune's fools: Why the rich go broke. *New York Times.*

36. American Society for Aesthetic Plastic Surgery. (2004). Cosmetic surgery. Quick facts: 2004 ASAPS statistics. Retrieved November 16, 2005, from the World Wide Web: http://www.surgery.org/press/statistics-2004.php.

37. Wengle, H. (1986). The psychology of cosmetic surgery: A critical overview of the literature 1960–1982. Part I. *Annals of Plastic Surgery,* 16: 435–43. Young, V. L., Nemecek, J. R., and Nemecek, D. A. (1994). The efficacy of breast augmentation: Breast size increase, patient satisfaction, and psychological effects. *Plastic and Reconstructive Surgery,* 94: 958–69. Indeed, women with cosmetic breast implants have been reported to have an increased risk of death from suicide. See McLaughlin, J. K., Wise, T. N., and Lipworth, L. (2004). Increased risk of suicide among patients with breast implants: Do the epidemiologic data support psychiatric consultation. *Psychosomatics,* 45: 277–80.

38. Schkade, D. A., and Kahneman, D. (1998). Does living in California make people happy?: A focusing illusion in judgments of life satisfaction. *Psychological Science,* 9: 340–46.

39. Diener, E., Wolsic, B., and Fujita, F. (1995). Physical attractiveness and subjective well-being. *Journal of Personality and Social Psychology*, 69, 120–29. See also another interesting study that found that fashion models are actually significantly *less* happy than their peers, possibly because they are more likely to be valued for their looks and have fewer opportunities to develop meaningful relationships or exert personal control within their jobs: Meyer, B., Enström, M. K., Harstveit, M., Bowles, D. P., and Beevers, C. G. (2007). Happiness and despair on the catwalk: Need satisfaction, well-being, and personality adjustment among fashion models. *Journal of Positive Psychology*, 2, 2–17.

40. Argyle, M. (1999). Causes and correlates of happiness. In Diener, Kahneman, et al., op. cit., and Schwarz, N., 353–75. Campbell, A., Converse, P. E., and Rodgers, W. L. (1976). *The Quality of American Life*. New York: Russell Sage Foundation. Lyubomirsky, S., and Tucker, K. L. (1998). Implications of individual differences in self-reported happiness for perceiving, thinking about, and recalling life events. *Motivation and Emotion*, 22, 155–86.

41. Frederick, S., and Loewenstein, G. (1999). Hedonic adaptation. In Kahneman et al., op. cit., 302–29.

42. Lyubomirsky, King, et al. (2005), op. cit.

43. Lucas, R. E., Clark, A. E., Georgellis, Y., and Diener, E. (2003). Reexamining adaptation and the set point model of happiness: Reactions to changes in marital status. *Journal of Personality and Social Psychology*, 84: 527–39.

44. Brickman, P., Coates, D., and Janoff-Bulman, R. (1978). Lottery winners and accident victims: Is happiness relative? *Journal of Personality and Social Psychology*, 36: 917–27.

45. Riis, J., Loewenstein, G., Baron, J., Jepson, C., Fagerlin, A., and Ubel, P. A. (2005). Ignorance of hedonic adaptation to hemodialysis: A study using ecological momentary assessment. *Journal of Experimental Psychology: General*, 134: 3–9.

46. Schneider, C. E. (1998). *The Practice of Autonomy*. New York: Oxford University Press, p. 71.

47. Lykken, D., and Tellegen, A. (1996). Happiness is a stochastic phenomenon. *Psychological Science*, 7: 186–89.

48. To protect confidentiality, names and identifying information about participants of research studies have been changed here and throughout the book.

49. Thomas Bouchard compiled and analyzed this fascinating sample.

50. Segal, N. (2000). *Entwined Lives.* New York: Plume.

51. Headey, B., and Wearing, A. (1989). Personality, life events, and subjective well-being: Toward a dynamic equilibrium model. *Journal of Personality and Social Psychology,* 57: 731–39.

52. Suh, E. M., Diener, E., and Fujita, F. (1996). Events and subjective well-being: Only recent events matter. *Journal of Personality and Social Psychology,* 70: 1091–1102.

53. Bilger, B. (2004, April 5). The height gap: Why Europeans are getting taller and taller—and Americans aren't. *New Yorker.*

54. Sternberg, R. J., Grigorenko, E. L., and Kidd, K. K. (2005). Intelligence, race, and genetics. *American Psychologist,* 60: 46–59.

55. Caspi, A., Sugden, K., Moffitt, T. E., Taylor, A., Craig, I. W., Harrington, H. L., McClay, J., Mill, J., Martin, J., Braithwaite, A., and Poulton, R. (2003). Influence of life stress on depression: Moderation by a polymorphism in the 5-HTT gene. *Science,* 301: 386–89.

56. For every single gene, each person has two alleles, one from the mother and one from the father. The short allele of the 5-HTTLPR gene decreases the brain supply of the neurotransmitter serotonin, a brain chemical that is needed to mitigate depression. Indeed, drugs like Prozac are called selective serotonin reuptake inhibitors (SSRIs) because they increase levels of serotonin and thereby lift depressive symptoms.

57. Taylor, S. E., Way, B. M., Welch, W. T., Hilmert, C. J., Lehman, B. J., and Eisenberger, N. I. (2006) Early family environment, current adversity, the serotonin transporter promoter polymorphism, and depressive symptomatology. *Biological Psychiatry,* 60: 671–76.

58. A typical participant in Davidson's experiments is outfitted with electrodes—metal conductors about the size of a dime—that envelop his head, looking like a great big shower cap. The electrodes are attached to wire leads and electric current runs through those leads from the participant's scalp to Davidson's measuring instruments. The current comes from biological electrical signals, called biopotentials.

59. Tomarken, A. J., Davidson, R. J., Wheeler, R. E., and Doss, R. C. (1992). Individual differences in anterior brain asymmetry and fundamental dimensions of emotion. *Journal of Personality and Social Psychology,*

62: 676–87. Urry, H. L., Nitschke, J. B., Dolski, I., Jackson, D. C., Dalton, K. M., Mueller, C. J., Rosenkranz, M. A., Ryff, C. D., Singer, B. H., and Davidson, R. J. (2004). Making a life worth living: Neural correlates of well-being. *Psychological Science,* 15: 367–72. See also van Honk, J., and Schutter, D. J. L. G. (2006). From affective valence to motivational direction: The frontal asymmetry of emotion revised. *Psychological Science,* 17: 963–65.

60. This remark was made by Nobel Prize winner and Princeton University professor Daniel Kahneman.

61. Mroczek, D. K., and Spiro, A., III. (2005). Change in life satisfaction during adulthood: Findings from the Veterans Affairs Normative Aging Study. *Journal of Personality and Social Psychology,* 88: 189–202.

62. Nolen-Hoeksema, S. (2005). *Eating, Drinking, Overthinking: The Toxic Triangle of Food, Alcohol, and Depression—and How Women Can Break Free.* New York: Henry Holt.

63. This quote is from English statesman Benjamin Disraeli. Disraeli, B. (2000). *Lothair.* Cambridge, UK: Chadwyck-Healey, vol. 3, p. 206.

## Chapter 3: How to Find Happiness Activities That Fit Your Interests, Your Values, and Your Needs

1. Harackiewicz, J. M., and Sansone, C. (1991). Goals and intrinsic motivation: You can get there from here. In Maehr, M. L., and Pintrich, P. R. (eds.). *Advances in Motivation and Achievement* (vol. 7, pp. 21–49). Greenwich, CT: JAI Press. Brunstein, J. C., Schultheiss, O. C., and Grässman, R. (1998). Personal goals and emotional well-being: The moderating role of motive dispositions. *Journal of Personality and Social Psychology,* 75: 494–508. Diener, E., and Fujita, F. (1995). Resources, personal strivings, and subjective well-being: A nomothetic and idiographic approach. *Journal of Personality and Social Psychology,* 68: 926–35. Higgins, E. T., (2005). Value from regulatory fit. *Current Directions in Psychological Science,* 14: 209–13. Brandstätter, H. (1994). Well-being and motivated person-environment fit: A time-sampling study of emotions. *European Journal of Personality,* 8: 75–93. Pervin, L. A. (1968). Performance and satisfaction as a function of individual-environment fit. *Psychological Bulletin,* 69: 56–68.

2. With the exception of the "natural" item, the measure of self-determined motivation presented here was based on a methodology developed by Ken Sheldon and his colleagues. The four reasons to engage in a happiness activity tap four kinds of motivation: (1) intrinsic motivation (assessed by the item "enjoy," though the item "natural" is closely related), defined as doing something because it is inherently interesting and enjoyable; (2) identified motivation ("value"), defined as doing something in order to express important values and beliefs; (3) introjected motivation ("guilty"), defined as acting to avoid guilt or anxiety; and (4) external motivation ("situation"), defined as doing something for a reward or to please others. According to Ed Deci and Rich Ryan, these four motivations lie along a continuum, from internal (or autonomous) to external (or controlled by others). Hence an aggregate self-determined motivation score is computed by averaging the identified and intrinsic ratings and subtracting the external and introjected ratings. This score assesses the extent to which a person's behavior is inspired by his or her lifelong interests and deeply held values. The greater the self-determined motivation for a particular goal (whether that goal is to become thinner, more productive, or more optimistic), the healthier, happier, and more successful is the person in attaining it. Relevant reading: Deci, E. L., and Ryan, R. M. (2000). The "what" and "why" of goal pursuits: Human needs and the self-determination of behavior. *Psychological Inquiry*, 4: 227–68. Sheldon, K. M., and Elliot, A. J. (1999). Goal striving, need-satisfaction, and longitudinal wellbeing: The Self-Concordance Model. *Journal of Personality and Social Psychology*, 76: 482–97. Sheldon, K. M., and Kasser, T. (1995). Coherence and congruence: Two aspects of personality integration. *Journal of Personality and Social Psychology*, 68: 531–43.

3. Sheldon, K. M., and Houser-Marko, L. (2001). Self-concordance, goal-attainment, and the pursuit of happiness: Can there be an upward spiral? *Journal of Personality and Social Psychology*, 80: 152–65. Ib. Sheldon and Kasser (1998), op. cit., Sheldon and Lyubomirsky (2006a), op. cit.

4. Dickerhoof (2007), op. cit.

5. For corroborating results with respect to the importance of fit in increasing well-being, see Fordyce (1977, 1983), op. cit. Sheldon and Lyubomirsky (2006a), op. cit.

6. Klem, M. L., Wing, R. R., McGuire, M. T., Seagle, H. M., and Hill, J. O. (1997). A descriptive study of individuals successful at long-term maintenance of substantial weight loss. *American Journal of Clinical Nutrition,* 66: 239–46.
7. Dickerhoof (2007), op. cit.


## Foreword to Part II: Before You Begin

1. The Oxford Happiness Questionnaire taps into several components of well-being, including self-esteem, sense of purpose, social interest, and humor, and has been successfully used in individuals of all ages. Reference: Hills, P., and Argyle, M. (2002). The Oxford Happiness Questionnaire: A Compact Scale for the Measurement of Psychological Well-being. *Personality and Individual Differences, 33,* 1073–1082.
2. Note that I have slightly altered the wording of a few items to enhance clarity.


## Chapter 4: Practicing Gratitude and Positive Thinking

1. Emmons, R. A., and Shelton, C. M. (2002). Gratitude and the science of positive psychology. In Snyder, C. R., and Lopez, S. J. (eds.). *Handbook of Positive Psychology* (pp. 459–71). Oxford: Oxford University Press.
2. McCullough, M. E., Emmons, R. A., and Tsang, J. (2002). The grateful disposition: A conceptual and empirical topography. *Journal of Personality and Social Psychology,* 82: 112–27. McCullough, M. E., Tsang, J., and Emmons, R. A. (2004). Gratitude in intermediate affective terrain: Links of grateful moods to individual differences and daily emotional experience. *Journal of Personality and Social Psychology,* 86: 295–309. Algoe, S., and Haidt, J. (2006). Witnessing excellence in action: The "other-praising" emotions of elevation, gratitude, and admiration. Manuscript under review. Bartlett, M. Y., and DeSteno, D. (2004). Gratitude: Helping when it really costs you. *Psychological Science,* 17: 319–25. For an accessible review, see Robert Emmons's recent book: Emmons, R. A. (2007). *THANKS! How the New Science of Gratitude Can Make You Happier.* New York: Houghton Mifflin.

3. Emmons, R. A., and McCullough, M. E. (2003). Counting blessings versus burdens: An experimental investigation of gratitude and subjective well-being in daily life. *Journal of Personality and Social Psychology,* 84: 377–89.

4. Emmons (2007), op. cit.

5. Fredrickson, B. L., Tugade, M. M., Waugh, C. E., and Larkin, G. R. (2003). What good are positive emotions in crises?: A prospective study of resilience and emotions following the terrorist attacks on the United States in September 11, 2001. *Journal of Personality and Social Psychology,* 84: 365–76.

6. Watkins, P. C., Grimm, D. L., and Kolts, R. (2004). Counting your blessings: Positive memories among grateful persons. *Current Psychology: Developmental, Learning, Personality, Social,* 23: 52–67.

7. Fredrickson et al. (2003), op. cit.

8. Malin, A. (2003, September). Maximum joy: 14 ways to feel lucky you're alive. *Prevention.*

9. Casey, M. J. (2006, October 20). A survivor's optimism. *New York Times.*

10. Bartlett, M. Y., and DeSteno, D. (2006). Gratitude and prosocial behavior: Helping when it costs you. *Psychological Science,* 17: 319–25.

11. McCullough et al. (2001), op. cit. Emmons and McCullough (2003), op. cit.

12. Algoe, S. B., Haidt, J., Gable, S. L., and Strachman, A. (2007). Beyond reciprocity: Gratitude and relationships in everyday life. Manuscript under review.

13. Lyubomirsky, King, et al. (2005), op. cit.

14. McCullough et al. (2002), op. cit.

15. Quote from psychiatrist Roger Walsh.

16. See the "What I Know to Be True" exercise in MacDonald, L. (2004). *Learn to Be an Optimist.* San Francisco: Chronicle Books, 51.

17. Miller, T. (1995). *How to Want What You Have.* New York: Avon.

18. Tkach (2005), op. cit.

19. Seligman, M. E., Steen, T. A., Park, N., and Peterson, C. (2005). Positive psychology progress: Empirical validation of interventions. *American Psychologist,* 60: 410–21.

20. Dickerhoof (2007), op. cit.

21. This distinction comes from the most thoughtful paper on optimism that

I've ever read: Peterson, C. (2000). The future of optimism. *American Psychologist,* 55: 44–55.

22. Franken, A. (1992). *I'm Good Enough, I'm Smart Enough, and Doggone it, People Like Me!: Daily Affirmations by Stuart Smalley.* New York: Dell. Personal disclosure: I love Al Franken.

23. Tiger, L. (1979). *Optimism: The Biology of Hope.* New York: Simon & Schuster. Scheier, M. F., and Carver, C. S. (1993). On the power of positive thinking: The benefits of being optimistic. *Current Directions in Psychological Science,* 2: 26–30.

24. Scheier and Carver (1993), op. cit.

25. Abramson, L. Y., Seligman, M. E. P., and Teasdale, J. D. (1978). Learned helplessness in humans: Critique and reformulation. *Journal of Abnormal Psychology,* 87: 49–74. Peterson, C. (1991). Meaning and measurement of explanatory style. *Psychological Inquiry,* 2: 1–10.

26. Snyder, C. R. (1994). *The Psychology of Hope: You Can Get There from Here.* New York: Free Press.

27. King, L. A. (2001). The health benefits of writing about life goals. *Personality and Social Psychology Bulletin,* 27: 798–807.

28. Sheldon and Lyubomirsky (2006a), op. cit.

29. For the benefits of writing, see Pennebaker, J. W., and Graybeal, A. (2001). Patterns of natural language use: Disclosure, personality, and social integration. *Current Directions in Psychological Science,* 10: 90–93. Singer, J. A. (2004). Narrative identity and meaning making across the adult lifespan: An introduction. *Journal of Personality,* 72: 437–59.

30. Segerstrom, S. C. (2001). Optimism, goal conflict, and stressor-related immune change. *Journal of Behavioral Medicine,* 24: 441–67.

31. Snyder, C. R., Harris, C., Anderson, J. R., Holleran, S. A., Irving, L. M., Sigmon, S. T., Yoshinobu, L., Gibb, J., Langelle, C., and Harney, P. (1991). The will and the ways: Development and validation of an individual-differences measure of hope. *Journal of Personality and Social Psychology,* 60: 570–85.

32. Scheier, M. F., Weintraub, J. K., and Carver, C. S. (1986). Coping with stress: Divergent strategies of optimists and pessimists. *Journal of Personality and Social Psychology,* 51: 1257–64. Nes, L. S., and Segerstrom, S. C. (2006). Disposi-

tional optimism and coping: A meta-analytic review. *Personality and Social Psychology Review,* 10: 235–51.

33. Scheier and Carver (1993), op. cit.
34. Helweg-Larsen, M., Sadeghian, P., and Webb, M. A. (2002). The stigma of being pessimistically biased. *Journal of Social and Clinical Psychology,* 21: 92–107.
35. This general suggestion about how to develop hope and analysis of "barrier hopes" has been made by the late psychologist C. R. Snyder.
36. See the "Look for the Silver Lining" exercise in MacDonald (2004), op. cit.
37. Gillham, J. E., and Reivich, K. J. (1999). Prevention of depressive symptoms in school children: A research update. *Psychological Science,* 10: 461–62.
38. This technique is called ABCDE disputation and is described in greater detail in Chapter 8. A = adversity (the issue that you face). B = belief (the negative belief engendered by the adversity). C = consequence (how you feel in response to the adversity). D = disputation (challenging the negative belief). E = Energize (note how more optimistic explanations can give you more energy and make you feel better). References: Seligman's (1991) *Learned Optimism* and (2002) *Authentic Happiness,* op. cit.
39. Aspinwall, L. G., and Brunhart, S. M. (1996). Distinguishing optimism from denial: Optimistic beliefs predict attention to health threats. *Personality and Social Psychology Bulletin,* 22: 993–1003.
40. Seligman, M. (1991). *Learned Optimism.* New York: Free Press, p. 292.
41. For reviews, see Lyubomirsky, S., and Tkach, C. (2003). The consequences of dysphoric rumination. In Papageorgiou, C., and Wells, A. (eds.). *Rumination: Nature, Theory, and Treatment of Negative Thinking in Depression* (pp. 21–41). Chichester, UK: John Wiley. Nolen-Hoeksema, S. (2003). *Women Who Think Too Much.* New York: Henry Holt.
42. Lyubomirsky, S., Dickerhoof, R., Kasri, F., and Zehm, K. (2007). The cognitive and hedonic costs of unwarranted dwelling. Manuscript under review.
43. Lyubomirsky et al. (2007), op. cit. See also Lyubomirsky, S., Kasri, F., and Zehm, K. (2003). Dysphoric rumination impairs concentration on academic tasks. *Cognitive Therapy and Research,* 27: 309–30.
44. Festinger, L. (1954). A theory of social comparison processes. *Human Relations,* 7: 114–40. Taylor, S. E., and Lobel, M. (1989). Social comparison

activity under threat: Downward evaluation and upward contacts. *Psychological Review,* 96: 569–75. Major, B., Testa, M., and Bylsma, W.H. (1991). Responses to upward and downward social comparisons: The impact of esteem-relevance and perceived control. In Suls, J., and Wills, T. A. (eds). *Social Comparison: Contemporary Theory and Research* (pp. 237–60). Hillsdale, NJ: Erlbaum. Affleck, G., and Tennen, H. (1991). Social comparison and coping with major medical problems. In Suls and Wills, op. cit., (pp. 369–93).

45. Lyubomirsky, S., and Ross, L. (1997). Hedonic consequences of social comparison: A contrast of happy and unhappy people. *Journal of Personality and Social Psychology,* 73: 1141–57.

46. Unscrambled, they are *basis, snowy, and toxin.*

47. Nolen-Hoeksema (2003), op. cit.

48. Fredrickson, B. L. (2001). The role of positive emotions in positive psychology: The broaden-and-build theory of positive emotions. *American Psychologist,* 56: 218–26.

49. Carlson, R. (1997). *Don't Sweat the Small Stuff—and It's All Small Stuff.* New York: Hyperion.

50. Tedeschi, R. G., Park, C. L., and Calhoun, L. G. (eds.). (1998). *Posttraumatic growth: Positive changes in the aftermath of crisis.* Mahwah, NJ: Erlbaum.

## Chapter 5: Investing in Social Connections

1. Berscheid, E. (2003). The human's greatest strength: Other humans. In Aspinwall, L. G., and Staudinger, U. M., (eds.). *A Psychology of Human Strengths: Fundamental Questions and Future Directions for a Positive Psychology* (pp. 37–47). Washington, DC: American Psychological Association. The quote appears on p. 39.

2. Lyubomirsky, King, et al. (2005), op. cit.

3. For review, see ibid.

4. This study is described in Lyubomirsky, Sheldon, et al. (2005), op. cit.

5. Tkach (2005), op. cit.

6. All the studies conducted in my laboratory (and described in this book) include at least one control group. The control group in this particular study consisted of participants who didn't perform any extra acts of kindness

but were instructed simply to list various events that happened to them weekly.

7. Williamson, G. M., and Clark, M. S. (1989). Providing help and desired relationship type as determinants of changes in moods and self-evaluations. *Journal of Personality and Social Psychology,* 56: 722–34.

8. Clark, M. C., (ed.). *Prosocial Behavior: Review of Personality and Social Psychology* (vol. 12, pp. 238–64). Newbury Park, CA: Sage.

9. Trivers, R. (1971). The evolution of reciprocal altruism. *Quarterly Review of Biology,* 46: 35–57.

10. For a review of the literature on volunteering and well-being, see Piliavin, J. A. (2003). Doing well by doing good: Benefits for the benefactor. In Keyes, C. L. M., and Haidt, J., (eds.). *Flourishing: Positive Psychology and the Life Well-Lived* (pp. 227–47). Washington, DC: American Psychological Association.

11. Schwartz, C. E., and Sendor, M. (1999). Helping others helps oneself: Response shift effects in peer support. *Social Science and Medicine,* 48: 1563–75.

12. Unfortunately, five participants are too few a number ("too small a sample size," in scientific terms) to allow researchers to generalize their findings to the community at large. In all the studies that I have done with my students and collaborators—indeed, in almost all the research cited in this book—the sample sizes have been large enough to permit such generalization and large enough to permit comparisons across groups (e.g., to answer such questions as: Is the kindness group happier than the control group?) and across time (e.g., Is the kindness group happier in May than it was in January?).

13. Here's a sampling: Pay the toll of the car behind you or put change into an expired parking meter; pick up litter in your neighborhood, beach, or park; paint a neighbor's home; volunteer at a food pantry, homeless shelter, or church/temple/mosque; teach an illiterate adult to read; cook a special meal for a busy family member, neighbor, or friend; spend time with an elderly relative or neighbor, or visit a nursing home; give up your seat on the bus or train; do a household chore even when it's not your turn; rescue an animal; open the door for someone or let somebody ahead of you in line; help someone carry a bag or package; donate to a charity your money, your time, or your blood; call, write, or travel to see a friend in need; tutor or be a mentor to a younger person; and leave a thank-you note

for your mail carrier, trash collector, or any other individual who simplifies your life.

14. Some of these suggestions are borrowed from Carlson (1997), op. cit.

15. Algoe and Haidt (2006), op. cit.

16. Glynn, S. A., Busch, M. P., Schreiber, G. B., Murphy, E. L., Wright, D. J., Tu, Y., Kleinman, S. H., and NHLBI REDS study group (2003). Effect of a national disaster on blood supply and safety: The September 11 experience. *Journal of the American Medical Association,* 289: 2246–53.

17. Esterling, B. A., Kiecolt-Glaser, J. K., Bodnar, J. C., and Glaser, R. (1994). Chronic stress, social support, and persistent alterations in the natural killer cell response to cytokines in older adults. *Health Psychology,* 13: 291–98.

18. Weitzenkamp, D. A., Gerhart, K. A., Charlifue, S. W., Whiteneck, G. G., and Savic, G. (1997). Spouses of spinal cord injury survivors: The added impact of caregiving. *Archives of Physical Medicine and Rehabilitation,* 78: 822–27.

19. Specter, M. (2005, October 24). What money can buy. *New Yorker.*

20. For review, see Lyubomirsky, King, et al. (2005), op. cit. See also Myers (2000), op. cit.

21. Baumeister, R. F., and Leary, M. R. (1995). The need to belong: Desire for interpersonal attachments as a fundamental human motivation. *Psychological Bulletin,* 117: 497–529.

22. House, J. S., Landis, K. R., and Umberson, D. (1988). Social relationships and health. *Science,* 241: 540–45. Kaplan, R. M., and Toshima, M. T. (1990). The functional effects of social relationships on chronic illnesses and disability. In Sarason, B. R., Sarason, I. G., and Pierce, G. R., (eds.). *Social Support: An Interactional View* (pp. 427–53). Oxford, UK: John Wiley. Verbrugge, L. M. (1979). Marital status and health. *Journal of Marriage and the Family,* 41: 267–85. Lynch, J. J. (1977). *The Broken Heart: The Medical Consequences of Loneliness.* New York: Basic Books.

23. The other three factors the Sardinians, Okinawans, and Seventh-Day Adventists had in common were "Don't smoke," "Stay physically active," and "Eat a plant-based diet." Buettner, D. (2005, November). "New wrinkles on aging." *National Geographic,* 2–27.

24. Berscheid, E., and Reis, H. T. (1998). Attraction and close relationships. In Gilbert, D. T., Fiske, S. T., and Lindzey, G., (eds.). *The Handbook of Social Psychology*, 4th ed. (vol. 2, pp. 193–281). New York: McGraw-Hill.

25. Rainwater, L. (1994). Family equivalence as a social construction. In Ekert-Jaffe, D. (ed.). *Standards of Living and Families: Observation and Analysis* (pp. 25–39). Montrouge, France: John Libbey Eurotext.

26. Easterlin, R. A. (2005). A puzzle for adaptive theory. *Journal of Economic Behavior and Organization,* 56: 513–21.

27. Gottman, J. M., and Silver, N. (1999). *The Seven Principles for Making Marriage Work*. New York: Three Rivers Press.

28. Gottman, J. M. (1994). *What Predicts Divorce: The Relationship Between Marital Processes and Marital Outcomes*. Hillsdale, NJ: Erlbaum.

29. Ibid.

30. Drigotas, S. M., Rusbult, C. E., Wieselquist, J., and Whitton, S. W. (1999). Close partner as sculptor of the ideal self: Behavioral affirmation and the Michelangelo phenomenon. *Journal of Personality and Social Psychology,* 77: 293–323. Drigotas, S. M. (2002). The Michelangelo phenomenon and personal well-being. *Journal of Personality,* 70: 59–77.

31. Murray, S. L., Holmes, J. G., and Griffin, D. W. (1996). The self-fulfilling nature of positive illusions in romantic relationships: Love is not blind, but prescient. *Journal of Personality and Social Psychology,* 71: 1155–80.

32. This compelling work has been conducted by Shelly Gable, Harry Reis, and their colleagues: Gable, S. L., Reis, H. T., Asher, E. R. and Impett, E. A. (2004). What do you do when things go right?: The intrapersonal and interpersonal benefits of sharing positive events. *Journal of Personality and Social Psychology,* 87: 228–45.

33. Schueller, S. M. (2006). Personality fit and positive interventions. Is extraversion important? Unpublished manuscript, Department of Psychology, University of Pennsylvania.

34. Gottman and Silver (1999), op. cit.

35. Keil, C. P. (1998). Loneliness, stress, and human-animal attachment among older adults. In Wilson, C. C., and Turner, D. C., (eds.). *Companion Animals in Human Health* (pp. 123–34). Thousand Oaks, CA: Sage.

36. These studies on singles were compiled in a recent influential piece by

psychologists Bella DePaulo and Wendy Morris, who challenge what they call the ideology of marriage and family: DePaulo, B. M., and Morris, W. L. (2005). Singles in society and in science. *Psychological Inquiry,* 16: 57–83. See also DePaulo, B. (2006). *Singled Out: How Singles Are Stereotyped, Stigmatized, and Ignored, and Still Live Happily Ever After.* New York: St. Martin's Press.

37. A number of these suggestions are from McGinnis, A. L. (1979). *The Friendship Factor.* Minneapolis: Augsburg. The magic number of "three" was suggested by Stanford University professor Laura Carstensen.

38. A Russian proverb.

39. Argyle, M., and Henderson, M. (1984). The rules of friendships. *Journal of Social and Personal Relationships,* 1: 211–37.

40. Clipman, J. M. (1999, March). A hug a day keeps the blues away: The effect of daily hugs on subjective well-being in college students. Paper presented at the Seventieth Annual Meeting of the Eastern Psychological Association, Boston.

41. In a subsequent study, Jane Marie Clipman gave students the opportunity to wink or to give compliments, instead of hug. Winking and complimenting also increased well-being.

42. Doehring, K. M. (1989). Relieving pain through touch. *Advancing Clinical Care,* 4: 32–33.

## Chapter 6: Managing Stress, Hardship, and Trauma

1. Ozer, E. J., and Weiss, D. S. (2004). Who develops post-traumatic stress disorder? *Current Directions in Psychological Science,* 13: 169–72.

2. Billings, A. G., and Moos, R. H. (1984). Coping, stress, and social resources among adults with unipolar depression. *Journal of Personality and Social Psychology,* 46: 887–91.

3. Carver, C. S., Scheier, M. F., and Weintraub, J. K. (1984). Assessing coping strategies: A theoretically based approach. *Journal of Personality and Social Psychology,* 56: 267–83.

4. Nolen-Hoeksema, S., and Morrow, J. (1991). A prospective study of depression and posttraumatic stress symptoms after a natural disaster: The 1989

Loma Prieta earthquake. *Journal of Personality and Social Psychology*, 61: 115–21.

5. Schut, H. A. W., Stroebe, M. S., van den Bout, J., and de Keijser, J. (1997). Intervention for the bereaved: Gender differences in the efficacy of two counselling programmes. *British Journal of Clinical Psychology*, 36: 63–72.

6. McQueeney, D. A., Stanton, A. L., and Sigmon, S. (1997). Efficacy of emotion-focused and problem-focused group therapies for women with fertility problems. *Journal of Behavioral Medicine*, 20: 313–31.

7. Lynn's story was profiled by the *Los Angeles Times:* Foreman, J. (2006, January 16). "The mystery that is mourning." *Los Angeles Times*, F4.

8. Tennen, H., and Affleck, G. (1999). Finding benefits in adversity. In Snyder, C. R., (ed.). *Coping: The Psychology of What Works* (pp. 279–304). New York: Oxford University Press.

9. Nolen-Hoeksema, S., and Davis, C. G. (2002). Positive responses to loss: Perceiving benefits and growth. In Snyder and Lopez, op. cit., 598–606. New York: Oxford University Press.

10. Taylor, S. E., Lichtman, R. R., and Wood, J. V. (1984). Attributions, beliefs about control, and adjustment to breast cancer. *Journal of Personality and Social Psychology*, 46: 489–502. See also Collins, R. L., Taylor, S. E., and Skokan, L. A. (1990). A better world or a shattered vision?: Changes in life perspectives following victimization. *Social Cognition*, 8: 263–85.

11. For a review, see Taylor, S. E., and Armor, D. A. (1996). Positive illusions and coping with adversity. *Journal of Personality*, 64: 873–98.

12. The quotes in this subsection are from bereaved participants in a study reported in Davis, C. G., Nolen-Hoeksema, S., and Larson, J. (1998). Making sense of loss and benefiting from the experience: Two construals of meaning. *Journal of Personality and Social Psychology*, 75: 561–74.

13. Shearer, L. (2001, September). When the friendly skies are not so friendly. *Georgia Magazine*, 80.

14. Affleck, G., Tennen, H., Croog, S., and Levine, S. (1987). Causal attributions, perceived benefits, and morbidity after a heart attack: An 8 year study. *Journal of Consulting and Clinical Psychology*, 55: 29–35.

15. Nolen-Hoeksema and Davis (2002), op. cit., 602.

16. Tedeschi, R. G., and Calhoun, L. G. (1995). *Trauma and transformation: Growing in the Aftermath of Suffering.* Thousand Oaks, CA: Sage. O'Leary, V. E., and

Ickovics, J. R. (1995). Resilience and thriving in response to challenge: An opportunity for a paradigm shift in women's health. *Women's Health: Research on Gender, Behavior, and Policy,* 1: 121–42.

17. There are many good descriptions of this work, but a particularly good reference is Tedeschi, R. G., and Calhoun, L. G. (2004). Posttraumatic growth: Conceptual foundations and empirical evidence. *Psychological Inquiry,* 15: 1–18.

18. O'Leary & Ickovics (1995), op. cit.

19. Ibid.

20. Langer, L. L. (1990). *Holocaust Testimonies: The Ruins of Memory.* New Haven: Yale University Press, p. 59. Quoted in O'Leary and Ickovics (1995), op. cit.

21. Engh, A. L., Beehner, J. C., Bergman, T. J., Whitten, P. L., Hoffmeier, R. R., Seyfarth, R. M., and Cheney, D. L. (2006) Behavioural and hormonal responses to predation in female chacma baboons (*Papio hamadryas ursinus*). *Proceedings of the Royal Society B,* 273: 707–12. Dreilinger, R. (2006, April). "No monkey, no cry." *Observer,* 12.

22. Pennebaker, J. W., and O'Heeron, R. C. (1984). Confiding in others and illness rate among spouses of suicide and accidental-death victims. *Journal of Abnormal Psychology,* 93: 473–76.

23. Levy, S. M., Herberman, R. B., Whiteside, T., Sanzo, K., Lee, J., and Kirkwood, J. (1990). Perceived social support and tumor estrogen/progesterone receptor status as predictors of natural killer cell activity in breast cancer patients. *Psychosomatic Medicine,* 52: 73–85. See also Kiecolt-Glaser, J. K., Dura, J. R., Speicher, C. E., Trask, O. J., and Glaser, R. (1991). Spousal caregivers of dementia victims: Longitudinal changes in immunity and health. *Psychosomatic Medicine,* 53: 345–62.

24. Spiegel, D., Bloom, J. R., Kraemer, H. C., and Gottheil, E. (1989). Effect of psychosocial treatment on survival of patients with metastatic breast cancer. *Lancet,* 2: 888–91.

25. Gilligan, C. (1982). *In a Different Voice: Psychological Theory and Women's Development.* Cambridge, MA: Harvard University Press.

26. Rook, K. S. (1984). The negative side of social interaction: Impact on psychological well-being. *Journal of Personality and Social Psychology,* 46: 1097–1108. Windholz, M. J., Marmar, C. R., and Horowitz, M. J. (1985). A

review of the research on conjugal bereavement: Impact on health and efficacy of intervention. *Comprehensive Psychiatry,* 26: 433–47.

27. Janoff-Bulman, R. (1992). *Shattered Assumptions: Towards a New Psychology of Trauma.* New York: Free Press.

28. Lerner, M. J. (1980). *The Belief in a Just World.* New York: Plenum.

29. Quotes are from Davis et al. (1998), op. cit.

30. Ibid.

31. Bower, J. E., Kemeny, M. E., Taylor, S. E., and Fahey, J. L. (1998). Cognitive processing, discovery of meaning, CD4 decline, and AIDS-related mortality among bereaved HIV-seropositive men. *Journal of Consulting and Clinical Psychology,* 66: 979–86.

32. A wonderfully readable summary of this work is in Pennebaker, J. W. (1997). *Opening Up: The Healing Power of Expressing Emotions.* New York: Guilford.

33. For reviews, see Pennebaker, J. W. (1997). Writing about emotional experiences as a therapeutic process. *Psychological Science,* 8: 162–66. Frattaroli, J. (2006). Experimental disclosure and its moderators: A meta-analysis. *Psychological Bulletin,* 132: 823–65.

34. Pennebaker, J. W., Mayne, T. J., and Francis, M. E. (1997). Linguistic predictors of adaptive bereavement. *Journal of Personality and Social Psychology,* 72: 863–71.

35. Pennebaker, J. W., and Seagal, J. D. (1999). Forming a story: The health benefits of narrative. *Journal of Clinical Psychology,* 55: 1243–54. Quote appears on p. 1244.

36. Seligman (1990), op. cit.

37. McCullough, M. E., and Witvliet, C. V. (2002). The psychology of forgiveness. In Snyder and Lopez, op. cit., 446–58.

38. McCullough, M. E., Pargament, K. I., and Thoresen, C. T. (eds.). (2000). *Forgiveness: Theory, Research, and Practice.* New York: Guilford.

39. McCullough, M. E., Rachal, K. C., Sandage, S. J., Worthington, E. L., Jr., Brown, S. W., and Hight, T. L. (1998). Interpersonal forgiving in close relationships. II. Theoretical elaboration and measurement. *Journal of Personality and Social Psychology,* 75: 1586–1603.

40. For excellent reviews of this research, see McCullough and Witvliet (2002), op. cit., and McCullough, M. E. (2001). Forgiveness: Who does it and how do they do it? *Current Directions in Psychological Science,* 10: 194–97.

41. Hebl, J. H., and Enright, R. D. (1993). Forgiveness as a psychotherapeutic goal with elderly females. *Psychotherapy: Theory, Research, Practice, Training,* 30: 658–67.

42. Worthington, E. L., Jr., Sandage, S. J., and Berry, J. W. (2000). Group interventions to promote forgiveness: What researchers and clinicians ought to know. In McCullough, M. E., Pargament, K. I., and Thoresen, C. T. (eds.). *Forgiveness: Theory, Research, and Practice* (pp. 228–53). New York: Guilford. Harris, A. H. S., and Thoresen, C. E. (2006). Extending the influence of positive psychology interventions into health care settings: Lessons from self-efficacy and forgiveness. *Journal of Positive Psychology,* 1: 27–36.

43. Karremans, J. C., Van Lange, P. A. M., and Holland, R. W. (2005). Forgiveness and its associations with prosocial thinking, feeling, and doing beyond the relationship with the offender. *Personality and Social Psychology Bulletin,* 31: 1315–26.

44. This exercise is adapted from one developed by Martin Seligman and Tracy Steen.

45. Witvliet, C. V., Ludwig, T. E., and Vander Laan, K. L. (2001). Granting forgiveness or harboring grudges: Implications for emotion, physiology, and health. *Psychological Science,* 12: 117–23.

46. See http://www.forgivenessday.org/hero.htm for examples of such "heroes of forgiveness," including both famous individuals and extraordinary ordinary people.

47. McCullough, M. E., Worthington, E. L., and Rachal, K. C. (1997). Interpersonal forgiving in close relationships. *Journal of Personality and Social Psychology,* 73: 321–36.

48. Shapiro, D. L. (1991). The effects of explanations on negative reactions to deceit. *Administrative Science Quarterly,* 36: 614–30.

49. McCullough et al. (1997), op. cit., McCullough et al. (1998), op. cit.

50. McCullough, M. E., Bellah, C. G., Kilpatrick, S. D., and Johnson, J. L. (2001). Vengefulness: Relationships with forgiveness, rumination, well-being, and the Big Five. *Personality and Social Psychology Bulletin,* 27: 601–10.

51. Remnick, D. (2006, September 18). The wanderer. *New Yorker.*

## Chapter 7: Living in the Present

1. Gregory, A. (2005, March 21). "(Man at work thinking about golf, golfing thinking about sex, having sex, thinking about work.)" *New Yorker.*
2. The best treatment of flow, in my opinion, is in Csikszentmihalyi, M. (1990). *Flow: The Psychology of Optimal Experience.* New York: Harper & Row.
3. Nakamura, J., and Csikszentmihalyi, M. (2002). The concept of flow. In Snyder, and Lopez, op. cit., 89–105.
4. Csikszentmihalyi, M., Rathunde, K., and Whalen, S. (1993). *Talented Teenagers.* Cambridge, UK: Cambridge University Press.
5. Csikszentmihalyi (1990), op. cit., 10.
6. LeFevre, J. (1988). Flow and the quality of experience during work and leisure. In Csikszentmihalyi, M., and Csikszentmihalyi, I. (eds.). *Optimal Experience* (pp. 307–18). New York: Cambridge University Press.
7. Csikszentmihalyi, M. (2000). *Beyond Boredom and Anxiety.* San Francisco: Jossey-Bass. (Original work published in 1975.)
8. This exercise was developed by Marty Seligman and Tracy Steen.
9. Wrzesniewski, A., McCauley, C., Rozin, P., and Schwartz, B. (1997). Jobs, careers, and callings: People's relations to their work. *Journal of Research in Personality,* 31: 21–33.
10. Wrzesniewski, A., and Dutton, J. E. (2001). Crafting a job: Revisioning employees as active crafters of their work. *Academy of Management Review,* 26: 179–201.
11. In addition, some people find flow in vandalism, physical violence, or exerting tyrannical control over a group, an organization, or a nation. Others experience flow while risk taking in reckless driving, gambling, shoplifting, or committing fraud. Therein lies another potential negative side of flow. Although these activities might make you feel joyful and self-possessed in the short term, the long-term costs are very high, and the happiness will not endure. Use good judgment.
12. David Lodge coined a wonderful term for this phenomenon: *future nostalgia.*
13. Fred Bryant and Joseph Veroff were the first to study and describe the phenomenon of savoring. For an updated and accessible overview, see Bryant, F. B., and Veroff, J. (2006). *Savoring: A New Model of Positive Experience.* Mahwah, NJ: Erlbaum. Their work is also described in the following papers: Bryant,

F. B. (1989). A four-factor model of perceived control: Avoiding, coping, obtaining, and savoring. *Journal of Personality,* 57: 773–97. Bryant, F. B. (2003). Savoring beliefs inventory (SBI): A scale for measuring beliefs about savoring. *Journal of Mental Health,* 12: 175–96.

14. Bryant (2003), op. cit.
15. Ibid.
16. Seligman, M. E. P., Rashid, T., and Parks, A. C. (2006). Positive psychotherapy. *American Psychologist,* 61: 774–88.
17. Schueller (2006), op. cit.
18. Attributed to Robert Brault.
19. Pasupathi, M., and Carstensen, L. L. (2003). Age and emotional experience during mutual reminiscing. *Psychology and Aging,* 18: 430–42.
20. Havighurst, R. J., and Glasser, R. (1972). An exploratory study of reminiscence. *Journal of Gerontology,* 27: 245–53.
21. Bryant, F. B., Smart, C. M., and King, S. P. (2005). Using the past to enhance the present: Boosting happiness through positive reminiscence. *Journal of Happiness Studies,* 6: 227–60.
22. Bryant et al. (2005), op. cit.
23. Ibid, 237.
24. Humphrey Bogart says this to Ingrid Bergman in the last scene of *Casablanca,* before she boards a plane to Lisbon, never to see him again.
25. Lyubomirsky, Sousa, et al. (2006), op. cit.
26. Langston, C. A. (1994). Capitalizing on and coping with daily-life events: Expressive responses to positive events. *Journal of Personality and Social Psychology,* 67: 1112–25. See also Gable et al. (2004), op. cit.
27. Bryant and Veroff (2006), op. cit.
28. Haidt, J., and Keltner, D. (2004). Appreciation of beauty and excellence [Awe, Wonder, Elevation]. In Peterson, C., and Seligman, M.E.P. (eds.). *Character Strengths and Virtues: A Handbook and Classification* (pp. 537–51). Washington, DC: American Psychological Association.
29. This wonderful example was cited by Haidt and Keltner (2004), op. cit., 537.
30. Brown, K. W., and Ryan, R. M. (2003). The benefits of being present: Mindfulness and its role in psychological well-being. *Journal of Personality and Social Psychology,* 84: 822–48.

31. James, W. (1924). *Memories and Studies.* New York: Longmans, Green, & Co. (Original work published in 1911.)

32. Jon Kabat-Zinn, founder of the Stress Reduction Clinic at the University of Massachusetts Medical Center, has been a pioneer in this field. For an overview of these studies, see Kabat-Zinn, J. (2005). *Full Catastrophe Living: Using the Wisdom of Your Body and Mind to Face Stress, Pain, and Illness,* 15th anniversary ed. New York: Bantam Dell.

33. Bryant and Veroff (2006), op. cit.

34. LeBel, J. L., and Dubé, L. (2001, June). The impact of sensory knowledge and attentional focus on pleasure and on behavioral responses to hedonic stimuli. Paper presented at the thirteenth annual American Psychological Society Convention, Toronto.

35. This story is quoted in Kubovy, M. (1999). On the pleasures of the mind. In Kahneman, Diener, and Schwarz, op. cit., pp. 134–54.

36. This idea was suggested by social psychologist Jaime Kurtz.

37. Kurtz, J. L., and Wilson, T. D. (2007). "Looking to the future to appreciate the present: The function of bittersweet emotions." Manuscript in preparation.

38. Boehm, J. K., Dickerhoof, R., and Lyubomirsky, S. (2007). "Endowing versus contrasting life events: The relationship between thought perspective and well-being." Unpublished data, Department of Psychology, University of California, Riverside.

39. Attributed to Jim Holliday. Caen, H. (1975, April 15). [Editorial]. *San Francisco Chronicle.*

40. Wildschut, T., Sedikides, C., Arndt, J., and Routledge, C. (2006). Nostalgia: Content, triggers, functions. *Journal of Personality and Social Psychology,* 91: 975–93.

41. Lyubomirsky, Sousa, et al. (2006), op. cit.

42. Epel, E. S., Bandura, A., and Zimbardo, P. G. (1999). Escaping homelessness: The influences of self-efficacy and time perspective on coping with homelessness. *Journal of Applied Social Psychology,* 29: 575–96.

43. Kessler, L. (2004, August 22). Dancing with Rose: A strangely beautiful encounter with Alzheimer's patients provides insights that challenge the way we view the disease. *Los Angeles Times Magazine,* 29.

44. For reviews, see Zimbardo, P. G., and Boyd, J. N. (1998). Putting time in perspective: A valid, reliable individual-difference metric. *Journal of Personality and Social Psychology,* 77: 1271–88. Boyd, J. N., and Zimbardo, P. G. (2005). Time perspective, health, and risk taking. In Strathman, A., and Joireman, J. (eds.). *Understanding Behavior in the Context of Time: Theory, Research, and Application* (pp. 85–107). Mahwah, NJ: Erlbaum.

45. For evidence that people are capable of doing both—that is, living in the present and being oriented toward the future—see Liu, W., and Aaker, J. (2007). Do you look to the future or focus on today?: The impact of life experience on intertemporal decisions. *Organizational Behavior and Human Decision Processes,* 102: 212–25.

46. The quote is from former president Bill Clinton. Remnick (2006, September 18), op. cit., 53.

## Chapter 8: Happiness Activity No. 10: Committing to Your Goals

1. Wolfe, W. B. (2001). *How to Be Happy Though Human.* London: Routledge. (Original work published in 1932.)

2. For a review, see Cantor, N., and Sanderson, C. A. (1999). Life task participation and well-being: The importance of taking part in daily life. In Kahneman, Diener, and Schwarz, op. cit., 230–43.

3. Brunstein, J. C. (1993). Personal goals and subjective well-being: A longitudinal study. *Journal of Personality and Social Psychology,* 65: 1061–70.

4. Swed, M. (2004, June 7). At Disney, a soaring tribute; Esa-Pekka Salonen's "Wing on Wing" is a stirringly heartfelt work honoring Frank Gehry. *Los Angeles Times,* E1.

5. Cantor, N. (1990). From thought to behavior: "Having" and "doing" in the study of personality and cognition. *American Psychologist,* 45: 735–50.

6. For a review, see Ryan, R. M., and Deci, E. L. (2000). Self-determination theory and the facilitation of intrinsic motivation, social development, and well-being. *American Psychologist,* 55: 68–78.

7. Kasser, T., and Ryan, R. M. (1993). A dark side of the American dream: Correlates of financial success as a central life aspiration. *Journal of Personality and Social Psychology,* 65: 410–22. Kasser, T., and Ryan, R. M. (1996). Further examining the American dream: Differential correlates of intrinsic and extrin-

sic goals. *Personality and Social Psychology Bulletin,* 22: 280–87. Sheldon, K. M., and Kasser, T. (1995). Coherence and congruence: Two aspects of personality integration. *Journal of Personality and Social Psychology,* 68: 531–43.

8. For two excellent reviews, see Sheldon, K. M. (2002). The self-concordance model of healthy goal-striving: When personal goals correctly represent the person. In Deci, E. L., and Ryan, R. M. (eds.). *Handbook of self-determination theory* (pp. 65–86). Rochester, NY: University of Rochester Press. Sheldon, K. M., and Elliot, A. J. (1999). Goal striving, need satisfaction, and longitudinal well-being: The self-concordance model. *Journal of Personality and Social Psychology,* 76: 546–57.

9. Elliot, A. J., and Sheldon, K. M. (1998). Avoidance personal goals and the personality-illness relationship. *Journal of Personality and Social Psychology,* 75: 1282–99. Elliot, A. J., Sheldon, K. M., and Church, M. A. (1997). Avoidance personal goals and subjective well-being. *Personality and Social Psychology Bulletin,* 23: 915–27.

10. Elliot, A. J., and McGregor, H. A. (2001). A 2 × 2 achievement goal framework. *Journal of Personality and Social Psychology,* 80: 501–19.

11. Strachman, A., and Gable, S. L. (2006). What you want (and do not want) affects what you see (and do not see): Avoidance social goals and social events. *Personality and Social Psychology Bulletin,* 32: 1446–58.

12. This phenomenon is essentially what happens in a rebound effect, when you are trying so hard *not* to think about or do something that you end up thinking or doing it. For a review, see Wegner, D. M. (1994). Ironic processes of mental control. *Psychological Review,* 101: 34–52.

13. Sheldon and Kasser (1995), op. cit. Emmons, R. A., and King, L. A. (1988). Conflict among personal strivings: Immediate and long-term implications for psychological and physical well-being. *Journal of Personality and Social Psychology,* 54: 1040–48.

14. Cantor and Sanderson (1999), op. cit.

15. Carstensen, L. L., Isaacowitz, D. M., and Charles, S. T. (1999). Taking time seriously: A theory of socioemotional selectivity. *American Psychologist,* 54: 165–81.

16. Fredrickson, B. L., and Carstensen, L. L. (1990). Choosing social partners: How old age and anticipated endings make people more selective. *Psychology and Aging,* 5: 335–47.

17. Sheldon, K. M., and Lyubomirsky, S. (2006b). Achieving sustainable gains in happiness: Change your actions, not your circumstances. *Journal of Happiness Studies,* 7: 55–86.

18. The instructions for this task are adapted from Kaiser, R. T., and Ozer, D. J. (1997). Emotional stability and goal-related stress. *Personality and Individual Differences,* 22: 371–79.

19. Kahneman, D., Krueger, A. B., Schkade, D., Schwarz, N., and Stone, A. A. (2004). A survey method for characterizing daily life experience: The Day Reconstruction Method. *Science,* 306: 1776–80.

20. Csikszentmihalyi et al. (1993), op. cit.

21. These suggestions were adapted from two exercises developed by Martin Seligman and Tracy Steen.

22. Quote by Robert Peter Tristram Coffin.

23. Sheldon, K. M., Kasser, T., Smith, K., and Share, T. (2002). Personal goals and psychological growth: Testing an intervention to enhance goal attainment and personality integration. *Journal of Personality,* 70: 5–31.

24. Bearman, P. S., and Brückner, H. (2001). Promising the future: Virginity pledges and first intercourse. *American Journal of Sociology,* 106: 859–912.

25. Greenwald, A. G., Carnot, C. G., Beach, R., and Young, B. (1987). Increasing voting behavior by asking people if they expect to vote. *Journal of Applied Psychology,* 72: 315–18.

26. Norcross, J. C., Mrykalo, M. S., and Blagys, M. D. (2002). Auld Lang Syne: Success predictors, change processes, and self-reported outcomes of New Year's resolvers and nonresolvers. *Journal of Clinical Psychology,* 58: 397–405. See also Brunstein (1993), op. cit.

27. Norcross, J. C., Ratzin, A. C., and Payne, D. (1989). Ringing in the New Year: The change processes and reported outcomes of resolutions. *Addictive Behaviors,* 14: 205–12.

28. For an excellent review, see David Myer's social psychology textbook: Myers, D. G. (2005). *Social Psychology.* New York: McGraw-Hill.

29. Sheldon and Houser-Marko (2001), op. cit.

30. Norcross, J. C., and Vangarelli, D. J. (1989). The resolution solution: Longitudinal examination of New Year's change attempts. *Journal of Substance Abuse,* 1: 127–34.

31. Brandtstädter, J., and Renner, G. (1990). Tenacious goal pursuit and flexible goal adjustment: Explication and age-related analysis of assimilative and accommodative strategies of coping. *Psychology and Aging,* 5: 58–67.

32. Heckhausen, J., and Schulz, R. (1995). A life-span theory of control. *Psychological Review,* 102: 284–304.

33. Lepper, M. R., Greene, D., and Nisbett, R. E. (1973). Undermining children's intrinsic interest with extrinsic reward: A test of the "overjustification" hypothesis. *Journal of Personality and Social Psychology,* 28: 129–37.

34. Gollwitzer, P. M. (1999). Implementation intentions. *American Psychologist,* 54: 493–503.

35. Dubé, M., Lapierre, S., Bouffard, L., and Alain, M. (in press). Impact of a personal goals management program on the subjective well-being of young retirees. *European Review of Applied Psychology.* For a similar study that confirmed these findings, see Green, L. S., Oades, L. G., and Grant, A. M. (2006). Cognitive-behavioral, solution-focused life coaching: Enhancing goal striving, well-being, and hope. *The Journal of Positive Psychology,* 1: 142–49.

36. Dubé et al., op. cit., The case study of Mrs. M is presented on pp. 17–20.

## Chapter 9: Taking Care of Your Body and Your Soul

1. For an excellent review, see Ellison, C. G., and Levin, J. S. (1998). The religion-health connection: Evidence, theory, and future directions. *Health Education and Behavior,* 25: 700–20. Another very readable review is Myers (2000), op. cit.

2. McIntosh, D. N., Silver, R. C., and Wortman, C. B. (1993). Religion's role in adjustment to a negative life event: Coping with the loss of a child. *Journal of Personality and Social Psychology,* 65: 812–21.

3. Examples of studies showing that religion is related to superior health include Oman, D., and Reed, D. (1998). Religion and mortality among the community dwelling elderly. *American Journal of Public Health,* 88: 1469–75. Koenig, H. G., Hays, J. C., George, L. K., Blazer, D. G., Larson, D. B., and Landerman, L. R. (1997). Modeling the cross-sectional relationships between religion, physical health, social support, and depressive symptoms.

*American Journal of Geriatric Psychology,* 5: 131–44. Oxman, T. E., Freeman, D. H., and Manheimer, E. D. (1995). Lack of social participation or religious strength and comfort as risk factors for death after cardiac surgery in the elderly. *Psychosomatic Medicine,* 57: 5–15. Strawbridge, W. J., Cohen, R. D., Shema, S. J., and Kaplan, G. A. (1997). Frequent attendance at religious services and mortality over 28 years. *American Journal of Public Health,* 87: 957–61.

4. Oxman et al. (1995), op. cit.

5. Koenig et al. (1997), op. cit.

6. Ellison and Levin (1998), op. cit.

7. This finding comes from analyses of National Opinion Research Center General Social Survey data. Myers (2000), op. cit.

8. Ellison and Levin (1998), op. cit.

9. Pollner, M. (1989). Divine relations, social relations, and well-being. *Journal of Health and Social Behavior,* 30: 92–104.

10. Koenig, H. G., George, L. K., and Siegler, I. C. (1988). The use of religion and other emotion-regulating coping strategies among older adults. *Gerontologist,* 28: 303–10.

11. Quoted in Pargament, K. I., and Mahoney, A. (2002). Spirituality: Discovering and conserving the sacred. In Snyder and Lopez, op. cit., pp. 646–59.

12. Jenkins, R. A., and Pargament, K. I. (1988). Cognitive appraisals in cancer patients. *Social Science and Medicine,* 26: 625–33.

13. Baumeister, R. F. (1991). *Meanings of Life.* New York: Guilford.

14. McCullough, M. E., and Worthington, E. L. (1999). Religion and the forgiving personality. *Journal of Personality,* 67: 1141–64.

15. Vaillant, G. E. (in press). *Spiritual Evolution: A Scientific Defense of Faith.* New York, Broadway Books.

16. Saucier, G. and Skrzypińska, K. (2006). Spiritual but not religious? Evidence for two independent dispositions. *Journal of Personality,* 74: 1257–92.

17. Pargament, K. I. (1999). The psychology of religion and spirituality?: Yes and no. *International Journal for the Psychology of Religion,* 9: 3–16.

18. Pargament and Mahoney (2002), op. cit.

19. Pollner, M. (1989). Divine relations, social relations, and well-being. *Journal of Health and Social Behavior,* 30: 92–104.

20. Pargament and Mahoney (2002), op. cit.

21. Poloma, M. M., and Gallup, G. H., Jr. (1991). *Varieties of Prayer: A Survey Report*. Philadelphia: Trinity Press International.

22. For a review of this research, see Compton, W. C. (2004). Religion, spirituality, and well-being. In *An Introduction to Positive Psychology* (pp. 196–216). Belmont, CA: Wadsworth.

23. Freud, S. (1964). *The Future of an Illusion*. Garden City, NY: Doubleday, p. 71. (Original work published in 1928).

24. For example, see Klonoff, E. A., and Landrine, H. (1996). Belief in the healing power of prayer: Prevalence and health correlates for African-Americans. *Western Journal of Black Studies,* 20: 207–10.

25. For example, see Koenig, H. G., Pargament, K. I., and Nielsen, J. (1998). Religious coping and health status in medically ill hospitalized older adults. *Journal of Mental and Nervous Disease,* 186: 513–21.

26. Glock, C. Y., and Stark, R. (1966). *Christian Beliefs and Anti-Semitism*. New York: Harper & Row.

27. Altemeyer, B., and Hunsberger, B. (1992). Authoritarianism, religious fundamentalism, quest, and prejudice. *International Journal for the Psychology of Religion,* 2: 113–33.

28. Compton (2004), op. cit.

29. Blanton, D. (2005, December 1). 12/01/05 FOX poll: Courts driving religion out of public life; Christianity under attack. Retrieved June 26, 2006, from the World Wide Web: http://www.foxnews.com/story/0,2933,177355,00. html.

30. Hoge, D. R. (1996). Religion in America: The demographics of belief and affiliation. In Shafranske, E. P., (ed.). *Religion and the Clinical Practice of Psychology* (pp. 21–42). Washington, DC: American Psychological Association. Johnson, B., Bader, C., Dougherty, K., Froese, P., Stark, R., Mencken, C., and Park, J. (2006, September 11). Losing my religion? No, says Baylor religion survey. Retrieved September 16, 2006, from the World Wide Web: http://www.baylor.edu/pr/news.php?action=story& story=41678.

31. Shapiro, S. L., Schwartz, G. E. R., and Santerre, C. (2002). Meditation and positive psychology. In Snyder and Lopez, op. cit., 632–45.

32. Kabat-Zinn, J. (1990). *Full Catastrophe Living*. New York: Delacorte Press.

33. Many of these studies, described in this section, are well reviewed in Shapiro et al. (2002), op. cit.

34. Davidson, R. J., Kabat-Zinn, J., Schumacher, J., Rosenkranz, M., Muller, D., Santorelli, S. F., Urbanowaki, F., Harrington, A., Bonus, K., and Sheridan, J. F. (2003). Alterations in brain and immune function produced by mindfulness meditation. *Psychosomatic Medicine,* 65: 564–70.

35. Smith, W. P., Compton, W. C., and West, W. B. (1995). Meditation as an adjunct to a happiness enhancement program. *Journal of Clinical Psychology,* 51: 269–73.

36. See also a study that found that a sixteen-week training program in Transcendental Meditation led to improved blood pressure, insulin resistance, and the reduction of other risk factors for coronary heart disease: Paul-Labrador, M., Polk, D., Dwyer, J. H., Velasquez, I., Nidich, S., Rainforth, M., Schneider, R., and Merz, N. B. (2006). Effects of a randomized controlled trial of transcendental meditation on components of the metabolic syndrome in subjects with coronary heart disease. *Archives of Internal Medicine,* 166: 1218–24.

37. Fredrickson, B. L., Cohn, M. A., Coffey, K. A., Pek, J., and Finkel, S. (2007). Open hearts build lives: Positive emotions, induced through meditation, build consequential personal resources. Manuscript under review.

38. Blumenthal, J. A., Babyak, M. A., Moore, K. A., Craighead, E., Herman, S., Khatri, P., Waugh, R., Napolitano, M. A., Forman, L. M., Appelbaum, M., Doraiswamy, P. M., and Krishnan, K. R. (1999). Effects of exercise training on older patients with major depression. *Archives of Internal Medicine,* 159: 2349–56.

39. Babyak, M. A., Blumenthal, J. A., Herman, S., Khatri, P., Doraiswamy, M., Moore, K., Craighead, W. E., Baldewicz, T. T., and Krishnan, K. R. (2000). Exercise treatment for major depression: Maintenance of therapeutic benefit at 10 months. *Psychosomatic Medicine,* 62: 633–38.

40. See numerous sources, including Biddle, S. J. H., Fox, K. R., and Boutcher, S. H. (eds.). (2000). *Physical Activity and Psychological Well-being.* London: Routledge. Kahn, E. B., Ramsey, L. T., Brownson, R. C., Heath, G. W., Howze, E. H., and Powell, K. E., Stone, E. J., Rajab, M. W., Corso, P., and the Task Force on Community Preventive Services (2002). The effectiveness of interventions to increase physical activity: A systematic review. *American Journal of Preventive Medicine,* 22: 73–107. Centers for Disease Control and Prevention. (1999, November 17). Physical activity and health: A report of

the surgeon general. Retrieved June 27, 2006, from the World Wide Web: http://www.cdc.gov/nccdphp/sgr/sgr.htm.

41. Motl, R. W., Konopack, J. F., McAuley, E., Elavsky, S. Jerome, G. J., and Marquez, D. X. (2005). Depressive symptoms among older adults: Long-term reduction after a physical activity intervention. *Journal of Behavioral Medicine,* 28: 385–94.

42. Thayer, R. E., Newman, J. R., and McClain, T. M. (1994). Self-regulation of mood: Strategies for changing a bad mood, raising energy, and reducing tension. *Journal of Personality and Social Psychology,* 67: 910–25. Biddle, S. J. H. (2000). Emotion, mood, and physical activity. In Biddle, S. J. H., Fox, K. R., and Boutcher, S. H. (eds.). *Physical Activity and Psychological Well-being* (pp. 63–87). London: Routledge.

43. Bahrke, M. S., and Morgan, W. P. (1978). Anxiety reduction following exercise and meditation. *Cognitive Therapy and Research,* 2: 323–33. Harte, J. L., Eifert, G. H., and Smith, R. (1995). The effects of running and meditation on beta-endorphin, corticotrophin-releasing hormone, and cortisol in plasma, and on mood. *Biological Psychology,* 40: 251–56.

44. Carter-Morris, P., and Faulkner, G. (2003). A football project for service users: The role of football in reducing social exclusion. *Journal of Mental Health Promotion,* 2: 24–30. (Quote on p. 27.)

45. Meeusen, R., and De Meirleir, K. (1995). Exercise and brain neurotransmission. *Sports Medicine,* 20: 160–88.

46. Biddle, S. J. H., and Ekkekakis, P. (2006). Physically active lifestyles and well-being. In Huppert, F. A., Baylis, N., and Keverne, B. (eds.). *The Science of Well-being* (pp. 141–68). New York: Oxford University Press.

47. Mutrie, N., and Faulkner, G. (2004). Physical activity: Positive psychology in motion. In Linley, A., and Joseph, S. (eds.). *Positive Psychology in Practice* (pp. 146–64). Hoboken, NJ: John Wiley. Quotation on p. 146.

48. To measure your heart rate during exercise without disrupting your workout too much, stop what you're doing and take a six-second pulse in your wrist or neck—that is, count the number of times you feel a pulse during a precise six-second period. Multiply by ten and you have your heart rate. To increase accuracy, use a longer time period—for example, take a ten-second pulse (then multiply by six) or a thirty-second pulse (then multiply by two).

49. Bailey, C. (1994). *Smart Exercise.* New York: Houghton Mifflin.

50. Stanford University School of Medicine professor William Dement: Dement, W. C., and Vaughan, C. (2000). *The Promise of Sleep.* New York: Dell.

51. Lyubomirsky, King, et al. (2005), op. cit.

52. Darwin, C. R. (1896). *The Expression of Emotions in Man and Animals.* New York: Appleton. Quotation on p. 365.

53. Strack, F., Martin, L. L., and Stepper, S. (1988). Inhibiting and facilitating conditions of the human smile: A nonobtrusive test of the facial feedback hypothesis. *Journal of Personality and Social Psychology,* 54: 768–77.

54. Levenson, R. W., Ekman, P., and Friesen, W. V. (1990). Voluntary facial action generates emotion-specific autonomic nervous system activity. *Psychophysiology,* 27: 363–84.

55. Cole, J. (1998). *About Face.* Cambridge, MA: MIT Press. Quotation on p. 127.

56. Finzi, E., and Wasserman, E. (2006). Treatment of depression with botulinum toxin A: A case series. *Dermatologic Surgery,* 32: 645–50.

57. Fromm, E. (1956). *The Art of Loving.* New York: Harper & Row. Quotation on p. 49. The other findings described in this paragraph are reviewed in Lyubomirsky, King, et al. (2005), op. cit.

58. Keltner, D., and Bonanno, G. A. (1997). A study of laughter and dissociation: Distinct correlates of laughter and smiling during bereavement. *Journal of Personality and Social Psychology,* 73: 687–702.

59. Berk, L. S., Tan, S. A., and Westengard, J. (2006, April). Beta-Endorphin and HGH increase are associated with both the anticipation and experience of mirthful laughter. Paper presented at the annual Experimental Biology meeting, San Francisco.

## Chapter 10: The Five Hows Behind Sustainable Happiness

1. Diener, E., Sandvik, E., and Pavot, W. (1991). Happiness is the frequency, not the intensity, of positive versus negative affect. In Strack, F., Argyle, M., and Schwarz, N. (eds.). *Subjective Well-being: An Interdisciplinary Perspective* (pp. 119–39). Elmsford, NY: Pergamon. Urry, H. L., Nitschke, J. B., Dolski, I., Jackson, D. C., Dalton, K. M., Mueller, C. J., Rosenkranz, M. A., Ryff, C.

D., Singer, B. H., and Davidson, R. J. (2004). Making a life worth living: Neural correlates of well-being. *Psychological Science,* 15: 367–72.

2. Fredrickson (2001), op. cit.

3. Proust, M. (1982). *Remembrance of Things Past, Vol. 1: Swann's Way and Within a Budding Grove,* trans. C. K. S. Moncrieff and T. Kilmartin. New York: First Vintage. (Original work published 1913–1918.)

4. Davidson, R. J. (1993). The neuropsychology of emotion and affective style. In Lewis, M., and Haviland, J. M. (eds.). *Handbook of Emotion* (pp.143–54). New York: Guilford. Watson, D., Clark, L. A., and Carey, G. (1988). Positive and negative affectivity and their relations to anxiety and depressive disorders. *Journal of Abnormal Psychology,* 97: 346–53.

5. MacLeod, A. K., Tata, P., Kentish, J., and Jacobsen, H. (1997). Retrospective and prospective cognitions in anxiety and depression. *Cognition and Emotion,* 11: 467–79. MacLeod, A. K., Pankhania, B., Lee, M., and Mitchell, D. (1997). Depression, hopelessness and future-directed thinking in parasuicide. *Psychological Medicine,* 27: 973–77. MacLeod, A. K., and Byrne, A. (1996). Anxiety, depression and the anticipation of future positive and negative experiences. *Journal of Abnormal Psychology,* 105: 286–89. For a review, see MacLeod, A. K., and Moore, R. (2000). Positive thinking revisited: Positive cognitions, well-being, and mental health. *Clinical Psychology and Psychotherapy,* 7: 1–10.

6. Joormann, J., Siemer, M., and Gotlib, I. H. (2006). Mood regulation in depression: Differential effects of distraction and recall of happy memories on sad mood. Manuscript under review.

7. Brown, G. W., Lemyre, L., and Bifulco, A. (1992). Social factors and recovery from anxiety and depressive disorders: A test of specificity. *British Journal of Psychiatry,* 161: 44–54. See also Taylor et al. (2006), op. cit.

8. Fredrickson, B. L., and Levenson, R. W. (1998). Positive emotions speed recovery from the cardiovascular sequelae of negative emotions. *Cognition and Emotion,* 12: 191–220. Fredrickson, B. L., Mancuso, R. A., Branigan, C., and Tugade, M. M. (2000). The undoing effect of positive emotions. *Motivation and Emotion,* 24: 237–58.

9. Fredrickson & Levenson (1998), op. cit.; Fredrickson et al. (2000), op. cit.

10. Dickerhoof (2007), op. cit.

11. Fredrickson (2001), op. cit. See also Ong, A. D., Bergeman, C. S., Bisconti, T. L., and Wallace, K. A. (2006). Psychological resilience, positive emotions, and successful adaptation to stress in later life. *Journal of Personality and Social Psychology,* 91: 730–49.

12. Namely, cognitive theory and hopelessness theory.

13. Dickerhoof (2007), op. cit.

14. Behavioral therapy, which aims at getting the depressed person to increase the number of pleasant experiences in his or her daily life, is a clear exception.

15. Keyes (2005), op. cit.

16. Lyubomirsky, King, et al. (2005), op. cit.

17. King, L. A., Hicks, J. A., Krull, J. L., and Del Gaiso, A. K. (2006). Positive affect and the experience of meaning in life. *Journal of Personality and Social Psychology,* 90: 179–96.

18. Lyubomirsky, Sheldon, et al. (2005), op. cit.

19. It's relevant here to consider the work of Leaf Van Boven at the University of Colorado, who has found that people are happier if they invest their money and resources in experiences (which of course include a wide variety of activities) rather than *possessions.* He posits three reasons for this: (1) Experiences, relative to material things, are more likely to improve with time; (2) people are less likely to compare unfavorably their experiences (as opposed to their possessions) with those of more fortunate others; and (3) experiences have more social value and are more likely to promote relationships. I would add a fourth benefit: Experiences (including activities) are relatively less prone to hedonic adaptation. For a review, see Van Boven, L. (2005). Experientialism, materialism, and the pursuit of happiness. *Review of General Psychology,* 9: 132–42.

20. Berlyne, D. (1970). Novelty, complexity, and hedonic value. *Perception and Psychophysics,* 8: 279–86. McAlister, L. (1982). A dynamic attribute satiation model of variety-seeking behavior. *Journal of Consumer Research,* 9: 141–50. Ratner, R. K., Kahn, B. E., and Kahneman, D. (1999). Choosing less-preferred experiences for the sake of variety. *Journal of Consumer Research,* 26: 1–15. Berns, G. (2005). *Satisfaction: The Science of Finding True Fulfillment.* New York: Henry Holt.

21. Tkach, 2005, op. cit.

22. Robert Jeffery, Division of Epidemiology and Community Health, University of Minnesota. Personal communication, July 17, 2006.

23. Eugenides, J. (2003). *Middlesex*. New York: Picador. Quotation is on p. 69.

24. Brown, G. W., and Harris, T. (1978). *Social Origins of Depression: A Study of Psychiatric Disorder in Women*. New York: Free Press.

25. Dubé et al. (in press), op. cit.

26. Gladwell, M. (2005, September 12). The cellular church: How Rick Warren's congregation grew. *New Yorker*.

27. Friedman, H. S. (2002). *Health Psychology*, 2nd ed. Upper Saddle River, NJ: Prentice Hall.

28. Caplan, R. D., Robinson, E.A.R., French, J.R.P., Jr., Caldwell, J. R., and Shinn, M. (1976). *Adhering to Medical Regimens: Pilot Experiments in Patient Education and Social Support*. Ann Arbor: Research Center for Group Dynamics, Institute for Social Research, University of Michigan.

29. Norcross & Vangarelli (1989), op. cit.

30. Wing, R. R., and Jeffery, R. W. (1999). Benefits of recruiting participants with friends and increasing social support for weight loss and maintenance. *Journal of Consulting and Clinical Psychology*, 67: 132–38.

31. Dickerhoof (2007), op. cit.

32. Sheldon and Lyubomirsky (2006a), op. cit.

33. Seligman et al. (2005), op. cit.; Sheldon and Lyubomirsky (2006a), op. cit.

34. Attributed to seventeenth-century scholar and mathematician Isaac Barrow: "Nothing of worth or weight can be achieved with half a mind, with a faint heart, and with a lame endeavor."

35. Oishi, S., Diener, E., and Lucas, R. E. (in press). Optimum level of well-being: Can people be too happy? *Perspectives in Psychological Science*.

36. Lyubomirsky, King, et al. (2005), op. cit.; Fredrickson (2001), op. cit.

37. For example, Wood, W., Tam, L., and Witt, M. G. (2005). Changing circumstances, disrupting habits. *Journal of Personality and Social Psychology*, 88: 918–33. For a review of the psychological literature on habits, see Neal, D. T., Wood, W., and Quinn, J. M. (2006). Habits: A repeat performance. *Current Directions in Psychological Science*, 15: 198–202.

38. Shiffrin, R. M., and Schneider, W. (1977). Controlled and automatic human information processing: II. Perceptual learning, automatic attending and a general theory. *Psychological Review*, 84: 127–90.

39. Centers for Disease Control. (1993). Smoking cessation during previous year among adults—United States, 1990 and 1991. *MMWR,* 42: 504–7. McGuire, M., Wing, R., and Hill, J. (1999). The prevalence of weight loss maintenance among American adults. *International Journal of Obesity,* 23: 1314–19. Kassirer, J., and Angell, M. (1998). Losing weight: An ill-fated New Year's resolution. *New England Journal of Medicine,* 338: 52–54.

40. Schachter, S. (1982). Recidivism and self-cure of smoking and obesity. *American Psychologist,* 37: 436–44.

41. Klem et al. (1997), op. cit.

## Postscript: If You Are Depressed

1. American Psychiatric Association. (2000). *Diagnostic and Statistical Manual of Mental Disorders,* 4th ed., text rev. Washington, DC: American Psychiatric Association.

2. Kessler, R. C. (2005, August). Population perspectives on the epidemiology and use of services for behavioral health disorders. Paper presented at the annual convention of the American Psychological Association, Washington, DC.

3. Schatzberg, A. F. (2000). New indications for antidepressants. *Journal of Clinical Psychiatry,* 61: 9–17.

4. Kessler, R. C., Michelson, K. D., Barber, C. B., and Wang, P. (2001). The association between chronic medical conditions and work impairment. In Rossi, A. S. (ed.). *Caring and Doing for Others: Social Responsibility in the Domain of the Family, Work, and Community* (pp. 403–26). Chicago: University of Chicago Press.

5. Greenberg, P., Kessler, R. C., Nells, T., Finkelstein, S., and Berndt, E. R. (1996). Depression in the workplace: An economic perspective. In Feighner, J. P., and Boyer, W. F. (eds.). *Selective Serotonin Reuptake Inhibitors: Advances in Basic Research and Clinical Practice* (pp. 327–63). New York: John Wiley.

6. This is called the diathesis–stress model. Diathesis represents a genetic susceptibility or predisposition. Stress represents an environmental trigger or precipitating event.

7. Kendler, K., Neale, M., Kessler, R., Heath, A., and Eaves, L. (1992). Major depression and generalized anxiety disorder. *Archives of General Psychiatry,* 49: 716–22.

8. Sullivan, P. F., Neale, M. C., and Kendler, K. S. (2000). Genetic epidemiology of major depression: Review and meta-analysis. *American Journal of Psychiatry,* 157: 1552–62.

9. Thase, M. E., Jindal, R., & Howland, R. H. (2002). Biological aspects of depression. In Gotlib and Hammen, op. cit., 192–218. See also Carlson, P. J., Singh, J. B., Zarate, C. A., Drevets, W. C., and Manji, H. K. (2006). Neural circuitry and neuroplasticity in mood disorders: Insights for novel therapeutic targets. *Journal of the American Society for Experimental NeuroTherapeutics,* 3: 22–41.

10. Mayberg, H. S., Lozano, A. M., Voon, V., McNeeley, H. E., Seminowicz, D., Hamani, C., Schwalb, J. M., and Kennedy, S. H. (2005, March 3). Deep brain stimulation for treatment-resistant depression. *Neuron,* 45: 651–60.

11. Monroe, S. M., and Hadjiyannakis, K. (2002). The social environment and depression: Focusing on severe life stress. In Gotlib and Hammen, op. cit., 314–40.

12. Abramson, L. Y., Alloy, L. B., Hogan, M. E., Whitehouse, W. G., Donovan, P., Rose, D., Panzarella, C., and Raniere, D. (1999). Cognitive vulnerability to depression: Theory and evidence. *Journal of Cognitive Psychotherapy: An International Quarterly,* 13: 5–20. Alloy, L. B., Abramson, L. Y., Whitehouse, W. G., Hogan, M. E., Tashman, N., Steinberg, D., Rose, D. T., and Donovan, P. (1999). Depressogenic cognitive styles: Predictive validity, information processing and personality characteristics, and developmental origins. *Behaviour Research and Therapy,* 37: 503–31.

13. National Institute of Mental Health. Depression. Bethesda (MD): National Institute of Mental Health, National Institutes of Health, U.S. Department of Health and Human Services; 2002 [updated 2004]. (NIH Publication Number: 02-3561.) 25 pages. Available from: http://www.nimh.nih.gov/publicat/depression.cfm.

14. Nolen-Hoeksema, S. (2003). *Women Who Think Too Much.* New York: Henry Holt; Lyubomirsky and Tkach (2003), op. cit.

15. Hollon, S. D., Haman, K. L., and Brown, L. L. (2002). Cognitive-behavioral treatment of depression. In Gotlib and Hammen, op. cit., 383–403.

16. DiMascio, A., Weissman, M. M., Prusoff, B. A., Neu, C., Zwilling, M., and Klerman, G. L. (1979). Differential symptom reduction by drugs and psychotherapy in acute depression. *Archives of General Psychiatry,* 36: 1450–56. Weissman, M. M., Prusoff, B. A., DiMascio, A., Neu, C., Goklaney, M., and Klerman, G. L. (1979). The efficacy of drugs and psychotherapy in the treatment of acute depressive episodes. *American Journal of Psychiatry,* 136: 555–58. Elkin, I., Shea, M. T., Watkins, J. T., Imber, S. D., Sotsky, S. M., Collins, J. F., Glass, D. R., Pilkonis, P. A., Leber, W. R., Docherty, J. P., Fiester, S. J., and Parloff, M. B. (1989). National Institute of Mental Health Treatment of Depression Collaborative Research Program: General effectiveness of treatments. *Archives of General Psychiatry,* 46: 971–82.

17. Whisman, M. A. (2001). The association between depression and marital dissatisfaction. In Beach, S. R. H. (ed.). *Marital and Family Processes in Depression: A Scientific Foundation for Clinical Practice* (pp. 3–24). Washington, DC: American Psychological Association.

18. Lovejoy, M. C., Gracyk, P. A., O'Hare, E., and Neuman, G. (2000). Maternal depression and parenting behavior: A meta-analytic review. *Clinical Psychology Review,* 20: 561–92.

19. Stress-generation theory was developed by Constance Hammen of the University of California, Los Angeles. Hammen, C. (1991). *Depression Runs in Families: The Social Context of Risk and Resilience of Children of Depressed Mothers.* New York: Springer-Verlag.

20. Beach, S. R. H., and Jones, D. B. (2002). Marital and family therapy for depression in adults. In Gotlib and Hammen, op. cit., 422–40.

21. Markman, H., Stanley, S., and Blumberg, S. I. (1994). *Fighting for Your Marriage.* San Francisco: Jossey-Bass.

22. Patterson, G. R. (1982). *Coercive Family Processes.* Eugene, OR: Castilia.

23. Beach, S. R. H., and O'Leary, K. D. (1992). Treating depression in the context of marital discord: Outcome and predictors of response for marital therapy versus cognitive therapy. *Behavior Therapy,* 23: 507–28. Jacobson, N. S., Dobson, K., Fruzzetti, A. E., Schmaling, K. B., and Salusky, S. (1991). Marital therapy as a treatment of depression. *Journal of Consulting and Clinical Psychology,* 59: 547–57.

24. Beach and Jones (2002), op. cit.

25. IMS Health, Inc. (2006, February). 2005 Year-end U.S. prescription and sales information and commentary. Retrieved September 29, 2006, from http://www.imshealth.com/ims/portal/front/articleC/0,2777,6599_18731_77056778,00.html.

26. Klein, D. F., Gittelman-Klein, R., Quitkin, F. M., and Rifkin, A. (1980). *Diagnosis and Drug Treatment of Psychiatric Disorders.* Baltimore: Williams & Wilkins.

27. Gelenberg, A. J., and Chesen, C. L. (2000). How fast are antidepressants? *Journal of Clinical Psychiatry,* 61: 712–21. However, in the most recent major published study on the effectiveness of antidepressants, half of approximately three thousand patients did not show benefits until eight to ten weeks. Reference: Rush, A. J., Trivedi, M. H., Wisniewski, S. R., Stewart, J. W., Nierenberg, A. A., Thase, M. E., Ritz, L., Biggs, M. M., Warden, D., Luther, J. F., Shores-Wilson, K., Niederehe, G., Fava, M., and STAR*D Study Team. (2006). Bupropion-SR, Sertraline, or Venlafaxine-XR after failure of SSRIs for depression. *New England Journal of Medicine,* 354: 1231–42.

28. Moffitt, T. E., Caspi, A., and Rutter, M. (2006). Measured gene-environment interactions in psychopathology. *Perspectives on Psychological Science,* 1: 5–27. McMahon, F. J., Buervenich, S., Charney, D., Lipsky, R., Rush, A. J., Wilson, A. F., Sorant, A. J., Papanicolaou, G. J., Laje, G., Fava, M., Trivedi, M. H., Wisniewski, S. R., and Manji, H. (2006). Variation in the gene encoding the serotonin 2A receptor is associated with outcome of antidepressant treatment. *American Journal of Human Genetics,* 78: 804–14.

29. In most states, only medical doctors (who have M.D. degrees) can prescribe medication. Psychotherapists cannot but will refer you to someone who can.

30. It's worth noting that because new scientific data about antidepressant drugs are arriving at a dizzying pace, you'll want to be sure that your doctor's knowledge is absolutely current.

31. Rush et al. (2006), op. cit. See also Trivedi, M. H., Fava, M., Wisniewski, S. R., Thase, M. E., Quitkin, F., Warden, D., Ritz, L., Nierenberg A. A., Lebowitz, B. D., Biggs, M. M., Luther, J. F., Shores-Wilson, K., Rush, A. J., and STAR*D Study Team. (2006). Medication augmentation after the failure of SSRIs for depression. *New England Journal of Medicine,* 354: 1243–52.

32. Frank, E., Kupfer, D. J., Perel, J. M., Cornes, C., Jarrett, D. B., Mallinger, A. G., Thase, M. E., McEachran, A. B., and Grochocinski, V. J. (1990). Three-year outcomes for maintenance therapies in recurrent depression. *Archives of General Psychiatry,* 47: 1093–99. Kupfer, D. J., Frank, E., Perel, J. M., Cornes, C., Mallinger, A. G., Thase, M. E., McEachran, A. B., and Grochocinski, V. J. (1992). Five-year outcome for maintenance therapies in recurrent depression. *Archives of General Psychiatry,* 49: 769–73.

33. Keller, M. B., Gelenberg, A. J., Hirschfeld, R. M. A., Rush, A. J., Thase, M. E., Kocsis, J. H., Markowitz, J. C., Fawcett, J. A., Koran, L. M., Klein, D. N., Russell, J. M., Kornstein, S. G., McCullough, J. P., Davis, S. M., and Harrison, W. M. (1998). The treatment of chronic depression: Part 2. A double-blind randomized trial of sertraline and imipramine. *Journal of Clinical Psychiatry,* 59: 598–606. Kocsis, J. H., Friedman, R. A., Markowitz, J. C., Leon, A. C., Miller, N. L., Gniwesch, L., Parides, M. Kupfer, D. J., and Frank, E. (1996). Maintenance therapy for chronic depression: A controlled clinical trial of desipramine. *Archives of General Psychiatry,* 53: 769–74.

34. Linde, K., Ramirez, G., Mulrow, C. D., Pauls, A., Weidenhammer, W., and Melchart, D. (1996). St. John's wort for depression: An overview and meta-analysis of randomized clinical trials. *British Medical Journal,* 313: 253–58.

35. Shelton, R. C., Keller, M. B., Gelenberg, A., Dunner, D. L., Hirschfield, R., Thase, M. E., Russell, J., Lydiard, R. B., Crist-Christoph, P., Gallop, R., Todd, L., Hellerstein, D., Goodnick, P., Keitner, G., Stahl, S. M., and Halbreich, U. (2001). Effectiveness of St. John's wort in major depression: A randomized controlled-trial. *JAMA,* 285: 1978–86.

36. National Institute of Mental Health, op. cit. Covi, L., and Lipman, R. S. (1987). Cognitive behavioral group psychotherapy combined with imipramine in major depression. *Psychopharmacology Bulletin,* 23: 173–77.

37. Hough, R. L., Landsverk, J. A., Karno, M., Burnam, M. A., Timbers, D. M., Escobar, J. I., and Regier, D. A. (1987). Utilization of health and mental health services by Los Angeles Mexican-Americans and Non-Hispanic Whites. *Archives of General Psychiatry,* 44: 702–09.

38. Seligman, Rashid, and Parks (2006), op. cit.

39. Fava, G. A., Rafanelli, C., Cazzaro, M., Conti, S., and Grandi, S. (1998). Well-being therapy: A novel psychotherapeutic approach for residual symptoms of affective disorders. *Psychological Medicine,* 28: 475–80. For an overview

of well-being therapy, see Fava, G. A., and Ruini, C. (2003). Development and characteristics of a well-being enhancing psychotherapeutic strategy: Well-being therapy. *Journal of Behavior Therapy and Experimental Psychiatry,* 34: 45–63.

40. Frisch, M. B. (2005). *Quality of Life Therapy: Applying a Life Satisfaction Approach to Positive Psychology and Cognitive Therapy.* New York: John Wiley.

41. Hope therapy was developed over a number of years by the late C. R. Snyder. See Lopez, S. J., Snyder, C. R., Magyar-Moe, J. L., Edwards, L. M., Pedrotti, J. T., Janowski, K., Turner, J. L., and Pressgrove, C. (2004). Strategies for accentuating hope. In Linley and S. Josephs, op. cit., pp. 388–404.

42. Positive psychotherapy was developed by Nossrat Peseschkian, and personal growth therapy by Christine Robitschek. For brief descriptions of these positively focused therapies, see Compton, W. C. (2004). Positive psychology interventions. In *An introduction to positive psychology* loc. cit., 182–95.

43. Lucas et al. (2003), op. cit. Masten, A. S. (2001). Ordinary magic: Resilience processes in development. *American Psychologist,* 56: 227–38.

44. Edwards, J. (2004). *Four Trials.* New York: Simon & Schuster.

# INDEX

# Index

# ABOUT THE AUTHOR

Sonja Lyubomirsky is a professor of psychology at the University of California, Riverside. She received her B.A. from Harvard University and her Ph.D. in social psychology from Stanford University. Lyubomirsky and her research have been the recipients of many honors, including the 2002 Templeton Positive Psychology Prize and a multiyear grant (with Ken Sheldon) from the National Institute of Mental Health to conduct research on the possibility of permanently increasing happiness. She lives in Santa Monica, California, with her husband and two young children.